RELIGION IN THE 21ST CENTURY

In spite of the debate about secularization or de-secularization, the existential-bodily need for religion is basically the same as always. What have been changed are the horizons within which religions are interpreted and the relationships within which religions are integrated.

This book explores how religions continue to challenge secular democracy and science, and how religions are themselves being challenged by secular values and practices. All traditions – whether religious or secular – experience a struggle over authority, and this struggle seems to intensify with globalization, as it has brought people around the world in closer contact with each other. In this book internationally leading scholars from sociology, law, political science, religious studies, theology and the religion and science debate, take stock of the current interdisciplinary research on religion and open new perspectives at the cutting edge of the debate on religion in the 21st century.

Religion in the 21st Century
Challenges and Transformations

Edited by

LISBET CHRISTOFFERSEN
University of Roskilde, Denmark
University of Copenhagen, Denmark

HANS RAUN IVERSEN
University of Copenhagen, Denmark

HANNE PETERSEN
University of Copenhagen, Denmark

MARGIT WARBURG
University of Copenhagen, Denmark

ASHGATE

© Lisbet Christoffersen, Hans Raun Iversen, Hanne Petersen, Margit Warburg and contributors 2010

All rights reserved. No part of this publication may be reproduced, stored in a retrieval system or transmitted in any form or by any means, electronic, mechanical, photocopying, recording or otherwise without the prior permission of the publisher.

Lisbet Christoffersen, Hans Raun Iversen, Hanne Petersen and Margit Warburg have asserted their right under the Copyright, Designs and Patents Act, 1988, to be identified as the editors of this work.

Published by
Ashgate Publishing Limited
Wey Court East
Union Road
Farnham
Surrey, GU9 7PT
England

Ashgate Publishing Company
Suite 420
101 Cherry Street
Burlington
VT 05401-4405
USA

www.ashgate.com

British Library Cataloguing in Publication Data
Religion in the 21st century: challenges and transformations.
  1. Church history – 21st century. 2. Secularism.
  I. Christoffersen, Lisbet.
  200.9'05–dc22

Library of Congress Cataloging-in-Publication Data
Religion in the 21st century: challenges and transformations / [edited by] Lisbet Christoffersen ... [et al.].
   p. cm.
   Includes index.
   ISBN 978-1-4094-0398-2 (hardcover: alk. paper) – ISBN 978-1-4094-0399-9 (ebook)
   1. Religion and sociology. I. Christoffersen, Lisbet.
   BL60.R345 2010
   306.609'0511–dc22

2009050048

ISBN 9781409403982 (hbk)
ISBN 9781409403999 (ebk)

Mixed Sources
Product group from well-managed forests and other controlled sources
www.fsc.org Cert no. SA-COC-1565
© 1996 Forest Stewardship Council

Printed and bound in Great Britain by
MPG Books Group, UK

Contents

About the Contributors   *vii*
Foreword   *xi*
Preface   *xiii*

Introduction   1
Hanne Petersen

PART I: CHALLENGES

Political And Intellectual Challenge

1. Religion Challenging the Myth of Secular Democracy   19
   José Casanova

2. 'Fundamentalism' and the Pluralization of Value-Orientations   37
   Peter Beyer

3. Intellectual Challenges from Religion   51
   Sven-Eric Liedman

4. Political and Intellectual Challenges: A Sociological Response   67
   Grace Davie

5. Political and Intellectual Challenges: A Theological Response   73
   Niels Henrik Gregersen

The Religion and Science Debate

6. Challenges in the 21st Century: Religion and Science   85
   Philip Clayton

7. Religions and the Natural Sciences: Appeals to Science as Religious Advocacy?   103
   Willem B. Drees

8. The Need of Real Doubt in Religion and Science   111
   Jesper Hoffmeyer

PART II: TRANSFORMATIONS

Islam and State Politics

9   'Systemically closed, cognitively open'? A Critical Analysis of Transformative Processes in Islamic Law and Muslim State Practice   119
Shaheen Sardar Ali

10   Clashes and Encounters: Challenges in Nordic Legal Cultures Related to Law and Religion   141
Kjell Å Modéer

11   Law and Religion in Europe   149
Silvio Ferrari

Secularism and State Politics

12   Republicisation of Religion in France   163
Sébastien Tank-Storper

13   The Meaning of Privatization and De-privatization   177
Martin Riesebrodt

Denmark and the Cartoons

14   The Settled Secularity of Happy Denmark   183
David Martin

15   Background of the Cartoon Crisis in Danish Mentality   191
Hans Raun Iversen

16   The Politics of Lutheran Secularism: Reiterating Secularism in the Wake of the Cartoon Crisis   207
Anders Berg-Sørensen

17   Globalisation and Religious Diasporas: A Reassessment in the Light of the Cartoon Crisis   215
Margit Warburg

Index   229

About the Contributors

Shaheen Sardar Ali is currently serving as Professor of Law at the University of Warwick, UK; Professor II at the University of Oslo, Norway; and Member of the United Nations Working Group on Arbitrary Detention. She has written on international law of human rights, women's human rights and Islamic law. Among her publications are Anne Hellum, Shaheen Sardar Ali, Julie Stewart and Amy Tsanga (eds), *Human Rights, Plural Legalities and Gendered Realities: Paths are Made by Walking* (Weaver Books, 2007); *Conceptualising Islamic Law, CEDAW and Women's Human Rights in Plural Legal Settings: A Comparative Analysis of application of CEDAW in Bangladesh, India and Pakistan* (UNIFEM Regional Office, 2006); *Gender and Human Rights in Islam and International Law: Equal before Allah, Unequal before Man?* (Kluwer Law International, 2000); and with Javaid Rehman, *Indigenous Peoples and Ethnic Minorities of Pakistan Constitutional and Legal Perspectives* (Curzon, 2001).

Anders Berg-Sørensen is Associate Professor in Political Science at the University of Copenhagen. He has written the doctoral dissertation *Paradiso-Diaspora: Reframing the Question of Religion in Politics*, and essays in Danish, Scandinavian and international journals such as *Political Theory*, *Journal of International Affairs* and *Krisis: Journal for Contemporary Philosophy* on secularism, religion and politics. He is currently researching the democratic negotiations of religion and politics in European political thinking and public cultures, and he is editing the forthcoming book *Contesting Secularism: Comparative Perspectives*.

Peter Beyer is Professor of Religious Studies at the University of Ottawa. He has written primarily on globalization and the role of religion in the global society. Among his publications are *Religions in a Global Society* (Routledge, 2006) and *Religion and Globalization* (Sage Publications, 1994).

José Casanova is currently serving as Professor of Sociology and Senior Fellow at the Berkeley Center for Religion, Peace, and World Affairs at Georgetown University. He has written on religion, democratization, transnational migration, and globalization. Among his publications, Casanova has authored 'Rethinking Secularization: A Global Comparative Perspective' (*The Hedgehog Review*, vol. 8, nos. 1–2, 2006) and *Public Religions in the Modern World* (University of Chicago Press, 1994).

Philip Clayton is Ingraham Professor at Claremont School of Theology, and Professor of Philosophy and Religion at the Claremont Graduate University in

Los Angeles. He is the author or editor of 17 books on philosophy of science, philosophy of religion, and reconstructive theology, including the *Oxford Handbook of Religion and Science* (Oxford University Press, 2006) and *In Quest of Freedom: The Emergence of Spirit in the Natural World* (Vandenhoeck & Ruprecht, July 2008).

Grace Davie is Professor of Sociology at the University of Exeter, UK. Her research interest lies in patterns of religion in Europe as well as the new theoretical paradigms such as the notion of 'multiple modernities'. Among her recent publications are *The Sociology of Religion* (SAGE, 2007) and *Predicting Religion: Christian, Secular, and Alternative Futures* (Ashgate, 2003).

Willem B. Drees is Professor of Philosophy of Religion and Ethics at Leiden University, Netherlands. His research deals with the impact of science, technology and philosophy of science on religion, theology and religious studies. Among his recent publications are the edited volumes *The Study of Religion and the Training of Muslim Clergy in Europe: Academic and Religious Freedom* (Leiden University Press, 2008) and *Creation's Diversity: Voices from Theology and Science* (T&T Clark Continuum, 2008).

Silvio Ferrari is Professor of Canon Law at the University of Milan and Professor of Church–State relations at the University of Leuven, Belgium. His research is on Church and State in Europe and on Comparative Law of Religions. Among his recent publications are *Laws on Religion and the State in Post-Communist Europe* (Peeters, 2003) and *Islam and European Legal Systems* (Ashgate, 2000).

Niels Henrik Gregersen is Professor of Systematic Theology at the University of Copenhagen. His research is primarily on science & religion and constructive theology, including philosophy of religion. He is part of the conference committee, contributed to *Gudebilleder. Ytringsfrihed og religion i en globaliseret verden* (Tiderne Skifter, 2006), and is co-editor with Paul Davies of *Information and the Nature of Reality: From Physics to Metaphysics* (Cambridge University Press, 2010).

Jesper Hoffmeyer is Associate Professor of Molecular Biology at the University of Copenhagen and a member of the steering committee for Religion in the 21st Century. His main field of research is biosemiotics, which is concerned with the sign-aspects of the processes of life. Recently he published his doctoral dissertation *Biosemiotik – en afhandling om livets tegn og tegnenes liv* (Ries' Forlag, 2005) and edited *A Legacy for Living Systems: Gregory Bateson as Precursor to Biosemiotics* (Springer Verlag, 2008)

Hans Raun Iversen is Associate Professor of Practical Theology at the University of Copenhagen and Chairman of the steering committee for Religion in the

21st Century. Among his recent books are *Gudstro i Danmark* [*Faith in God in Denmark*] (Forlaget Anis, 2005), edited with Morten Højsgaard, and *At the Heart of Denmark: Institutions and Mentalities*, authored with Peter Gundelach and Margit Warburg (forthcoming).

Sven-Eric Liedman is Emeritus Professor in the Humanistic Faculty at the University of Gothenburg, Sweden. His research focus is on theory of knowledge, ethics and democracy. He is editor of *The Postmodernist Critique of the Project of Enlightenment* (Poznan Studies, Rodopi, 1997) and author of *Stenarna i själen. Form och materia från antiken till idag* (Albert Bonniers förlag, 2006) [*The Stones in the Soul: Form and Matter from Antiquity until Today*].

David Martin is Emeritus Professor of Sociology at the London School of Economics. His work is on the critique of secularization as a theory of social process and on Pentecostalism in Latin America. Among his recent publications are *Pentecostalism: The World Their Parish* (Blackwell, 2002) and *On Secularization: Towards a Revised General Theory* (Ashgate, 2005).

Kjell Å. Modéer is Emeritus Professor of Legal History at the University of Lund, Sweden. His current research is on the desacralization and retraditionalization in late-modern perspectives on Law. In his honour was recently published *Liber Amicorum Kjell Å Modeer* (Juristförlaget i Lund, 2007), and he has contributed to *Law and Religion in the 21st Century: Nordic Perspectives* (Peeters, 2010).

Hanne Petersen is Professor of Law. She has worked and written widely on legal pluralism and legal polycentricism in relation to women's law and indigenous peoples, and recently also to religious norms. She has been Professor of Law in Greenland and is part of the management group for a new centre for Studies of Legal Culture at the University of Copenhagen.

Martin Riesebrodt is Professor of Sociology of Religion at both the Divinity School and the University of Chicago. His academic interests are in social theory, the historical and comparative sociology of religion, and the relationship between religion, politics and secular culture. Among his recent publications is *Cultus und Heilsversprechen* (C.H. Beck, 2007).

Sébastien Tank-Storper is Associate Scientist at the National Center for Scientific Research, France, and a member of the Center for Social Anthropology at the University of Toulouse. His research is on sociology of religions and most specifically on sociology and anthropology of contemporary Judaism. He recently published *Juifs d'élection. Se convertir au judaïsme* (Sociologie, CNRS Éditions, 2007).

Margit Warburg is a sociologist of religion and professor at the University of Copenhagen. Her research is on religious minorities, migration, globalization and religious change. She recently published *Citizens of the World: A History and Sociology of the Baha'is from a Globalisation Perspective* (Brill, 2006), and she has co-authored *At the Heart of Denmark: Institutions and Mentalities* (forthcoming). She is part of the conference committee, and she is co-editor of five books on the book panels.

Foreword

No one can be in any doubt that religion has returned to the public space in a major way over the last couple of decades. It has been most visible in the high-profile presence of Islam in the media and politics of Europe, but we see it also in a new reflection, breaking out into the political arena, about the relationship between the religious and the secular in Europe, the role of the 'values' debate in US politics, and the rise of publicly assertive religious movements in Judaism, Hinduism and Buddhism in various parts of the world.

But how much of this is new, and how much is the reappearance of traditions temporarily marginalized or suppressed during a period of post-colonial enthusiasm for western-style modernity? And if it is a reappearance, how has the tradition been re-expressed or transformed both by the period of marginalization and by the interaction with a now changed environment? And how have the processes of globalization and technological change affected the role of the individual believer in relation to the social and religious community? Where does this leave the traditional religious authorities? And what are the challenges for society at large?

The University of Copenhagen Research Priority 2003–2007 'Religion in the 21st Century' provided a framework within which these and related issues could be explored in an international and thoroughly interdisciplinary fashion. It provided an opportunity for a variety of leading thinkers in the field to meet and to develop their ideas further. And Scandinavian, and especially Danish, scholars were able to place their peculiarly Scandinavian experiences into a creative discussion with colleagues from around the world.

It was fortuitous that, as the project was approaching its completion, Denmark was hit by the crisis sparked by the publication of the now notorious cartoons. The experience of working across disciplines and institutions accumulated during the project meant that at very short notice the expert resources of the university could be mobilized to produce a full one-day public seminar to insert a degree of balance and depth into a fraught public debate.

As members of the Scientific Advisory Board we, together with our colleagues in that group, can only commend the university, the coordinators and the contributors to the project for the extent and quality of the achievement.

Ingvild Sælid Gilhus
University of Bergen, Norway and University of Oslo, Norway

Jørgen S. Nielsen
University of Copenhagen, Denmark and University of Birmingham, UK

Preface

In 2003 – after 9/11 had become a symbolic date indicating a dramatic shift, and after the Danish involvement in both the wars against 'religious terrorism' in Afghanistan and in Iraq – Linda Nielsen, the first female Vice Chancellor of the University of Copenhagen, which was established in 1479 after Papal authorization, decided to support an application for an interdisciplinary research priority area on *Religion in the 21st Century* lasting from 2003 to 2007. Individual researchers and PhD students coming from departments of Theology and Sociology of Religion constituted a major part in this project. Like most other modern universities, the University of Copenhagen considers itself a secular institution. Partners from other fields thus had to re-establish contact with and awareness of the religious and moral history and heritage of their fields of knowledge. The research priority area provided an opportunity for the university, its students and teachers to be updated in a field many felt quite uneasy about. Religion as a priority area was clearly also a challenge to a secular identity. During the five years of the research program almost one hundred individual researchers from all faculties involved themselves in the quest of scrutinizing this historical heritage and facing contemporary challenges, reflecting on and investigating impact and consequences in the new era of the new century. The Cartoon Crisis – in Denmark called 'the Mohammed Crisis' – at the beginning of 2006 demonstrated the crucial importance of increased insight in and knowledge of relations among religion, society, politics, law and globalizations.

Most of the articles in this book were presented in their first versions at the final conference of the research priority area, which took place in September 2007, aiming to present and take stock of some of the issues investigated during the program period, as well as to raise questions for the future. The overarching themes of the conference were the concepts of challenges and transformations connected to religion, which also structure the content of this book. Of the 35 books planned to publish results from the research priority area and the 27 major conferences arranged by the research priority area, 24 have already been published; cf. www.ku.dk/satsning/religion. Whereas these books present specialized studies on specific cross-disciplinary topics, the present book attempts to paint some principal scenery in the complicated picture of Religion in the 21st century.

The editors wish to express their sincere thanks for the efforts and patience by the renowned international as well as local Danish scholars who helped us to bring together the material in this book. A special word of thanks goes to Master in Sociology of Religion Laura Maria Schütze, who did the bulk of the practical work in correspondence with the authors after the 2007 conference.

Lisbeth Christoffersen, Research Coordinator of *Religion in the 21st Century*
Hans Raun Iversen, Chair of the Board of *Religion in the 21st Century*
Hanne Petersen, Member of the Board of *Religion in the 21st Century*
Margit Warburg, Vice Chair of the Board of *Religion in the 21st Century*

University of Copenhagen, April 2010

Introduction

Hanne Petersen

The Berlin Conference that divided up the African continent took place towards the end of the 19th century, in 1884–85. To this conference came representatives from the states considered important at the time – fourteen in total, including roughly all the states of Europe except Switzerland plus the United States of America. At that time they were considered 'the international community' – or at least the important part of it. These were states that were – apart from the Ottoman Empire – all Christian nations.[1] Two years earlier Nietzsche had declared God dead in his book *Die fröhliche Wissenschaft – The Gay Science*.

The 20th century started and ended with a collapse of values. World War I demonstrated that Christian 'civilized' nations would go to war against each other, and thousands upon thousands of young men were killed. The century of secularism had begun. When the League of Nations was formed in 1920 a minority of the founding 42 countries were not Christian: China, Persia, Iraq, Siam, Turkey and Afghanistan. They were not considered modern either. Secularism and modernism moved high on the agenda of the 20th century, not only of the newly established Soviet Union.

The end of the Cold War ended the binary categorization of the growing number of world states into followers of the ideologies of either capitalism or communism. Hardly anybody had envisioned that 'The Wall' would come tumbling down in 1989, that communism would collapse, and that secularism with its strong links to socialist and communist ideologies would thus also experience a significant loss of credibility.

With the collapse of the Twin Towers at the beginning of the 21st century this shift from a dominance of secular to post-secular or religiously inspired ideologies in a globalized world gradually dawned on the shocked television viewers of the world. The world of the 21st century would not necessarily be a world governed by one hegemonic set of modern liberal values. The global stage was set for new actors – or perhaps old actors returning to the scenes. The characters of the globalized play to be watched on the screens put on show by the rapidly growing cable networks were the 'bad and dangerous guys' – the terrorists and extremist religious leaders – on the one side against the 'good guys', that is, the martial and

---

[1] Austro-Hungarian Empire, Belgium, Denmark, France, Germany, Great Britain, Italy, the Netherlands, Portugal, Russia, Spain, Sweden & Norway (in union), and the United States of America.

political guardians of modern and mainly western primarily secular values such as democracy and human rights.

Conflicts make for good stories on both local and global scenes, and villains and lawbreakers always generate the dynamics of both real and fabricated stories, as do the players representing religious ideas and values. Conflicts also sell stories, whether on the screen or on the stage, in the streets or in the printed media. The return to the stage of the 'repressed', 'religious' ideas and actors meant that other actors and audiences had to take them seriously also. It remains to be seen what value-changes will follow in the wake of the collapse of the financial markets primarily in the secularized Western parts of world society in October 2008.

This book presents some of the challenges and transformations facing both the world and Danish society due to these paradigmatic value-shifts, which have taken place on both global and local levels and which have made themselves felt strongly at the beginning of this century. The state of Denmark may perhaps be said to have undergone a shift from a 20th-century 'autonomous' nation state to a 'province of the world'. Part of this process of 'provincializing' earlier central players – such as states and regions, including not least Europe – may also be that 'Western secular modernity' is challenged.[2]

It is claimed by some contributing authors to this book to be a myth that European democracy is intrinsically linked to secularization. What we are witnessing is a contemporary 'European exceptionalism' where Europe is an exception as *the* secular continent in a world where religion still plays an important role for both society and the individual. Other authors underline similarities among 'fundamentalisms', be they Christian or Islamist. Both forms have difficulties accepting value pluralism, and fight against loss and transformation of authority. Both are religio-nationalist in character, and often anti-intellectualist. All religion, however, is not fundamentalist. It is necessary to note the differences within traditions and communities, be they religious or scientific. Further, there is a need and a movement towards a re-enchantment of modern science as well. In the late modern world religion satisfies vital needs and seems better equipped to face some of the problems challenging societies and individuals in this period. It is in fact entirely normal to be both 'fully modern' and 'fully religious', as Grace Davie writes – or to be a modern and 'secular believer' in a situation where loss of certainty is felt by both religious and modern scientific knowledge.

All traditions, whether religious or secular, experience a struggle over authority and replacement of former elites. However, these traditions have also had alliances, notably in their view of nature as a passive realm, that they may now be challenged to give up.

The return of religion and tradition also challenges the Western concept – or tradition – of law, which is defined as a largely formal, black letter construct. At the same time, a veneer of immutability is often cast over the Islamic legal tradition

---

[2] See Dipesh Chakrabarty's *Provincializing Europe: Postcolonial Thought and Historical Difference*, Princeton, NJ: Princeton University Press, 2000 and 2008.

despite the full knowledge that this is no longer appropriate under conditions of 'fractured' modernities. Some struggles over authority seem to concern issues of generational and minority power, and of identity recognition in the public sphere of societies considering themselves secular.

Lutheranism seems to mutate into semi-secular Social Democracy – especially in Denmark, where 'overlapping membership' of several faith communities is not necessarily considered a problem, and where conversion implies transformation of identity involving bodily and ritual aspects that are important in the process of identity-making. Knowledge of Christianity and Christian practice is limited among ethnic Danes, and few immigrants in the Scandinavian countries are practicing Muslims. The escalation of the Cartoon Crisis and the patterns of its course were characteristic of globalization, as demonstrations and disturbances erupted simultaneously in unrelated places, demonstrating simultaneity and deterritorialization. Before presenting these challenges and transformations, we provide a more detailed overview of the articles in this anthology.

Political and Intellectual Challenge

According to Spanish–American **José Casanova**, the challenge coming from religion towards the secular is related to what he calls 'de-privatization', 'confessional de-territorialization' and 'global denominationalism'. What is being challenged for him is secularism, but this process also provides conditions and opportunity structures for religions to be transformed. In western Europe, secular modernity has become hegemonic and taken for granted to a degree, where we suffer from a 'secularist prejudice' that has excluded religion from the public sphere. According to Casanova, 'the "secular" nature of the modern European state and the "secular" character of European democracy serve as one of the foundational myths of the contemporary European identity.' In Casanova's – modern – understanding of myth, this is a false story. He reminds us that the drastic secularization of most western European societies came after the consolidation of democracy, not before. It would therefore be irrelevant to present the secularization of state, politics and society as a condition of democracy. He also reminds us that the EU was fundamentally a Christian-Democratic project sanctioned by the Vatican at a time of general religious revival in post-World War II Europe 'in the geopolitical context of the World War when the "free world" and "Christian civilization" had become synonymous'. The European secular foundational myth overlooks that modern early states were in fact confessional states and not secular states, built as they were on the principle of *cuius regio eius religio* – a principle that was particularly strong in the Nordic Lutheran societies. Anders Berg-Sørensen in a later article writes about 'The Politics of Lutheran Secularism', describing the importance of this principle and of contemporary but still Lutheran-influenced understanding of the relation between state and church for current Danish understandings of 'true secularism'.

Casanova suspects that the function of the selective European historical memory is to safeguard the perception of the progressive achievements of Western secular modernity, offering a self-validating justification of the secular separation of religion and politics as the condition for modern liberal democratic politics. For him, what constitutes the truly novel aspect of the present global condition is the fact that all world religions can be reconstituted for the first time truly as de-territorialized global imagined communities, detached from the civilizational settings in which they have been traditionally embedded. We are witnessing the end of hegemonic European Christianity due to a dual process of advanced secularization in post-Christian Europe and the increasing globalization of a de-territorialized and de-centered Christianity. Cosmopolitanism as a faithful child of the Enlightenment is still based on a rigid dichotomous contraposition of tradition and modernity.

It is time to revise our teleological conceptions of a global cosmopolitan secular modernity against which we can characterize the religious 'other' as 'fundamentalist'. We need to make room for more complex, nuanced and reflexive categories, which will help us to understand better the already-emerging global systems of multiple modernities, he claims. Every universalism and every modernity is particularistic.

Canadian **Peter Beyer** moves from religion's challenge to secularism to its challenges to politics and the framework of the state, where it leads to a combination of 'fundamentalism' and a pluralization of value-orientations of 'modern' societies. He also underlines the differences in religion – some expressions are fundamentalist, while other expressions may be more liberal. Thus the 'fundamentalist' challenges for politics and state include a challenge of the 'secular' character of the world's dominant systems of power and influence, particularly the state. They represent certain value-orientations, which contradict others. Fundamentalism is an explicitly religious challenge that has modes of expression leading more often than not to violence and war, and it further challenges cultural, moral and religious pluralism. Since the focus has been especially on Islam, Beyer asks what it might be about this sort of Islam that is so challenging, specifically politically challenging. Protestant Christian Fundamentalism, which coined the concept, has not had the aim of 'de-secularizing' society, but its core can be understood as the assertion of a different set of primarily religious *values* in comparison with those that were and are still deemed to be dominant in American society. Beyer suggests that there are significant and strong parallels between Christian and Islamist 'fundamentalisms'. In the American Christian Right one focus is on 'family values', including highly gendered bodily control issues and those having to do with child-rearing and education. Here the moral aspect is critical. Another focus according to Beyer is 'free enterprise', including advocacy of fairly unfettered American capitalism and corresponding opposition to 'big government'. The global relevance of the American Protestant fundamentalism is the third value-dimension, the need to 'make America great again'. What this kind of fundamentalism opposes is 'secular humanism' and its external manifestation, 'one-worldism'. According to Beyer, the political challenge of religion that the American Christian Right exemplifies is the wish to use the state as an instrument to protect a locally imagined and religio-national particularism, but in such a way as to allow the continued and self-interested participation in global power systems.

In terms of content, this religio-political movement is deeply troubled by religio-moral plurality and its attendant value of pluralism, which asserts the formally equal value or 'rights' of those worldviews, religions, cultures and individual orientations that constitute the plurality. Beyer suggests that this is a concern shared by different forms of fundamentalism including that of Osama bin Laden. Most 'fundamentalist' religio-political movements are religio-nationalist in character. The political challenge exists in the wish to construct and assert the internal uniformity that is the aim of the movement, in part through the deliberate exclusion of the pluralizing 'other'. The only alternative to exclusion becomes conversion.

Moving from the 'fundamentalist' to the 'liberal' political challenges from religion, Beyer writes that 'liberal' religious critiques in many ways resonate rather precisely with so-called 'secularist' values and oppose the so-called 'fundamentalist' ones: they favour pluralism, whether religious, cultural or individual. Taking this into consideration, the 'challenge' from religion 'becomes the sort of opposition attendant upon the construction of a fundamentally pluralized social world, and from that perspective, something rather ordinary that can have a religious basis or not'.

The 'dis-identification' of the religious and the 'fundamentalist' could to a certain extent also be said to lie behind the contribution by self-declared – Lutheran – atheist, Swedish **Sven-Eric Liedman**. He discusses the intellectual challenges from religion in the 21st century, informing the reader at the outset that at the end of his article he will sketch the outlines of an atheism that does not come across as gloomy, 'while avoiding insensitivity and lack of tolerance for the great aesthetic and cultural values that religion represents', and informing us at the end of the article that he is highly skeptical of what he calls 'belligerent atheism'. Liedman underlines the common traits of the expanding Christian and Muslim movements of the past few decades, which include a clearly fundamentalist orientation and a good measure of anti-intellectualism as manifested in an aversion to traditional religious ideology and science. Central to the discourse on modernity are the opposites of 'disenchantment' and 're-enchantment'. The notion that the world is heading towards an increasingly deeper religious re-enchantment has one major exception, Europe, which is far more de-Christianized than other parts of the world. Nonetheless, the social sciences and philosophy also have witnessed a remarkably renewed interest in traditional theological questions among many European intellectuals normally associated with irreligious currents.

Liedman claims that in certain – not least technological – areas the enchantment of modernity is alive and well: 'What can't be solved today will be solved tomorrow'. But classical believers in progress strike us as naïve, he writes, when they assert that the human race is improving on the moral plane. The belief in the death of religion seems to be obsolete these days, where religion often goes hand in hand with the solid components of modernity. It is spread in the new media; many of its adherents are technologically or scientifically knowledgeable; and it is closely linked to the global economy. Religion clearly satisfies vital needs in a late modern world.

One of its challenges is anti-intellectual, while the other challenge involves a serious, intellectually responsible discussion about how religion relates to secular philosophy, contemporary science, and late modern society. The secular thinking of today offers insufficient avenues for expression and is insensitive to the problem of wayward lives, unreasonable aspirations, and perverted social conditions. Religion is better equipped for the challenge, Liedman writes, in a discussion of the dialogue between former cardinal Ratzinger and Jürgen Habermas.

The fascination with the Apostle Paul for a number of secularized European intellectuals, including Žižek, is a fascination with a project about the worldly potential of religion. Paul is seen as the founder of something new – a church, a community that transcends borders, with all the power of eschatology. But as Liedman warns us in one of his last sentences, 'Human beings are just as much destroyers as they are creators'.

Grace Davie, from Britain, in her 'sociological response' to the political and intellectual challenges treated by Casanova, Beyer and Liedman underlines the importance of language – related to the issue of values, the importance of context – drawing attention to the 'European exceptionalism' and the issue of plurality in relation to modernity, to multiple modernities. The form of – secular – modernity that has emerged in Europe is only one among many, not necessarily the global prototype, she stresses. Additionally, she raises the following important question for economic, political and social scientists, whether interested in religion or not: 'What are the consequences of taking seriously the fact that, for the great majority of the world's populations in the 21st century, it is not only possible, but entirely "normal", to be both fully modern and fully religious?'

Niels Henrik Gregersen from Denmark in his 'theological response' to Casanova, Beyer and Liedman proposes the terms 'foundationalism' and 'communitarian ideals' as alternatives to 'fundamentalism' and 'liberalism', and presents his reflections on these terms. Foundationalism represents a view about how to justify beliefs and ethical stances, and all fundamentalists are foundationalists, but not all foundationalists are fundamentalists. The distinction between liberals and conservatives is a category within the political sciences, which are probably not apt with regard to religiously motivated challenges to politics in all relations. Political 'citizens' are not identical to (Christian) 'neighbours'. Gregersen raises the general question concerning in what sense secular notions of religion-free domains can be imagined from a religious perspective, and suggests a certain connection and overlap between Darwinism and Lutheranism. And finally he claims that, in spite of all secularity, the world still affords the presence of events and processes that continue to trigger a religious sensibility.

The Religion and Science Debate

In his reflections on the relation between religion and science, American **Philip Clayton** asks whether a productive religion–science dialogue is possible, claiming that so far each side in this dialogue has emphasized the virtues of its own particular perspectives – either the merit of science or the value of religion. He suggests that the world's various 'wisdom traditions', which serve as repositories both for human values and for justifying stories and arguments, and which go beyond the ideology of nation-states, if updated and interpreted may offer guidance 'at least in formulating the ecological and bioethical dilemmas of contemporary science', certainly if an open-minded spirit is shown also in the approach to religion on the part of believers. But a religion–science partnership would also question the traditional claim that detachment is the precondition for any adequate empirical study of religion. If belief and critical questioning be combined, it would also require that a life of faith include doubt and radical questioning and sometimes even despair. In what seems to be in line with both Liedman and Davie, he suggests the term 'secular believer'. This believer might perhaps think it reasonable 'that certain religious beliefs should be revised or even discarded as a result of new scientific discoveries.' The possibility of this combination of different orders of knowledge seems to Clayton to be present in various developments in the theory of knowledge in the 20th century, which has challenged the strict separation that underlies positivism and neo-Enlightenment thinking. A loss of certainty seems to be felt by both religious and modern scientific knowledge.

The comment by Dutch **Willem B. Drees** underlines that the most significant struggle is taking place not between traditions – including religious traditions – but *within* traditions: this is a struggle over authority. He sees Clayton's contribution as a plea for a particular, liberal attitude in religion in contrast with certain orthodox stances that, as a believer, he shares. However, he sees that which is presented as 'religion and science' as serving at least three other purposes: apologetics for science, apologetics for religion, and apologetics for religious studies and theology in the modern research university. The real struggle over evolution is not about biology. The fear is that with the acceptance of evolution a whole cluster of social values would be put at stake. Controversies over evolution are controversies over social issues, Drees claims. He also asks why it would not be legitimate to see how far one gets by understanding religious belief as delusions. 'Religion and science' is a major battle ground between revisionists and traditionalists in each tradition. The Galileo affair provided the context of a struggle over authority in exegetical matters, the outcome affirming the authority of the Pope and Church officials over lay reading of Scripture in the aftermath of the Protestant Reformation and the Council of Trent. In the reception of Darwin's ideas in the 19th century, the issue was not just evolution, but also the replacement of an elite of gentleman-naturalists by scientific professionals, doing science for a living. This question of authority is also central in Islam, where the issue is who speaks for the true faith.

Jesper Hoffmeyer, from Denmark, replies to Clayton among others by relating his experience that 'real doubt is perhaps as rare in university life as it is among religious believers'. As somebody who has dealt with biosemiotics for more than a decade, he claims that 'the prevailing scientific conceptions of evolution are unnecessarily flat.' Darwin established a cosmology that allowed humans to belong in the world without having to invoke any supernatural causes or beings. Biosemiotics re-establishes the conception of living beings as *intentional creatures* whose activities are governed by internal models of their surroundings. Hoffmeyer refers to a movement in science itself, which asks: 'Was the universe an orderly place from the very beginning? Or is the lawful behaviour of things in the world, that now seems so pronounced, instead the result of an emergent process?' One of the important consequences of a scientific movement in the direction of emergentist conceptions is that the sharp fact–value distinction separating science and humanities or theology cannot be upheld. 'Maybe it is now time that science and religion give up the old alliance they formed with each other back in Galilee's century on the conception of Nature as an irreparably passive realm to be ruled by God or by natural laws (given by Him)', Hoffmeyer suggests.

Islam, Law and State Politics

The reconsideration of knowledge presented in the fields of religion and science so far is continued in the discussion of the field of law, specifically in the Islamic legal tradition presented by Pakistani **Shaheen Sardar Ali**, who currently resides in Britain. She sets out to indicate evidence of transformative processes both in Islamic law and in Muslim state practice. Western scholarship defines law as largely a formal, black letter, written construct. In contrast, *Shari'a* is the overarching umbrella of rules regulations, values and normative framework covering all aspects and spheres of life for Muslims. It constitutes the Divine injunctions of God (the *Qur'an*) and the divinely inspired *Sunna* (words and deeds of the Prophet Muhammad), as well as the human articulation and understanding of these sources. *Shari'a* is thus 'the embodiment of a rich, dynamic, responsive living organism of norms, legal and non-legal; hence transformative over time and place.' Sardar Ali discusses some of the important and dynamic concepts that have contributed to this transformation. Concepts and principles are not unknown in a Western and European understanding of law, but their importance has decreased in the modern era. But the Islamic tradition demonstrates a reluctance and sometimes a total denial of the fact that it is susceptible to transformation. The interaction of Muslims with notions of 'modernity' – the nation-state, its structures and institutions, the international community and its organizations – has been for the most part an uneasy process. However, one of the fastest growing bodies of scholarship and practice consists of Islamic Banking and Finance, and its responsiveness to contemporary international issues. Sardar Ali discusses the role of Muslim diasporic communities as a discursive site for Islamic legal tradition, in a historical situation where millions of Muslims have made a conscious decision to adopt non-Muslim jurisdictions of their homes, voluntarily and permanently. One of the areas where issues of authority are at stake is Muslim family law, which is occasionally seen by some as 'the remaining bastion of a universal Muslim identity and governed solely by an unadulterated "Islamic" family law'. According to Sardar Ali, reality reflects that this type of law has evolved with tremendous alacrity especially over the past century. The legal tradition has progressively moved towards codification, and the resistance to polygamy has been expressed in a strategy conceived over centuries that stipulates an exorbitant amount as *mahr* (dower) to inhibit the husband from taking another wife.

The institution of the *ifta* – the practice of giving a *fatwa* or non-binding opinion by a *mufti* in response to a question – is one of the most powerful vehicles of interpretative and transformative processes within the Islamic legal tradition. *Fatwas* are perceived by many as the 'meeting point between legal theory and social practice', serving a number of functions ranging from a legal tool assisting the adjudication process, to functioning as social instruments (for example, questions by private persons within a community), political discourses, and devices for reform. Sardar Ali argues that, while the *fatwa* contributed to legal discourse within the Islamic legal tradition, it was also an important social instrument and helped in shaping societal views on issues from the mundane to the sublime. In view of the high rates of illiteracy among Muslim populations and their dependency on the mass media, reliance on 'verbal' *fatwas* delivered to an audience has increasingly become a popular offering on radio and television channels. They acquire increasing popularity as scores of troubled Muslims, young and old, lose faith in their respective governments and turns towards an '*ummatic*' response from scholars anywhere in the world so long as they belong to the Muslim *ummah*.

Sardar Ali submits that there appears to have evolved an invisible hierarchy within the Islamic legal tradition regarding its sources and techniques. Culture, custom, tradition, religion, as well as statute law and international laws, operate in a legally fluid environment, appearing as 'fractured modernities', negotiating ever-shifting boundaries of engagement within themselves and other spheres of legality and illegality. Muslim jurisdictions make selective use of Islamic injunctions. A veneer of immutability is often cast over the legal systems emanating from the Islamic religion, despite the full knowledge that this is no longer appropriate. What is not appreciated adequately is something that resonates with earlier presentations – namely, the complexities, values, norms and legal systems that Muslims negotiate today.

Kjell Å. Modéer, from Sweden, in his response discusses challenges in Nordic legal cultures related to law and religion. He notes initially that Sardar Ali's definition of *Shari'a* as a well and watering place is very similar to the metaphor used in the Old Testament by the prophet Amos, who describes justice as 'roll[ing] on like a river, righteousness like a never failing stream', a metaphor often used in the Western rhetorical legal tradition. He focuses upon the dynamic aspect of law, where the static historical argumentation is based on the religious text and the dynamic argument is based on the religious context, the culture and the tradition. In the Nordic countries also, the historical argument has changed into a more dynamic exchange concerning the late modern society of the early 21st century.

Nordic countries have been very homogenous both legally and religiously since their religious life was until the end of the 20th century dominated by Evangelical Lutheran State Churches. The state churches were identified not only with the state, but also with its political culture. This homogenous view, however, is today transformed and challenged both due to the EU and the European Council and to increasing multiculturalism and multi-religiosity. The *Shari'a* as a parallel norm system is in this situation more controversial for the humanist and atheist association than for the members of the Catholic congregations in the Nordic countries, for example. Modéer refers to the German law professor Mathias Rohe, who argues for the integration of what he terms 'Euro-Islam' into the European legal systems, as German judges have in a number of court cases accepted an adaptation of the Islamic law tradition. This process underlines the main focus of Shaheen Sardar Ali's contribution on the transformative processes of Islamic law in an international context.

Italian professor of Church and State law **Silvio Ferrari** also discusses the new religious plurality in Europe and its relation to legal change. Immigration and individualism are paving the way for the birth of a culturally and ethically plural society. These socio-religious transformations in Europe have been noticed by the national legal systems where there is a decline in regimes and where concordats and agreements with religious communities have been concluded. The legal systems based on a constitutionally dominant religion, which represents the Orthodox *pendant* of the Protestant Church of State, also show a parallel decline. Ferrari concludes that a process of convergence from the extremities towards the centre is taking place in Europe: modernization does not imply Church–State separation, but a moderate involvement of states with religions, as for instance in the Swedish case. Everywhere in Europe states regard the teaching of religion as part of their educative tasks, and even a secular state (such as France) cannot ignore the importance of religion as an instrument for understanding today's world. Pluralism and individualism have opened school doors to some religious minorities that in the past had been excluded. Simultaneously Islam is undergoing a transformation process from an immigrant's religion into a religion that by full right is part of the European reality. Ferrari writes – in line with Rohe and Modéer – that '[t]his process requires to be accompanied by appropriate legal initiatives aimed at fully integrating Muslim communities in the European model of relations between states and religions, or, in other words, at transforming this model so that it is able to accommodate the needs of Muslim communities. It is unlikely that a European Islam may take shape, substance and stability before this process is completed.' In this context the 'unchanging status of the *Qur'anic* texts – as well as that of the Bible or the Gospels – cannot be too lightly dismissed as something irrelevant, as it has an impact on the interpretative work and, therefore, on the evolution of the legal system'. The challenge for Europe is to identify an approach for this process.

Secularism and State Politics

The prototypical example of the distinction and division between secular and religious spheres and ideas in science, politics and law is 'The French Case' as presented by **Sébastian Tank-Storper**. His purpose is to describe how religion returns to the public sphere while becoming more private and individual – not according to a principle of domination, but rather according to the logic of identity recognition in the democratic public sphere. Privatization and individualization of religion undermine religious authority and the sense of obligation; '[t]he most important consequence of the process of individualisation and privatisation of religion is the radical switch from a religion conceived as a principle of heteronomy to a religion conceived as an identity and a support for individuals in an uncertain modern society'. Religion tends to become a frame for social identities and especially for minority identities, writes Tank-Storper, focusing specifically on young Muslims in France: 'Islam is a means to convey a serious and rigorous image of themselves'. Further, '[p]ublicising of Muslim identity by wearing an ostentatious sign such as *hidjab* enables one to express self-autonomy through conflict. This is a very modern way to build and publicise an authentic religious identity: a dominated population mobilises a depreciated sign of their culture to claim the material and symbolic exclusion that they feel by using in their own way the dominant values of individualism.' Bearing in mind the contribution by Sardar Ali, one might speculate whether what is at stake is generational authority both in relation to a religious Islamic tradition and a secular national tradition. Tank-Storper suggests the term 'republicisation of religious identity' rather than the expression 'deprivatisation of religions' used by Casanova. It is because religion stays private that it can find a new place in public space. Religion is incorporated in the democratic game rather than being a normative principle, he writes. This is partly due to a situation wherein politics no longer claims to have a monopoly on certain ethical subjects: '[w]hen religion stops being a political danger, that is, by not seeking to dominate society, it can be reintroduced in the public sphere as a legitimate actor of civil society ... religion becomes a "voice" beside other voices and loses its absolute character.'

In his comment on Tank-Storper's article, German–American **Martin Riesebrodt** writes that Tank-Storper fails to explain why people in growing numbers choose religion as a marker of identity. Riesebrodt also claims that religion is much more complex than other markers of identity, because it has a social dimension and a commitment to a certain conduct of life. Religion has never ceased to play a role in democratic politics, as the example of Christian parties in Europe shows. And all salvation religions have a private and individual dimension, since they have to be appropriated subjectively in order to be practiced.

Denmark and the Cartoons

The last part of the book deals with the challenges and transformations in the Danish setting, especially regarding the challenges presented by the Mohammed Cartoon Crisis. The contributors are Danish apart from **David Martin**, who remarks on 'the Settled Secularity of Happy Denmark' in his review of the study *At the Heart of Denmark*. Martin claims that the Nordic countries illustrate his belief that religious and political cultures mirror each other quite closely. The ensemble they represent has to be set in a geographical and geopolitical niche, both within the national boundaries and beyond them in the whole continental context. Martin notes the curious tendency of Lutheranism to mutate into semi-secular Social Democracy. Luther's stress on individual faith and trust is easily transformed into the idea that everyone is a Christian in his or her own way, while the priesthood of all believers downgrades hierarchy as such, not only the dogmatic deliverances of ecclesiastical hierarchy.

The last three articles deal with the impact, interpretations and context of the Cartoon Crisis. **Hans Raun Iversen** writes that it was about the handling of an actual multicultural situation, 'or rather the Danish lack of ability in this respect'. Ethnic Danes have a clear tendency to position themselves in relation to Muslims and thus to claim that they are Christian, or at any rate that they live in a Christian country, even though the content of their Christian knowledge and practice is modest. Danes keep to what they themselves have experienced. What we find in the Cartoon Crisis is a clash of different mentalities with a religious dimension yet not a crisis about religion, not to speak of a clash of civilizations. The dominant mentality in Denmark seems to be that 'affirming one's certitude and the depth of one's sincere conviction is sufficient to justify the claim of objective certainty.'

Anders Berg-Sørensen claims that when the cartoon controversy peaked in February 2006 a politics of *Lutheran* secularism was articulated in order to put religion in its place with reference to the Lutheran tradition of the majority of the Danish population, constituting a dominant social imaginary of the proper relationship between religion and politics. As an exercise of power, a politics of secularism operates by political-theologizing, and, thus, it produces the very paradoxes of secularism questioning its political ideals: liberty, equality, neutrality and impartiality. The state is not neutral in religious matters; rather, the reiteration of the impact of Lutheran theology on political institutions and the culture of Danish democratic society grants priority to one religious tradition on behalf of others. The sovereign operates as a political–theological authority whose power of lawgiving transcends the law.

Margit Warburg discusses both globalization and the usefulness of the concept of religious diasporas as a way of understanding the reactions of the Muslim community in Denmark in relation to the Cartoon Crisis, which temporarily united Danish Muslims to a hitherto-unseen degree, where they felt challenged as Muslims first and foremost, rather than as immigrants. In the Scandinavian countries, less than a quarter and probably far fewer of the immigrants from Muslim countries are practicing Muslims. The escalation of the crisis and the patterns of its course are characteristic of globalization. The demonstrations and disturbances abroad erupted simultaneously in several geographically unrelated places, demonstrating simultaneity and de-territorialization.

The debate about secularization and/or de-secularization is ongoing. One point of view is that the existential-bodily need for religion – for example, rituals – is basically the same as always. What have changed are the horizons and contexts within which religions are interpreted, and the relationships in which religions and rituals are integrated. There are more than twice as many states today as at the time of the Berlin Conference. The global landscape is changing both politically and normatively. This means, among other things, that religions and beliefs in various forms continue to challenge – and interact with – their surroundings, for instance secular democracy and science, by which religions are themselves being challenged. It also means that religions as well as the societies and communities in which they exist are being transformed in a continuing and sometimes very dynamic process.

PART I: CHALLENGES

Political and Intellectual Challenge

Chapter 1
Religion Challenging the Myth of Secular Democracy

José Casanova

For the last two to three centuries it was religion that was on the defensive, being constantly challenged by secular modernity. Today it is Western secular modernity, another of our mental constructs, that feels intellectually and politically challenged by religion. In this presentation, I would like to examine this political challenge coming from religion under three separate headings: the challenge of 'de-privatization', the challenge of 'confessional de-territorialization', and the challenge of 'global denominationalism'. It would be misleading, however, to view those challenges as if they were coming from religion per se. Rather, religions and the secular across the world are being transformed in multiform ways by global historical processes that we tend to conceptualize under the shorthand category of globalization. In other words, contemporary global historical processes are creating conditions of possibility and opportunity structures for religions to be transformed in manifold ways that challenge our received conceptions of Western secular modernity. This is particularly the case in Western Europe, where secular modernity as a construct had become hegemonic, a kind of 'unthought' *doxa*, the taken-for-granted assumption of elites as well as of ordinary people.

The Challenge of 'De-privatization'

It has been over a decade now since the publication of my book *Public Religions in the Modern World* (1994), and it can be asserted with some confidence that the thesis first presented there that we were witnessing a process of 'de-privatization' of religion as a relatively global trend has been amply confirmed. The most important contribution of the book, in my view, was not so much the relatively prescient empirical observation of such a new global trend, but the analytical–theoretical and normative challenge that my thesis presented to liberal theories of privatization claiming that religion in the modern world was and ought to remain an exclusively 'private' affair. I argued that such a claim was no longer defensible either empirically, as evidenced by global historical trends, or normatively, since there was no valid justification, other than secularist prejudice, to exclude religion from the democratic public sphere. In a certain sense, the best confirmation of the validity of the 'de-privatization' of religion can be found in the heartland of secularization, that is, in Western European societies. It is here that the challenge of 'de-privatization' is most keenly felt.

To be sure, there is very little evidence of any kind of religious revival among the European population, if one excludes the significant influx of new immigrant religions. At most one could say that the general precipitous decline in individual religious belief may have come to a halt throughout much of Europe and we may be witnessing a slight upward trend in 'belief' among the younger generations. But this is a form of 'private' religion, of 'believing without belonging', in Danièle Hervieu-Léger's apt characterization, that does not translate into greater participation in public religious ceremonies of any kind, much less does it present a political challenge to secular democratic structures.

But religion has certainly returned as a contentious political issue to the public sphere of European societies. It may be premature to speak of a post-secular Europe, but certainly one can sense a significant shift in the European zeitgeist. At first, the thesis of the de-privatization of religion found practically no resonance among Western European publics, academic and non-academic alike, with the exception of small groups within the sociology of religion or of small intellectual religious publics. The privatization of religion was simply taken too much for granted both as a normal empirical fact and as the norm for modern European societies. The concept of modern public religion was still too dissonant, and religious revivals elsewhere could simply be explained or rather explained away as the rise of fundamentalism in not yet modern societies. But recently, in the last four to five years at least, there has been a noticeable change in attitude and attention to religion throughout Europe. Every second week one learns of a new major conference on religion being planned somewhere in Europe, or of the establishment of some newly funded research center or research project on 'religion and politics' or on 'immigration and religion' or on 'religion and violence' or on 'inter-religious dialogue'. None of this would have been thinkable even a decade ago. Most tellingly, there are very few voices in Europe today simply defending the old thesis, unrevised and unadorned, that religion is and ought to remain an exclusively private affair. Even the self-assured French *laïcité* is on the defensive and ready to make some concessions. The question is no longer whether religion will remain private, but how to contain the de-privatization of religion within acceptable limits, so that it does not present a major threat to our modern secular liberal democratic structures.

The terrorist attacks of September 11th, successive terrorist bombings in London and Madrid, and the many foiled attempts elsewhere, as well as the resonance of the discourse of the clash of civilizations in light of the 'global war on terror' pursued by the Bush administration and the ongoing wars in Afghanistan and Iraq – all of these developments have certainly played an important role in focusing European attention on issues of religion. But it would be a big mistake to attribute this new attention solely or even mainly to the rise of so-called Islamic fundamentalism and the threats and challenges that *jihādist* terrorism poses to the West and particularly to Europe. Internal European transformations contribute equally to the new public interest in religion. General processes of globalization, the global growth of transnational migration and the very process of European integration, particularly the possibility of Turkey joining the European Union, are presenting crucial challenges not only to the European model of the national welfare state but also to the different kinds of religious–secular and church–state settlements that the various European countries had achieved in post-World War II Europe, as well as to the civilizational identity of Europe.

My own analysis of the de-privatization of religion tried to contain, at least normatively, public religions within the public sphere of civil society, without allowing them to spill over into political society or the democratic state. Today I must recognize my own modern Western secular prejudices and the particular hermeneutic Catholic and 'ecclesiastical' perspective on religion that I adopted in my comparative analysis of the relations between church, state, nation and civil society in Western Catholic and Protestant societies. The moment one adopts a global comparative perspective, one must admit that the de-privatization of religion is unlikely to be contained within the public sphere of civil society, within the territorial boundaries of the nation-state, and within the constitutional premises of ecclesiastical disestablishment and juridical separation of church and state. We need to go beyond the secularist discourse of separation and beyond the public sphere of civil society, in order to address the real issues of religious democratic politics across the world. Alfred Stepan's model of the 'twin tolerations' offers in my view one of the most fruitful approaches.

The 'secular' nature of the modern European state and the 'secular' character of European democracy serve as one of the foundational myths of the contemporary European identity. There is a frequently heard secular European narrative, usually offered as a genealogical explanation and as a normative justification for the secular character of European democracy, that has the following schematic structure: Once upon a time in medieval Europe there was, as is typical of pre-modern societies, a fusion of religion and politics. But this fusion, under the new conditions of religious diversity, extreme sectarianism, and conflict created by the Protestant Reformation, led to the nasty, brutish and long-lasting religious wars of the early modern era that left European societies in ruin. The secularization of the state was the felicitous response to this catastrophic experience, which apparently has indelibly marked the collective memory of European societies. The Enlightenment did the rest. Modern Europeans learned to separate religion, politics and science. Most importantly, they learned to tame the religious passions and to dissipate obscurantist fanaticism by banishing religion to a protected private sphere, while establishing an open, liberal, secular public sphere where freedom of expression and public reason dominate. Those are the favorable secular foundations upon which democracy grows and thrives. As the tragic stories of violent religious conflicts around the world show, the unfortunate de-privatization of religion and its return to the public sphere will need to be managed carefully if one is to avoid undermining those fragile foundations.

But how 'secular' are the European states? How tall and solid are the 'walls of separation' between national state and national church and between religion and politics across Europe? To what extent should one attribute the indisputable success of post-World War II Western European democracies to the triumph of secularization over religion, as is usually done? If one looks at the reality of 'really existing' European democracies rather than at the official secularist discourse, it becomes obvious that most European states are by no means strictly secular nor do they tend to live up to the myth of secular neutrality.[1]

Indeed, France appears to be the only Western European state that is officially and proudly 'secular,' that is, that defines itself and its democracy as regulated constitutionally by the principles of *laïcité*. By contrast, there are several European countries with long-standing democracies that have maintained established churches. They include England and Scotland within the United Kingdom, and all the Scandinavian Lutheran countries – Denmark, Norway, Iceland, Finland and, until the year 2000, Sweden. Of the new democracies, Greece has also maintained the establishment of the Greek Orthodox Church. This means that, with the exception of the Catholic Church, which paradoxically has eschewed establishment in every recent (post-1974) transition to democracy in Southern Europe (Portugal, Spain) and in Eastern Europe (Poland, Hungary, Czech Republic, Slovakia, Slovenia, Croatia), every other major branch of Christianity (Anglican, Presbyterian, Lutheran, Orthodox) is officially established somewhere in Europe, without apparently jeopardizing democracy in those countries.

Since on the other hand there are many historical examples of European states that have been secular and non-democratic, the Soviet-type communist regimes being the most obvious case, one can, therefore, safely conclude that the strict secular separation of church and state appears to be neither a sufficient nor necessary condition for democracy, despite the frequently repeated cautionary warnings directed didactically at non-Western cultures undergoing processes of democratization, as if implying 'do as we believe, not as we actually do'.

Indeed, one could advance the proposition that, of the two clauses of the First Amendment to the US Constitution, 'free exercise' of religion, rather than 'no establishment', is the one that appears to be a necessary condition for democracy. One cannot have democracy without freedom of religion. In fact, 'free exercise' stands out as a normative democratic principle in itself. The 'no-establishment' principle, by contrast, is defensible and necessary only as a means to free exercise and to equal rights. Disestablishment becomes politically necessary for democracy wherever an established religion claims monopoly over the state territory, impedes the free exercise of religion, and undermines the equal rights of all citizens. This was the case of the Catholic Church before it officially recognized the principle of 'freedom of religion' as an unalienable individual right. In other words, secularist

---

[1] In the following section I am going to rely heavily on Alfred Stepan's analysis of the 'Twin Tolerations' and democracy, particularly on the section 'Separation of Church and State? Secularism? Some Empirical Caveats', in Stepan 2001 (218–25).

principles per se may be defensible on instrumental grounds, as a means to the end of free exercise, but not as an intrinsically liberal democratic principle in itself.

Alfred Stepan has pointed out how the most important empirical analytical theories of democracy, from Robert Dahl to Juan Linz, do not include secularism or strict separation as one of the institutional requirements for democracy, as prominent normative liberal theories such as those of John Rawls or Bruce Ackerman tend to. As an alternative to secularist principles or norms, Stepan has proposed the model of the 'twin tolerations', which he describes as 'the minimal boundaries of freedom of action that must somehow be crafted for political institutions *vis-à-vis* religious authorities, and for religious individuals and groups *vis-à-vis* political institutions' (Stepan 2001: 213). Religious authorities must 'tolerate' the autonomy of democratically elected governments without claiming constitutionally privileged prerogatives to mandate or to veto public policy. Democratic political institutions, in turn, must 'tolerate' the autonomy of religious individuals and groups not only to complete freedom to worship privately, but also to advance publicly their values in civil society and to sponsor organizations and movements in political society, as long as they do not violate democratic rules and adhere to the rule of law. Within this framework of mutual autonomy, Stepan concludes, 'there can be an extraordinarily broad range of concrete patterns of religion–state relations in political systems that would meet our minimal definition of democracy' (ibid.: 217).

This is precisely the case empirically across Europe. Between the two extremes of French *laïcité* and Nordic Lutheran establishment, there is a whole range of very diverse patterns of church–state relations, in education, media, health and social services, and so on, that constitute very 'unsecular' entanglements, such as the consociational formula of pillarization in the Netherlands, or the corporatist official state recognition of the Protestant and Catholic churches in Germany (as well as of the Jewish community in some *Länder*).[2] One could of course retort that European societies are de facto so secularized and, as a consequence, what remains of religion has become so temperate that both constitutional establishment and the various institutional church–state entanglements are as a matter of fact innocuous, if not completely irrelevant. But one should remember that the drastic secularization of most Western European societies came after the consolidation of democracy, not before, and therefore it would be incongruent to present not just the secularization of the state and of politics, but also the secularization of society as a condition for democracy.

---

[2] John Madeley has developed a tripartite measure of church–state relations, which he calls the TAO of European management and regulation of religion–state relations by the use of Treasure (T: for financial and property connections), Authority (A: for the exercise of states' powers of command) and Organization (O: for the effective intervention of state bodies in the religious sphere). According to his measurement all European states score positively on at least one of these scales, most states score positively on two of them, and over one-third (16 out of 45 states) score positively on all three (Madeley 2007).

In fact, at one time or another most continental European societies developed confessional religious parties that played a crucial role in the democratization of those societies. Even those confessional parties that initially emerged as anti-liberal and at least ideologically as anti-democratic, as was the case with most Catholic parties in the 19th century, ended up playing a very important role in the democratization of their societies. This is the paradox of Christian Democracy so well analyzed by Stathis Kalyvas (1996). Catholic political mobilization emerged almost everywhere as a counter-revolutionary reaction against Liberalism and its anti-clerical assault on the Catholic Church. Political and even social Catholicism was in many respects fundamentalist, intransigent and theocratic. Focusing on Catholic ideology and doctrine, one was bound to conclude that Catholicism and democracy were indeed antithetical and irreconcilable, as the liberal and Protestant anti-Catholic discourse never tired of stressing throughout the 19th century (Casanova 2005). Yet, somehow, the dynamics of electoral competition led to the transformation of Catholic parties everywhere. Those parties, in turn, by embracing democratic politics made a fundamental contribution to the consolidation of democracy in their respective countries. With important variations the similar story repeats itself in Germany, Austria, Holland, Belgium and Italy, the countries where Christian Democracy became dominant after World War II.

Kalyvas's conclusions concerning the role of non-liberal Catholic parties and, as he also points out, the role of similarly non-liberal Social-Democratic parties in the democratization of Western European societies, are poignantly relevant at a time when the alleged incompatibility of Islam and democracy and the supposedly anti-democratic nature of Muslim parties are so frequently and publicly debated. Equally forgotten is the fact that the initial project of a European Union was fundamentally a Christian-Democratic project, sanctioned by the Vatican, at a time of a general religious revival in post-World War II Europe, in the geopolitical context of the Cold War when 'the free world' and 'Christian civilization' had become synonymous. Indeed, ruling or prominent Christian Democrats in the six signatory countries of the Treaty of Rome – Germany, France, Italy and Benelux – played a leading role in the initial process of European integration. But this is a history that secular Europeans, proud of having outgrown a religious past, from which they feel liberated, would apparently prefer not to remember.

When Europeans today observe with dismay different types of political religious mobilization elsewhere throughout the world, whether Muslim political parties in Turkey, religious mobilization in American electoral politics, or religious nationalism in India, to give some prominent examples, rather than remembering their own recent past recognizing in them typical historical European patterns that have become globalized along with many other aspects of European modernity, they prefer to view these phenomena as manifestations of the otherness of non-Western cultures that have not yet learned to live up to the standards of European secular modernity, or alternatively they prefer to recall the forgotten histories of their own religious wars centuries ago, finding solace in the fact that they at least have been able to overcome such irrational religious passions.

The Challenge of 'Confessional De-territorialization'

The most astounding aspect of the European secular foundational myth is the often repeated assertion that the secularization of the European state system was a felicitous response, a kind of positive learning from the catastrophic experience of confessional inter-religious warfare. It should be obvious that such a historical narrative, grounded in the self-understanding of the Enlightenment critique of religion, is indeed a historical myth. The religious wars of Early Modern Europe and particularly the Thirty Years' War (1618–48) did not ensue, at least not immediately, into the secular state, but rather into the confessional one. The principle *cuius regio eius religio*, established first at the Peace of Augsburg and reiterated at the Treaty of Westphalia, is not the formative standard of the modern secular democratic state, but rather that of the modern confessional territorial absolutist state. Nowhere in Europe did religious conflict lead to the secularization of state and politics, but rather to the confessionalization of the state and to the territorialization of religions and peoples. Moreover, this early modern dual pattern of confessionalization and territorialization was already well established before the religious wars and even before the Protestant Reformation. The Spanish Catholic state under the Catholic Kings serves as the first paradigmatic model of state confessionalization and religious territorialization. The expulsion of Spanish Jews and Muslims who refused to convert to Catholicism is the logical consequence of such a dynamic of state formation. Ethno-religious cleansing, in this respect, stands at the very origin of the early modern European state.

From such a perspective, the so-called 'religious wars' could also more appropriately be called the wars of early modern European state formation. Religious minorities caught in the wrong confessional territory were offered not secular toleration, much less freedom of religion, but the 'freedom' to emigrate. The Polish–Lithuanian Commonwealth, with its multi-confessional Catholic, Protestant-Lutheran and Orthodox ruling aristocracies, offers the unique exception of a major early modern state that resisted the general European dynamic of confessionalization and offered refuge to religious minorities and radical sects from all over Europe, well before North America and other overseas colonies offered a safer haven.

The pattern of confessionalization of European peoples, states and nations, and the pattern of territorialization that it entails, has lasted well into the 20th century. In many respects it is still present today throughout Europe despite its advanced secularization. The territorial confessional boundaries between Catholic and Protestant, Lutheran, Calvinist, Presbyterian and Anglican communities have remained basically stable until today, and peoples' identities throughout Europe remain confessional even after they cease believing. Thus, Danièle Hervieu-Léger's characterization 'belonging without believing' captures equally well the European religious–secular situation, and nowhere more so than in Nordic Lutheran Europe.

Denmark offers a perfect example. It combines one of the lowest rates of regular church attendance – in the single digits, as low as East Germany, and in this respect it is one of the most secular societies of Europe – with one of the highest rates of membership affiliation in the national established church and one of the highest rates of participation in religious rites of passage such as baptism, confirmation and burial of the dead, almost as high as those one finds in much more religious societies such as Catholic Poland or Ireland. It is not only that atheists in Denmark, like Professor Sven-Eric Liedman from neighboring Sweden, may recognize themselves to be Lutheran atheists, as a kind of cultural negative photograph that they unavoidably carry in their minds. More striking is the fact that, judging from the numbers of self-declared atheists and of self-declared affiliated members of the Danish Lutheran Church, at least one-third of Danish atheists still claim to be members of the Danish Church. One may retort that this is just the innocuous expression of an implicit national confessional identity, a residual manifestation of a long historical pattern of fusion of church, state and nation. But this is precisely my point, that this is a deeply sedimented European pattern of confessional territorialization that may not be so innocuous historically if one considers the serious problems that modern and supposedly secular nationalism throughout Europe had with the 'Jewish question' and if one considers the apparent problems that European societies have in integrating Muslim immigrants today.

This is the fundamental political challenge that Islam represents for European societies as well as for European secular and religious confessional identities today. Not the geopolitical territorial clash of confessional civilizations depicted by Samuel Huntington, but rather the challenges that both Muslim immigrants within Europe and a modern Muslim democratic Turkey hoping to join the European Union present to the European pattern of confessional territorialization as well as to the pattern of European secularization. Western European societies are deeply secular societies, shaped by the hegemonic knowledge regime of secularism. As liberal democratic societies, they tolerate and respect individual religious freedom. But due to the pressure towards the privatization of religion, which among European societies has become a taken-for-granted characteristic of the self-definition of a modern secular society, those societies have a much greater difficulty in recognizing some legitimate role for religion in public life and in the organization and mobilization of collective group identities.

Muslim organized collective identities and their public representations become a source of anxiety not only because of their religious otherness as a non-Christian and non-European religion, but more importantly because of their religiousness itself as the other of European secularity. In this context, the temptation to identify Islam and fundamentalism becomes the more pronounced. Islam, by definition, becomes the other of Western secular modernity. For that very reason, the prospect of Turkey's joining the European Union generates much greater anxiety among Europeans, Christian and post-Christian alike. The paradox and the quandary for modern secular Europeans, who have shed their traditional historical Christian identities in a rapid and drastic process of secularization that has coincided with the very success of the process of European integration, and who therefore identify European modernity with secularization, is that they observe with some apprehension the reverse process in Turkey. The more 'modern', or at least democratic, Turkish politics become, the more publicly Muslim and less secularist they also tend to turn out to be.

In its determination to join the EU, Turkey is adamantly staking its claim to be, or its right to become, a fully European country economically and politically, while simultaneously fashioning its own model of Muslim cultural modernity. It is this very claim to be simultaneously a modern European and a culturally Muslim country that baffles European civilizational identities, secular and Christian alike. It contradicts both the definition of a Christian Europe and the definition of a secular Europe. Turkey's claim to European membership becomes an irritant precisely because it forces Europeans to reflexively and openly confront the ambiguities and contradictions in their own civilizational identity.

Moreover, the question of the integration of Turkey in the EU is inevitably intertwined, implicitly if not explicitly, with the question of the failed integration of Muslim immigrants. What makes 'the immigrant question' particularly thorny in Europe, and entwined inextricably with 'the Turkish question', is the fact that, in continental Europe at least, until very recently immigration and Islam have been almost synonymous. This entails a superimposition of different dimensions of 'otherness' that exacerbates issues of boundaries, accommodation and incorporation. The immigrant, the religious, the racial and the socio-economic disprivileged 'other' all tend to coincide. Moreover, all those dimensions of 'otherness' now become superimposed upon Islam, so that Islam becomes the utterly 'other'. Anti-immigrant xenophobic naturism, the conservative defense of Christian culture and civilization, secularist anti-religious prejudices, liberal–feminist critiques of Muslim patriarchal fundamentalism, and the fear of Islamist terrorist networks, are being fused indiscriminately throughout Europe into a uniform anti-Muslim discourse that practically precludes the kind of mutual accommodation between immigrant groups and host societies that is necessary for successful immigrant incorporation.

I want to insist, however, that secularist anti-religious prejudices make the problem of Muslim immigrant integration particularly difficult. It is indeed astounding to observe how widespread is the view throughout Europe that religion is intolerant and creates conflict. According to the 1998 ISSP public opinion survey, the overwhelming majority of Europeans, practically over two-thirds of the population in every Western European country, holds the view that religion is 'intolerant' (Greeley 2003: 78, Table 5.2). Since people are unlikely to expressly recognize their own intolerance, one can assume that in expressing such an opinion Europeans are thinking of somebody else's 'religion' or, alternatively, present a selective retrospective memory of their own past religion, which fortunately they consider to have outgrown. It is even more telling that a majority of the population in every Western European country, with the significant exception of Norway and Sweden, shares the view that 'religion creates conflict'. Interestingly enough, the

Danes distinguish themselves clearly from their fellow Lutheran Scandinavians in both respects. They score higher than any other European country, as high as 86 per cent, on the view that religion creates conflict, and score the second highest (79 per cent) after the Swiss (81 per cent) on the belief that religion is intolerant. Along with most other former communist countries, the Poles score well below the Western European average on both issues, which is striking given the widespread perception of Polish Catholicism as 'intolerant' and the fact that religion in Poland has in fact been a source of conflict.

What would seem obvious is that such a widespread negative view of 'religion' cannot possibly be grounded empirically on the collective historical experience of European societies in the 20th century or on the actual personal experience of most contemporary Europeans. It can plausibly be explained, however, as a secular construct that has the function of positively differentiating modern secular Europeans from 'the religious other', either from pre-modern religious Europeans or from contemporary non-European religious people, particularly from Muslims. Most striking is the view of 'religion' in the abstract as the source of violent conflict, given the actual historical experience of most European societies in the 20th century. 'The European short century', from 1914 to 1989, using Eric Hobsbawm's apt characterization, was indeed one of the most violent, bloody and genocidal centuries in the history of humanity. But none of the horrible massacres – not the senseless slaughter of millions of young Europeans in the trenches of World War I; nor the countless millions of victims of Bolshevik and communist terror through Revolution, Civil War, collectivizations campaigns, the Great Famine in Ukraine, the repeated cycles of Stalinist terror and the Gulag; nor the most unfathomable of all, the Nazi Holocaust and the global conflagration of World War II, culminating in the nuclear bombing of Hiroshima and Nagasaki –, none of those terrible conflicts can be said to have been caused by religious fanaticism and intolerance. All of them were rather the product of modern secular ideologies.

Yet contemporary Europeans obviously prefer to selectively forget the more inconvenient recent memories of secular ideological conflict, retrieving instead the long-forgotten memories of the religious wars of early modern Europe to make sense of the religious conflicts they see today proliferating around the world and increasingly threatening them. Rather than acknowledging the common structural contexts of modern state formation, inter-state geopolitical conflicts, modern nationalism and the political mobilization of ethno-cultural and religious identities, processes central to modern European history that became globalized through the European colonial expansion, Europeans prefer seemingly to attribute those conflicts to 'religion' – that is, to religious fundamentalism and to the fanaticism and intolerance that are supposedly intrinsic to 'pre-modern' religion, an atavistic residue that modern secular enlightened Europeans have fortunately left behind. One may suspect that the function of such a selective historical memory is to safeguard the perception of the progressive achievements of Western secular modernity, offering a self-validating justification of the secular separation of religion and politics as the condition for modern liberal democratic politics.

The Challenge of Global Denominationalism

Processes of globalization are challenging simultaneously the patterns of European secularization as well as the patterns of confessional territorialization. Trans-societal migrations and the world religions, at times separately but often in conjunction with each other, have always served as important carriers of processes of globalization. In a certain sense, one could argue that the successive waves of migration of *homo sapiens* out of Africa some fifty thousand years ago and the subsequent settlements throughout the globe constitute the point of departure of the process of globalization. But these migrations had no subjective dimension of reflexive consciousness and can only now be reconstructed objectively thanks to advances in DNA and other scientific technologies. By contrast, the subjective dimension of imagining a single humanity sharing the same global space and the same global time was first anticipated in all universalistic world religions. Yet, these imaginary anticipations, while serving as a precondition for the civilizational expansion of the world religions, lacked a structural, that is, objective and material global base.

Until very recently, the civilizational *oikoumenē* of all world religions had very clear territorial limits, set both by the very world regimes in which those religions were civilizationally and thus territorially embedded, and by the geographically circumscribed limitations of the existing means of communication. What constitutes the truly novel aspect of the present global condition is precisely the fact that all world religions can be reconstituted for the first time truly as de-territorialized global imagined communities, detached from the civilizational settings in which they have been traditionally embedded. Paraphrasing Arjun Appadurai's image of 'modernity at large', one could say that the world religions, through the linking of electronic mass media and mass migration, are being reconstituted as de-territorialized global religions 'at large.'

For that very reason, Huntington's thesis of the impending clash of civilizations is simultaneously illuminating of the present global condition and profoundly misleading. It is illuminating insofar as it was one of the first prominent voices calling attention to the increasing relevance of civilizations and civilizational identities in the emerging global order and in global conflicts. But it is also profoundly misleading inasmuch as it still conceives of civilizations as territorial geopolitical units, akin to superpowers, having some world religion as its cultural core.

This process of dissociation of territory, religion and civilizational culture is by no means uniform or homogeneous across world religions and civilizations; indeed, it encounters much resistance on the part of states that still aspire not only to the monopolistic control of the means of violence but also to the administrative regulation of religious groups and cultural identities over their territories, as well as on the part of 'churches', in the broad Weberian sense of the term, as religious institutions or as religious imagined communities that claim or aspire to religious monopoly over their civilizational or national territories.

There is a fundamental tension in the modern world between two well-recognized principles. There is on the one hand the principle of the inalienable right of the individual person to freedom of conscience and therefore to freedom of religion, but also to freedom of conversion. This principle has assumed in all modern democratic societies the form of an unquestioned universal human right. Nobody should be coerced or forced to believe or not to believe any particular religious doctrine. Consequently, everybody has also the right to believe or not to believe any particular religious doctrine, including the right to conversion to any particular religion. On the other hand, there is also the increasing recognition of the collective rights of peoples to protect and preserve their traditions and their cultures from colonial, imperialist and predatory practices. Such recognition is enshrined primarily in United Nations documents on the rights of indigenous peoples. But it could easily be turned into a general principle of the reciprocal rights and duties of all peoples of the world to respect each others' traditions and cultures, constituting the basis of what could be called an emerging global denominationalism.

Actually, one finds practically everywhere similar tensions between the protectionist impulse to claim religious monopoly over national or civilizational territories and the ecumenical impulse to present one's own particular religion as the response to the universal needs of global humanity. Transnational migrations and the emergence of diasporas of all world religions beyond their civilizational territories make this tension visible everywhere. Of course, neither transnational migrations nor the resulting diasporas is a novel phenomenon per se. It is the general, almost universal character of the phenomenon under novel global conditions that makes it particularly relevant for all world religions.

For obvious historical reasons this process of dissociation of world religion, civilizational identity and geopolitical territory is most pronounced in the so-called 'Christian' West, but it is emerging as a general global phenomenon. We are accustomed to think of Western Christianity as a 2000-year-old civilization, but sociologically speaking the core institutions and social forms of Western European Christendom that form one of the foundations of modern Western civilization are only one thousand years old: the first five hundred years as Medieval European Christendom centered around the Papacy and the next five hundred years as modern Western Christianity both in its post-Reformation multi-denominational forms and in its expanded Western colonial and post-colonial forms. As we are entering the third millennium, however, we are witnessing the end of hegemonic European Christianity due to a dual process of advanced secularization in post-Christian Europe and the increasing globalization of a de-territorialized and de-centered Christianity. Thus, the thousand-year-old association between Christianity and Western European civilization is coming to an end. Western Europe is less and less the core of Christian civilization, and Christianity in its most dynamic forms today is less and less European or even Western.

The transplantation of Western Christianity beyond its European territories was at first a function of the European colonial expansion. European Christianity became re-territorialized overseas by displacing either the natives or their religions, in Catholic Latin America, in the Philippines, in Catholic Quebec, in Protestant North America, and in Afrikaans (Dutch Calvinist) South Africa, to name only the most obvious cases. Irish immigrants, themselves colonized by the British, further transplanted Catholicism throughout the Anglo-Saxon colonial world. Other European Catholic immigrants, Germans and Italians, Poles and other Slavs, would follow. But until the 20th century overseas Catholicism had been primarily a transplanted European institution. Today, however, world Catholicism has been reconstituted as a global religious regime 'at large' under papal supremacy.

Protestant Christianity is undergoing similar transformations throughout the globe. Following the Reformation and the consolidation of the European system of states, all the Protestant churches underwent similar processes of national territorialization. The dissident sects and all the branches of the English Reformation found a new home in North America. If the territorial parish is the naturalized form of the local church, the congregation is the characteristic form of the local sect. In America, the sectarian principle of voluntary, individualistic, religious association became generalized into the 'denomination'. It is the pluralist denominational structure of the American religious subsystem that transforms all religions in America, Christian and non-Christian alike, irrespective of their origins, doctrinal claims and ecclesiastical identities, into de-territorialized denominations. At the local level, all adopt the congregational form of a voluntary association.

As in the Americas, the growth of Christianity throughout Africa and Asia could have been viewed at first as simply the transplantation of European Christianity throughout the colonial world. But colonial Christianity soon underwent diverse processes of indigenization and acculturation. Indeed, it is in the religious sphere where it is most evident that to reduce cultural globalization in all its many-sided complexities to Westernization is simply short-sighted.

If the transformation of contemporary Catholicism illustrates the opportunities that the process of globalization offers to a transnational religious regime with a highly centralized structure and an imposing transnational network of human, institutional and material resources, which therefore feels confident in its ability to thrive in a relatively open global system of religious regimes, contemporary Pentecostalism may serve to illustrate the equally favorable opportunities that globalization offers to a highly decentralized religion, with no historical links to tradition and no territorial roots or identity, and that therefore can make itself at home anywhere in the globe where the Spirit moves.

We may take Brazil as a paradigmatic example. The transnational character of Brazilian Pentecostalism is inscribed in its very beginnings. It arrived from the United States as early as 1910, just a few years after the Azusa Street Revival, brought by European immigrants, by an Italian and two Swedish missionaries who had encountered Pentecostalism in Chicago. Yet almost immediately Pentecostalism assumed an indigenous Brazilian form. In this sense, Brazilian Pentecostalism represents a dual process of de-territorialization: North-American Christianity is de-territorialized by taking indigenous roots in Brazil, a Catholic territory, that therefore leads to the de-territorialization of Catholicism from Brazil.

This is the most important consequence of the explosive growth of Pentecostalism throughout Latin America. Latin America has ceased being Catholic territory, even if Catholicism continues to be for the foreseeable future the majority religion of all Latin American countries. It is estimated that currently two-thirds of all Latin American Protestants are Pentecostals–Charismatics. Latin America, particularly Brazil, has become in a very short time a world center of Pentecostal Christianity, wherefrom it has now begun to radiate in all directions, including back into the United States.

The growth of Pentecostal Christianity in sub-Saharan Africa (Ghana, Nigeria, Zimbabwe, South Africa) is no less explosive. Moreover, African Pentecostalism is as local, indigenous and autonomous as its Latin American counterpart. The same could be said about Pentecostalism in Korea or in China. Korean missionaries, for instance, are becoming ubiquitous in evangelical missions throughout Asia. Indeed, Pentecostalism's expansion must be seen as a multi-source diffusion of parallel developments across the globe. Pentecostalism is not a religion with a particular territorial center like the Mormon Church, which is rapidly gaining worldwide diffusion. Nor is it a transnational religious regime like Catholicism with global reach. As Paul Freston has pointed out, 'new churches are local expressions of a global culture, characterized by parallel invention, complex diffusion and international networks with multilateral flows.' Pentecostalism may be said to be the first truly global religion. Moreover, Pentecostalism is simultaneously global and local. In this respect, it is historically unique and unprecedented. It is the historically first and paradigmatic case of a de-centered and de-territorialized global culture.

Similar illustrations could be offered from other branches of Christianity and from other world religions. The dynamic core of Anglicanism no longer resides in post-Christian England. But today, immigrants from all over the British post-colonial world are reviving Anglicanism in secular England. The Patriarch of Constantinople is re-emerging, at least symbolically, as a de-territorialized global center of Eastern Christianity, in competition with the Moscow patriarchate and with the other territorial autocephalous national Orthodox churches. For the world religions globalization offers to all the opportunity to become for the first time truly world religions – that is, global –, but also the threat of de-territorialization. The opportunities are greatest for those world religions like Islam and Buddhism that always had a transnational structure. The threat is greatest for those embedded in civilizational territories like Islam and Hinduism. But through worldwide migrations they are also becoming global and de-territorialized. Indeed, their diasporas are becoming dynamic centers for their global transformation affecting their civilizational homes.

When it comes to Islam, we in the West are naturally obsessed with state Islamism and *khilafist jihādism* as the two contemporary dominant forms of globalized Islam. Yet the majoritarian currents of transnational Islam today and the ones likely to have the greatest impact on the future transformation of Islam are transnational networks and movements of Muslim renewal, equally disaffected from state Islamism and transnational *jihādism*. They constitute the networks of a loosely organized and pluralistic transnational *ummah*, or global Muslim civil society: from the 'evangelical' Tablighi Jama'at, a faith movement highly active throughout the Muslim world and in Muslim diasporas, whose annual conferences in India represent the second largest world gathering of Muslims after the *hajj*, and other transnational *dawa* networks, to the neo-Sufist Fethullah Gülen's educational network, active throughout Turkey, Turkish diasporas and the Turkic republics of Central Asia, and other Sufi brotherhoods such as the Mourides of West Africa who have also expanded their transnational networks into the Muslim diasporas of Europe and North America. One could make a similar analysis of the formation of a global Hindu *ummah* linking the civilizational home, 'Mother India', with old diasporic colonial Hindu communities across the former British Empire from South East Asia, to South Africa, to the Caribbean, and with new immigrant Hindu communities throughout the West, from the British Isles, to North America, and to Australia.

It is this proliferation of de-territorialized transnational global imagined communities, encompassing the old world religions as well as many new forms of hybrid globalized religions such as the Bahais, Moonies, Hare Krishnas, Afro-American religions, Falun Gong, and so on, that I call the emerging global denominationalism. To a certain extent, this global denominationalism is most clearly visible in the new global immigrant societies of North America, the United States and Canada. American religious pluralism is expanding and incorporating all the world religions in the same way as it previously incorporated the religions of the old European immigrants. A complex process of mutual accommodation is taking place. Like Catholicism and Judaism before, other world religions, Islam, Hinduism, Buddhism are being 'Americanized' and in the process they are transforming American religion, while the religious diasporas in America are simultaneously serving as catalysts for the transformation of the old religions in their civilizational homes, in the same way that American Catholicism had an impact upon the transformation of world Catholicism, and American Judaism has transformed world Judaism.

America is bound to become 'the first new global society' made up of all world religions and civilizations, at a time when religious civilizational identities are regaining prominence at the global stage. At the very same moment that political scientists like Samuel Huntington are announcing the impending clash of civilizations in global politics, a new experiment in intercivilizational encounters and accommodation between all the world religions is taking place at home. Indeed, this emerging pattern of global denominationalism within the United States presents a challenge not only to Huntington's vision of the clash of civilizations but also to his American nativist anti-immigrant and anti-multiculturalist posture, which tries to protect the Western civilizational purity of the United States from civilizational, particularly Latino-Mexican, hybridization.

But the pattern of global denominationalism presents equally frontal challenges to European models of secular cosmopolitanism. Cosmopolitanism is used here in the broad sense of any worldview that envisions the future global order as a single relatively homogeneous and unified global economic, political and cultural system or as a single human 'universal civilization'. To a certain extent, most theories of globalization share similar cosmopolitan assumptions insofar as they assume that economic and technological globalization will determine the shape of global society and of global culture. Though more complex, Luhmannian theories of 'world society' are based on similar assumptions.

Cosmopolitanism builds upon developmental theories of modernization that envision social change as a global expansion of Western modernity, which is understood not as the hegemonic expansion of a particular social formation, but as a universal process of human development. In most cosmopolitan accounts, religion either does not exist, or it is simply 'invisible' in Thomas Luckmann's sense of the term of being an individualized and privatized form of salvation or quest for meaning that is irrelevant to the functioning of the primary institutions of modern society. In its collective dimension, religion is simply reduced to just another form of cultural group identity. If and when religion emerges in the public sphere and has to be taken seriously, it is usually branded either as anti-modern fundamentalism resisting processes of secularization, or as a form of traditionalist collective identity reaction to the threat of globalization. In other words, religion in the eyes of cosmopolitan elites is either irrelevant or reactive. Indeed, when it comes to religion all forms of cosmopolitanism share at least implicitly the basic tenets of the theory of secularization that the social sciences and modern liberal political ideologies have inherited from the Enlightenment critique of religion. Cosmopolitanism remains a faithful child of the European Enlightenment.

It is time to revise our teleological conceptions of a global cosmopolitan secular modernity against which we can characterize the religious 'other' as 'fundamentalist'. It is time to make room for more complex, nuanced and reflexive categories that will help us to understand better the already-emerging global system of multiple modernities. As long as we maintain this concept of a single cosmopolitan modernity as a general process of secular differentiation, indeed as a normative global project, we are compelled to characterize all forms of religion we cannot accept as our own as threatening 'fundamentalism', and we become ourselves unwittingly partisans in a supposedly worldwide secular–religious conflict perhaps even helping to turn the so-called 'clash of civilizations' into a self-fulfilling prophecy. What is at stake, ultimately, is the recognition of the irremediable plurality of universalisms and the multiplicity of modernities – namely, that every universalism and every modernity is particularistic. We are moving from a condition of competing particularist universalisms to a new condition of global denominational contextualism.

Cosmopolitanism, like the theories of modernization of the 1960s, is still based on a rigid dichotomous contraposition of tradition and modernity, assuming that the more of the one leads to the less of the other. But in fact, it is well recognized today that societies can become ever more modern while simultaneously reproducing or reconstructing their traditions, or inventing new ones. The clash of civilizations, by contrast, emphasizes the essential continuity between tradition and modernity. Western modernity is assumed to be continuous with the Western tradition. As other civilizations modernize, rather then becoming ever more like the West they will also maintain an essential continuity with their respective traditions. Thus the inevitable clash of civilizations, as all modern societies basically continue their diverse and mostly incommensurable traditions.

The multiple modernities position rejects both the notion of a modern radical break with traditions and that of an essential modern continuity with tradition. All traditions and civilizations are radically transformed in the processes of modernization, but they also have the possibility of shaping in particular ways the institutionalization of modern traits. The model of *aggiornamento* is perhaps a more adequate image of the dynamic and reciprocal relations between tradition and modernity. Traditions are forced to respond to and adjust to modern conditions, but in the process of reformulating their traditions for modern contexts they also help to shape the particular forms of modernity. No modern culture is simply a continuation of pre-modern traditions, otherwise there would be no common modernity and no common modern traits. But modernity is not simply a homogeneous formation to which traditions have simply to adapt. There is a continuous dynamic relationship whereby multiple traditions help to shape multiple modernities while modernity radically alters all traditions.

Indeed, all world religions are forced to respond to the global expansion of modernity by reformulating their traditions in an attempt to fashion their own particular civilizational versions of modernity. Moreover, they are responding not only to the global challenge of secular modernity but also to their mutual and reciprocal challenges, as they all undergo multiple processes of *aggiornamento* and come to compete with one another in the emerging global system of religions. This is what I would call the emerging global denominationalism.

I repeat, what constitutes the truly novel aspect of the present global condition is precisely the fact that all religions, old and new, can be reconstituted for the first time truly as de-territorialized global imagined communities, detached from the civilizational settings in which they have been traditionally embedded. Through the linking of electronic mass media and mass migration, all world religions are being reconstituted as de-territorialized global religions 'at large'. In most instances, moreover, diaspora communities are playing a crucial role in the contemporary reconstitution of all world religions as competing global ummahs. Under conditions of globalization, moreover, the world religions draw not only upon their own traditions but increasingly upon one another. Intercivilizational encounters, cultural imitations and borrowings, diasporic diffusions, hybridity, creolization, and transcultural hyphenations are as much part and parcel of the global present as Western hegemony, cosmopolitan homogenization, religious fundamentalism or the clash of civilizations.

References

Appadurai, A. (1996). *Modernity at Large*, Minneapolis: University of Minnesota Press.

Casanova, J. (1994). *Public Religions in the Modern World*, Chicago, IL: University of Chicago Press.

Casanova, J. (2001). 'Religion, the New Millenium and Globalization', *Sociology of Religion*, 62:4, pp. 415–41.

Casanova, J. (2005). 'Catholic and Muslim Politics in Comparative Perspective', *The Taiwan Journal of Democracy*, 1:2 (December), pp. 89–108.

Greeley, A.M. (2003). *Religion in Europe at the End of the Second Millenium*, New Brunswick, NJ: Transaction Books.

Hervieu-Léger, D. (2000). *Religion as a Chain of Memory*, New Brunswick, NJ: Rutgers University Press.

Hobsbawm, E. (1994). *The Age of Extremes: The Short Twentieth Century, 1914–1991*, New York: Vintage.

Luckmann, T. (1967). *The Invisible Religion*, New York: Macmillan.

Kalyvas, S.N. (1996). *The Rise of Christian Democracy in Europe*, Ithaca, NY: Cornell University Press.

Madeley, J.T.S. (2007). 'Unequally Yoked: The Antinomies of Church–State Separation in Europe and the USA', unpublished paper presented at the Annual Meeting of the American Political Science Association, Chicago, 30 August to 2 September.

Stepan, A. (2001). 'The World's Religious Systems and Democracy: Crafting the "Twin Tolerations"', in *Arguing Comparative Politics*, Oxford: Oxford University Press, pp. 213–53.

Chapter 2
'Fundamentalism' and the Pluralization of Value-Orientations

Peter Beyer

I want to begin by quoting from the lyrics of a song by an artist from Texas, Eliza Gilkyson. The song is called 'Man of God', and its first two verses go like this:

> The cowboy came from out of the west
> With his snakeskin boots and his bulletproof vest
> Gang of goons and his big war chest
> Fortunate son he was doubly blessed
> Corporate cronies and the chiefs of staff
> Bowing to the image of the golden calf
> Startin' up wars in the name of God's son
> Gonna blow us all the way to kingdom come.
> *Refrain:*
> Man of God, man of God
> That ain't the teaching of a man of God
> Man of God, man of God
> That ain't the preaching of a man of God
>
> Coalition of the fearful and the judgmental
> Patricians, politicians, and the fundamentalists
> You never have to tell them how the money's spent
> You never have to tell them where their freedom went
> Homophobes in the high command
> Waitin' for the Rapture like it's Disneyland
> Hide all the bodies from out of view
> Channel all the treasure to the chosen few.
> Man of God …
> (Gilkyson 2005)

The song continues in this vein, using Christian religious symbolism and prophetic style to protest what it sees as political hubris and corruption, economic exploitation, and war. Much could be said about the form it takes, the cultural context out of which it speaks, and the specific references that it makes. Here I want to point to only two aspects that will inform my presentation: first, it styles itself as a *religious* critique of what it sees as the political misuse of religion; second, the central object of this critique is very obviously George W. Bush and, through him, the US Republican establishment and its supporters, including the Christian Right. Both of these features offer entry into an important dimension of the question at issue: what might be the political challenges from religion in the 21st century? And here I note that the phrase is political challenges *from* religion, which I interpret to mean the challenges religion is likely to pose in the realm of politics generally and the state specifically.

The fact that the song styles itself as a religious critique points immediately to the question of what we mean when we speak of the political challenges *from religion*. What do we mean by religion? And which manifestations of that religion are we talking about? These two questions are somewhat interrelated. They point to potentially implicit assumptions that we may or may not be making in this matter.

As regards the first, it seems to me that what is meant primarily is what is often called institutional religion and what I would call systemic religion (Beyer 2006). This very much includes the so-called 'world religions' like Islam, Christianity, Hinduism, Sikhism, Judaism, and the like. It also includes an array of more or less recognized religions like Baha'i or Candomblé; and especially New (and not-so-new) Religious Movements like Aum Shinrikyo, Scientology or Falun Gong. By contrast, what is thereby excluded is the vast panoply of non-institutionalized religious forms, things that sometimes fall under other labels like 'spirituality', 'personal cultivation', 'culture', or even 'popular religion'. Also excluded are social forms that may function like religion (whatever that function may be), but are usually not called religion, forms like nationalism (unless it is religious nationalism), neo-liberalism, 'civil religion', 'implicit religion', the 'religion of globalization', or 'secular humanism'. These religious or quasi-religious forms are not unimportant – quite the contrary – but I do not think that they are the target of our observation in posing the question about political challenges; and, in any case, to include them would be to deprive the question of any contours. Everything imaginable would be included. Summarizing, therefore, what we apparently mean by religion is in fact *the religions*: those social institutions that are generally, most often globally, recognized as 'one of the religions' or that claim such recognition; and ones that in most cases self-identify as such.

Within this range of socially recognized or recognizable religions, the question probably poses itself not so much to some rather than others – for instance, to Christianity, Islam or Aum Shinrikyo, and not to Buddhism, Daoism or Umbanda – but more to certain manifestations or movements within these religions than to others. And here we can refer to Eliza Gilkyson's song again. As concerns religion, the target of her critique is clearly what she and many others call 'fundamentalism', in this case the supposed Christian 'fundamentalism' of George W. Bush and the segments of the American population that he represents. In fact, although it is not explicit, the meaning of the term 'the fundamentalists' seems closely tied to what is objectionable – here, challenging – about them: they translate their religion into the exercise of political power, of government, in a way that results in exploitation, oppression, injustice, delusion, violence and destruction. 'Fundamentalism', one might conclude, is religion that, when it enters the political arena, does harm and generally has negative consequences. In other words, the objectionable or challenging character of the religion is not straightforwardly any religion that seeks to influence politics and government, although that is a point to which I shall turn in due course. It is also, and possibly much more, the content of that religion that is at issue: 'that ain't the teachings of a man of God', implying that a true 'man of God' in such a political position might be acceptable and even laudable; and that the difference would be in the moral consequences. Rather than injustice, oppression and exploitation, the aim would be justice, freedom and solidarity; rather than reckless delusion, war and destruction, the direction would be prudence, clarity and peace. We might then ask, if 'the fundamentalists' represent an unacceptable political challenge from religion, what other sort of religion would pose an acceptable and perhaps even a welcome challenge? Significantly, the possibilities are not nearly as obvious as is the case with those movements and people often labelled 'fundamentalist'; but they do exist. They might just possibly include, for example, Jimmy Carter, another American president who was of the same general religious stripe as George W. Bush, namely an evangelical Protestant. Carter was also a devout president who confessed to having 'sinned in his heart'; he also, probably from the same religious motivation, seriously tried to enforce better human rights standards on some of America's more authoritarian allies, notably the Shah of Iran. (Ironically, what happened in the wake of this policy was the 'best success' of a so-called 'fundamentalist' movement yet achieved, the Khomeinist Islamic Republic of Iran, even though it would be going too far to assume a straightforward causal relation between the two.) If Carter is a less than convincing example, we could perhaps point to Fernando D'Escoto or Ernesto Cardenal, liberation-theological priests who were members of the post-1979 Sandinista government in Nicaragua. And beyond them, we might include Cardinal Jaime Sin of the Philippines or Archbishop Desmond Tutu of South Africa, each in his own way publicly vocal in opposition to oppressive regimes in their respective countries, regimes that came to an end during their tenure. Going back just a little farther in history, the list might also include Mahatma Gandhi and Muhammad Iqbal, respectively instrumental in the political foundation of independent India and Pakistan back in 1947.

With these and perhaps various other possibilities in mind, the question of what sort of religion we are looking at when we ask about the political challenges from religion in the 21st century becomes somewhat ambiguous: is it also what I have elsewhere called the 'liberal' forays of religion into politics (Beyer 1994) that we are concerned about, the Gandhis and the Tutus; or is it the case that, if it weren't for the so-called 'fundamentalists', the Falwells and the Khomeinis, this topic might not even be on the agenda? My sense is that, when we hear the question, images of the latter arise in most of our minds far more easily than of the former, and that this imbalance has something to do with the *content* of the religion that each represents. Assuming I am correct – and I may not be – I want to rephrase the question to ask what it is about 'fundamentalist' *content* that seems to pose such a challenge, and what the prognosis for this challenge might be in the 21st century.

Several possibilities suggest themselves for understanding what precisely the 'fundamentalist' challenge might be.[1] The ones upon which I shall focus include:

1. that it challenges the 'secular' character of the world's dominant systems of power and influence, the state in particular;
2. that it represents certain value-orientations that challenge and contradict other value-orientations (for example, those held by Bush vs. those held by Gilkyson);
3. that its modes of political expression more often than not lead to violence and war;
4. that it challenges cultural, moral and religious pluralism;
5. and finally, that it is an explicitly religious challenge.

These five sorts of possible challenge are of course interrelated. In treating them separately, my aim is to show what is implicit – although probably not intended – in Gilkyson's lyrics: that 'fundamentalism' presents a challenge, not because it represents an anomaly in our contemporary globalized social world, but rather because it is a fundamental expression of that world, an intimate aspect of it. The challenge, in other words, is not so much a 'reaction against' as it is a 'manifestation of' the contemporary global circumstance. Referring to Gilkyson's lyrics, the association of 'fundamentalism' with rapacious capitalism and reckless warmongering is meant to be an organic connection, not an accidental one.

In considering the idea that 'fundamentalism' challenges the secular character of power systems such as the state and law, I think it is important at the outset to be careful not to confuse religious influence on the operation of formally secular institutions with de-secularization in the sense of de-differentiation. The difference is subtle but important. It is one sort of challenge if a prominent religious figure like Benedict XVI tries to pressure governments not to sanction gay and lesbian marriages because homosexuality is against God's will. It is quite another if the Ayatollah Khamane'i or his Guardianship Council vetoes a law passed by the Iranian Majles because it goes against the Qur'an. The former is using political lobbying, which is to say 'secular' means, to try to achieve political ends; his means are really no different from that of a business lobby pressuring a government for tariff protection or tax concessions. Similarly, a religious person acceding to

---

[1] For the sake of brevity I shall continue to use the word 'fundamentalist' to refer to this sort of religious challenge, but it should be understood that the word always appears in scare-quotes because of the pejorative connotations that it usually carries and the arbitrary way in which it is often used. For serious attempts to use the concept in a controlled and consistent fashion, see Marty and Appleby 1991–95; Almond, Appleby et al. 2000.

political power or a political party with a formally religious identity, such as the various Christian Democratic parties in Western Europe, does not by itself already constitute a de-secularizing challenge. Recent history is replete with examples, including the current Prime Minister of Canada and the current majority party in Germany. In the Iranian case, however, Khamane'i and the Guardianship Council are using programmatic religion *as* political process. The basis of their political power is explicitly religion, here Islam; their political decisions take the form of religious action; and both are deemed beyond ordinary, that is, differentiated, political process (cf. Bakhash 1990; Khosrokhavar and Roy 1999; Keddie 2003). That is much more clearly de-secularization.

The Iranian example thereby illustrates one sort of political challenge of 'fundamentalist' religion. Such a *structural* challenge to secularity is, however, only part of the picture; an important part, to be sure, because the current Islamic Republic serves as a kind of shining beacon of how far the de-secularizing political challenge of 'fundamentalism' can go. It is probably one reason for the profound distrust with which an array of 'secularists' treat any explicitly Islamist government, no matter if it is popularly elected. One thinks of the panic – not to mention violent response – that greeted the almost-election of an Islamist FIS government in Algeria in 1992; to some extent the quick rejection of the popularly elected Hamas government in Palestine in 2006; and the ongoing distrust and queasiness that the recent re-election of the AKP government in Turkey once again elicited. What 'secularists' who oppose these democratically elected governments seem at the very least to fear is that, once elected, these governments will 'show their true colours' and undo the political process that they used to attain power, subverting democracy and the 'popular will' to replace it with their version of 'Islamic authority'. Two aspects of this fear are particularly noteworthy. The first is that such an about-face has never actually happened anywhere. The Islamist political structure of Iran was put into place in the context of the post-revolutionary power struggle in 1979–82. The Taliban government in Afghanistan, another example of an explicitly religious regime that one hears mentioned in this context, came to power even more explicitly through 'the barrel of a gun'. And in the case of both the FIS and Hamas, neither was allowed to form a government and rule. The origins and fate of the Turkish AKP government illustrate a second, and I think more consequential, aspect. Not only has this regime had to demonstrate publicly and consistently that it has no Islamization plans, lest it suffer the fate of virtually every one of its Islamic party forebears in Atatürk's republic, that of dissolution, nowadays by the Constitutional Court; its room for enacting any policy that would allow Islam even only greater leeway for public expression is highly restricted by the same secularist forces (see Yavuz 2006). Although the specifics and reasons for this situation are peculiar to contemporary Turkey, it points to the blurred way in which those observers distrustful of the AKP's 'real' intentions view the challenge of 'de-secularization' of secular institutions. In effect, the distinction upon which I just insisted between religious influence and de-secularization is negated or obscured in a kind of 'reefer madness' orientation: any policy allowing religion greater public visibility – what José Casanova titles de-privatization (Casanova 1994) – is interpreted not, as it could be, as an attempt to remove hindrances from the 'free exercise' of religion, but rather as symptomatic of a slide down the slippery slope towards de-secularization. Moreover, it cannot escape anyone's attention that all of these examples have to do with the same religion, namely Islam. Not that the question of the de-secularizing political challenges of religion should be reduced to those posed through Islam, but I do not think it would be going at all too far to suggest that, without what has been happening in certain segments of contemporary Islam, the question would be far less urgent. That said, what might it be about this sort of Islam that is so challenging, specifically politically challenging? This observation brings us back to the issue of 'fundamentalist' content.

Islam is not the only religion that has of late been a source of 'fundamentalist' political challenge. Indeed, the extension of the word to Islamist movements in the wake of the 1979 Iranian Revolution occurred in light of the political resurgence of Protestant Christian Fundamentalism, properly so called, in the United States at about the same time (Haines 1979; Mehden 1980). Christian 'fundamentalists' in the United States of the late 20th- and very early 21st century have not sought the kind of de-secularization that amounts to significant de-differentiation; efforts have rather gone in the direction of electing, through differentiated political process, individuals and parties thought likely to pursue policies and legislation in tune with the Christian Right's agenda. In that context, unlike in the paradigmatic case of the Islamic Republic of Iran, little to no attempt has been made to meld religious and political authority, the effort by Pat Robertson to win the 1988 Republican presidential nomination being perhaps the outstanding exception that proves the rule. Robertson failed substantially because he was perceived as a religious authority in spite of his attempt not to appear that way (see Liebman & Wuthnow 1983; Bruce 1988; Wilcox 2000). Nonetheless, the Christian Right emerged very quickly as a substantial political challenge, not, as I say, in the form of a move to de-secularize the political system, to de-differentiate religion and politics, but rather through the programmatic content of the movement, which identified it as in continuity with the original Fundamentalist movement of the early 20th century. That content has of course been multi-faceted, but its core can be understood as the assertion of a different set of religious – but not just religious – *values* in comparison with those that were and are still deemed to be dominant in American society, and to some extent around the world. I can introduce these with reference to terms that the Christian Right itself has used: 'family values', 'free enterprise' and 'making America great again'; and, in negative terms, opposition to 'secular humanism' and 'one-worldism'.

In looking more closely at these three positive value-dimensions of the American Christian Right, as well as their negative 'other' side, we should constantly be keeping in mind the parallel content of other 'fundamentalisms', including but not limited to Islamist 'fundamentalisms'. There are, I want to suggest, significant and even strong parallels. The first heading, 'family values', indicates that portion of Christian Right content that is most clearly religious, but generally in the sense of religio-moral. The moral aspect is critical because it renders the religious into political or at least politicizable form. I include under this title highly gendered bodily control issues and those having to do with child-rearing and education. The list of specific manifestations is probably familiar: opposition to sexual relations outside monogamous heterosexual marriage, abortion, and homosexuality; advocacy of patriarchal family structure, Christian parental control of schools and schooling, and 'creationism' (now: 'intelligent design'). Most of this is explicitly and consistently justified in terms of 'biblical warrant' and is in that sense *religio-moral* content.

The other two value-dimensions generally have far more resonance with what one might call the secular American Right or the Republican right. Under the heading of 'free enterprise' comes advocacy of fairly unfettered American capitalism and corresponding opposition to 'big government', a stance that resonates with the 'family values' dimension since it includes not only opposition to 'welfarism' and taxation, but also to control of education by professional educators and 'interference' by government in the affairs of the individual, in this case represented by the patriarchal and heterosexual family. What gives the entire program its global relevance, however, is the third value-dimension, the need to 'make America great again' (Beyer 1994). What this item boils down to is not just projecting American power onto the rest of the world, making it safe for American 'free enterprise', but even more keeping out the rest of the world with its 'secularizing' and 'relativizing' values. Whereas before 1990 the issue was most often expressed in terms of a strong anti-Communism (opposition to 'godless Communism'), there seems since to have been a shift to opposition to 'one-worldism' and 'world government' (Durham 2000), and to some extent to Islam in particular; with a corresponding advocacy of protecting America, whether this be in terms of economic interests, borders and immigration, or from encroachment by 'world' institutions and processes like the United Nations and multilateralism. Included here would also be a strong pro-Israeli stance that relates in part to specifically biblical understandings. All these aspects are, of course, represented symbolically in Eliza Gilkyson's lyrics.

The 'other' side of all this, for the American Christian Right, falls under the moniker of 'secular humanism' and its external manifestation, 'one-worldism'. In other words, the conflicting value-orientations against which this movement sees itself pitted are those that are not explicitly based in (evangelical, fundamentalist, Christian) religion – and in that sense secularized – and those that would immerse America, or at least understand and accept America as immersed, in a relativizing and structurally global society where plurality and to some extent pluralism reign, where 'security' is a constant balancing act without guarantees and 'governance' is an elusive goal requiring recurring compromise and collaboration with 'others'. In this light, the political challenge of religion that the American Christian Right exemplifies is the wish to use the state as an instrument to protect a locally imagined and religio-national particularism, but in such a way as to allow the continued and self-interested participation in global power systems. In this respect, it has much in common with trends in various other countries, whether associated with specific religio-national movements or not. Put somewhat differently, this American 'fundamentalism', and I would suggest most other politicized 'fundamentalisms', is from one perspective a movement that wishes to use political power to promote its particular religious vision, its particular religious values. That is important. From another perspective, however, it is a movement that uses religious resources to pursue agendas and goals that others around the world pursue outside the confines of one of the religions. The political challenge from religion in this sense does not depend on religion, Christian, Islamic, Hindu, Jewish, Sikh, or otherwise. The question then becomes: Is there something peculiar about such movements when they do use religious resources in this fashion?

One answer that one hears not infrequently is that politicized 'fundamentalisms' lead to violence, violence principally turned against the external enemy or its supposed internal representatives. The argument might go like this: because religious interpretations tend to 'cosmicize' the oppositions at issue, so that one is opposing not just a human opponent but the earthly representation of cosmic evil itself, violent means are not only justified but positively enjoined because one cannot 'reason with the devil'. The enemy isn't just other human beings with different opinions and agendas, it is 'godless Communism' (or Reagan's 'Evil Empire' or Bush's 'Axis of Evil') or the 'Great American Satan'. Here Gilkyson's lyrics can again serve as illustration: 'Startin' up wars in the name of God's son. Gonna blow us all the way to kingdom come.' The perhaps most visible current example of such a combination of religious movement and violent means is that shadowy entity usually labelled al-Qaeda, and its symbolic leader Osama bin Laden. Unlike Sayyid Qutb, the intellectual godfather of this sort of Islamist movement, bin Laden and the movement associated with him does not have an internal aspect: it does not seek as a primary goal to take over the government of a particular state, for instance as a first step in a more global transformation (cf. Qutb n.d.). There is therefore no question of forming parties, influencing legislation, mass mobilization, eventually winning government as there is for virtually every other religio-political movement, Islamist movements included. It does not present that sort of political challenge. There is only globally extended violence that targets most states, especially Western and Muslim ones. In fact, al-Qaeda seems to have become a word, associated with political Islamism, that means little more than the violent means that it uses: the careful yet random staging of events whose purpose is to kill people who represent, or who are at the moment occupying places that represent, the evil enemy. Just because al-Qaeda has this character, it presents a peculiar sort of political challenge, one that has no conceivable end because it has no concrete goal other than to continue until ... well, until kingdom come. It may even be misleading to understand it as a 'political' challenge at all, if we mean by that engagement with the institution of the state. Its significance in terms of the question I am discussing may not lie in that it demonstrates how 'fundamentalist' political challenges tend towards violence, but rather the exact opposite. The 'fundamentalist' movements that do present effective political challenges are precisely those that eschew, overcome, or move beyond violent means in favour of finding ways of appropriating institutionalized political structures through which to carry out their religious and religiously legitimated programs. Ultimately, the more politically challenging movement is the one that manages to move from the use of military force to the exercise of political authority. Looking at the relation between 'fundamentalism' and violence in this way points to the parallel between this challenge and that of de-secularization: there are important examples of the 'fundamentalist' challenge taking these forms, de-secularizing and forming as a transnational movement of perpetual violence; but these are actually quite rare, liable by their spectacular visibility to detract from those sorts of challenge that have broader and longer-term prospects. Once again, this brings me back to the question of content.

When discussing the challenge of value-orientations a few moments ago, I noted that the American Christian Right is particularly concerned with the relativization attendant upon incorporation into global systems. In terms of content, this religio-political movement is deeply troubled by religio-moral plurality and its attendant value of pluralism, which asserts the formally equal value or 'rights' of those worldviews, religions, cultures and individual orientations that constitute the plurality. 'Fundamentalisms', I want to suggest, in fact share this concern. Although some 'fundamentalist' movements include the stated goal of 'converting' the whole world to their religion – one thinks, for instance, of Osama bin Laden's recent pronouncement inviting all those he opposes to convert to Islam, or of the close association of American evangelical Protestantism, the prime base of the American Christian Right, with worldwide Christian evangelism – their political agendas seem far more directed towards dominating and protecting particular national or regional societies. Most 'fundamentalist' religio-political movements, in other words, are religio-nationalist in character, at least to a significant degree, because that is the only practical hope for carving out a non-pluralist space in a globalized society characterized by pluralization. Islamist and Christian 'fundamentalisms' could be used to illustrate this point, but a more interesting example is a movement that often gets labelled 'fundamentalist' precisely because of its seeming opposition to specifically religious pluralism. This is the Hindu nationalist movement embodied in India's *Sangh Parivar*, including the BJP, the RSS and the VHP. The Hindu nationalists do to some extent advocate the kind of conservative moral value-orientation typical of movements like the Christian Right, including a gendered emphasis on bodily discipline and control; but the main content of their agenda concerns pluralism, religious pluralism in particular (Veer 1994; Jaffrelot 1996). Much like the Christian Right wants America to be determined by their version of evangelical Protestant Christianity, and Islamists typically advocate the 'Islamization' of their local and regional societies, in each case with other religions being effectively subordinated, so do Hindu nationalists want India to be a Hindu nation defined by Hinduness (*Hindutva*). The content of this Hinduness is typically rather vague because it seeks to include not just the tremendous variety of religious orientations that count as Hindu, but also any religion that is deemed to have been founded in 'Mother India', Hinduism, Buddhism, Sikhism and Jainism in particular. So a key part of its aim and challenge is to construct the non-pluralist religious, cultural and national identity that it seeks to further and protect. The difficulty of this project reveals itself in that far clearer than what constitutes the 'inside' of *Hindutva*, is the 'outside', again very clearly defined in religious terms, namely Islam and Christianity, religions deemed to be fundamentally 'foreign'. The political challenge is therefore this wish to construct and assert the internal uniformity that is the aim of the movement, in part through the deliberate exclusion of the pluralizing 'other'. Here again, as with other 'fundamentalisms', the alternative to exclusion for these 'others' is nothing short of 'conversion' – or more precisely, 'reversion' – to the inside. What the Hindu nationalist movement therefore shows, perhaps more clearly than others, is that the political challenge from 'fundamentalism' with relation to pluralism is at the same time the (not infrequently violent) exclusion of those defined as 'others' and the assertion of an internal, often national, 'self' that has to be constructed in the first place as the agent and beneficiary of that exclusion. From this perspective, 'fundamentalist' movements are simply a type of exclusivist nationalism that uses religious resources to circumscribe the nation and inform that nation's purpose. As such, the challenge that they present is no different in political consequences than formally 'secular' exclusivisms exemplified in countries like *juche*-dominated North Korea, Milosevic's Serbia, and various formally secular nationalist parties and currents in countries as varied as Austria, Russia, Japan and Turkey.

The final explicitly political challenge I want to treat has been somewhat implicit throughout my presentation thus far, and that is the challenge religion may be seen to present merely by asserting itself as a public presence, as a legitimate source and basis for public political action and involvement. There are two main reasons that I treat this one last and that it has remained for the most part implicit. On the one hand, if we mean by this the mere existence of religiously identified political parties or political action in other forms, then, by itself, this hardly constitutes a political challenge any more than does the existence of, for instance, socialist, liberal, conservative, populist or nationalist parties and movements. Any political agenda, no matter what its source and basis, would from such a perspective constitute a challenge. This is why I have been focussing on content, and on 'fundamentalist' content specifically: to get at what precisely might be politically 'challenging' from religion as religion. On the other hand, if we mean by this the mere public and assertive visibility of religion – de-privatization – then one has to ask why such visibility would be construed as a challenge generally, and a political challenge specifically. To illustrate, I return to the example of Turkey, but now with the addition of France. Both of these countries have institutionalized, including politically in the form of legislation, public policy, and even constitutional provisions, doctrines of *laïcité* or *laiklik*, which de-legitimate the visible presence of religion in public institutions such as schools, and especially in government and its attendant political process, including political parties (Yavuz 2006; Baubérot 2007; Weil 2007). In both cases, Islam has been a particular target of public rules and regulations in this regard, more recently in the case of France, since the founding of the Kemalist republic and even before in the case of Turkey. Public displays – and what exactly constitutes 'public' is itself an issue of political regulation – of strong religious identification and overtly seeking to introduce religiously inspired agendas into the political process are subject to a variety of disincentives, including expulsion from public institutions like schools and suppression of any overtly religious party or party political agenda. Religion as such, in both countries, is not suppressed so much as restricted in the range of activities in which it can be overtly displayed and thematized. The particulars of this situation in both countries are the outcome of their respective histories, but they bear more than a passing resemblance to the significantly more extreme attempted suppression of religion in various former socialist countries around the world, and largely for the same reasons: religion itself is deemed to be a mildly to strongly suspect activity and orientation, one that is perhaps harmless if kept inside the walls of private homes and designated spaces like mosques and churches, but that is dangerous if not so confined. And the reason for this danger of religion is that it is what the classic 19th-century critics said it was: irrational, illusory, benighted superstition, a mark of cultural backwardness – at best a crutch of the weak or a soporific for the downtrodden; at worst, a source of irrational violence and hatred. As such, it cannot really be 'reasonably accommodated' in the rational and enlightened atmosphere of public, by contrasting definition 'secular', institutions. An extreme formulation of this attitude appears, for example, in the works of recent 'radical atheists' such as Richard Dawkins (Dawkins 2006), Christopher Hitchens (Hitchens 2007), or Sam Harris (Harris 2004). If I may be permitted a paraphrase of their argument: religion is inherently 'fundamentalist', and 'liberal' religion, if not simply an oxymoron, is inconsistent, a manifestation of 'bad faith'. I will not be the first to observe that this interpretation is at root the 'fundamentalist' position turned on its head. It is the expression of a clash of value-orientations in which those deemed to be the supposed carriers of opposing values are reduced to simple stereotypes and caricatures of the 'other'. But then it is the clashing value-orientations that are at issue, and only as an expression of these, the supposed polar opposition between religion and secularism. Seeing de-privatization as a political challenge from religion therefore betrays the presence of just the sort of reduction of 'religion' to 'fundamentalism' that I have adopted here in order to get at what the challenges might possibly be. This final 'challenge' thus brings us full circle to the other challenges: de-secularization in the sense of de-differentiation of the religious and political systems, value-orientation conflicts, violence, and opposition to pluralism.

Even accepting this analysis of the nature of these political challenges from religion, there still remains the question of the 21st century: what are the future prospects for these challenges? It goes almost without saying that prediction is at best risky, and probably more or less futile. No one expected the theocratic Iranian revolution just as no one expected the Berlin Wall to fall when it did. Nonetheless, the way that I have presented the challenges does favour certain futures more than others. In a nutshell, the challenge of de-secularization probably does not have much of a future since, judging by past examples, the confluence of circumstances that allow for the stabilization over the longer term of religious movements of politico-religious de-differentiation is rare. Those circumstances evidently existed in Iran of the late 20th century, and the fact that Iran benefits in large part from a rentier economy based on oil production may well sustain the Khomeinist regime for the foreseeable future, as it is sustaining its Saudi neighbour to the west. The practical impossibility of 'exporting' this revolution even to countries where political Islamist forces and movements are quite strong seems, however, to be equally evident. The Taliban regime in Afghanistan, if it is to be taken as another example, came to power in a peculiar and temporary geopolitical vacuum (Rashid 2000) and quickly crumbled back to the form of at best a warring faction in the face of its first serious challenge. By contrast the value-orientation challenge appears to me to be the most significant perhaps precisely because it does not require de-secularization and can remain at the level of religious influence on political regulation; and because, in spite of often opposing religious and moral pluralism, it actually resonates with a global cultural environment that favours heterogeneity, a multiplicity of voices and identities, including 'fundamentalist' religious ones. As for the question of violence, we are unlikely in the 21st century to live in a more peaceable world even in comparison with a previous century that was, taken as a whole, one of the most, if not the most, violent in human history. Religious movements will undoubtedly continue to be one source of this violence, as they have been throughout human history. Regrettably, they will certainly not be alone in this role. That challenge, in other words, is not particularly religious, although it can be. And finally, as concerns pluralism, whether religious, moral, cultural or individual, given that today's global society is structured so as constantly to encourage and to enable pluralization in all of these dimensions, religious challenges against it fight a sharply uphill battle and can in that circumstance likely hope to constitute a serious challenge only at particular local levels at best.

In conclusion, I want to return very briefly to the question of possible political challenges from religion that is generally not labelled as 'fundamentalist'. These 'liberal' challenges do exist, whether in the form of religious groups that intervene in political venues in favour of marginalized people, groups that take up environmental and human rights issues, religious movements and groups that promote democracy in states ruled by dictatorial regimes, or those that present themselves at international fora to promote peace and international cooperation. If one asks why the challenges from these quarters are far less often mentioned in the context of discussions about religious challenges, then the answer lies probably again in the domain of value-orientations. 'Liberal' religious critiques in many ways resonate rather precisely with so-called 'secularist' values and oppose the so-called 'fundamentalist' ones: they favour pluralism, whether religious, cultural or individual. They positively promote, in their ecumenical endeavours, what the American Christian Right fears and opposes as 'one-worldism'. They work against aggressive foreign policies and are quite often mildly to severely critical of the excesses and inequalities attendant upon the operation of the global capitalist system. And they usually find themselves on the 'secularist' side when it comes to bodily control and personal morality issues, for instance favouring gender equality and accepting homosexuality and homosexual marriage. They almost invariably reject the de-secularization of secular institutions in the strong sense that I have been discussing here. In short, their political challenge becomes largely invisible if one reads 'political challenge from religion' as 'the challenge to secularity by religion'. In that case, really only 'fundamentalist' challenges count. More pointedly and in summary, the word 'fundamentalist' gains its purchase precisely from a presumed opposition between the 'religious' and the 'secular'; and that is the basis of its perceived 'challenge'. Remove that supposed opposition, reject the self-evidence of the opposition that both 'fundamentalists' and 'secularists' would have us assume, and the 'challenge', even if it does not disappear, becomes the sort of opposition attendant upon the construction of a fundamentally pluralized social world, and from that perspective, something rather ordinary that can have a religious basis or not.

References

Almond, G.A., R.S. Appleby and E. Sivan (eds) (2000). *Strong Religion: The Rise of Fundamentalisms around the World*, Chicago, IL: Chicago University Press.

Bakhash, S. (1990). *The Reign of the Ayatollahs: Iran and the Islamic Revolution*, rev. edn, New York: Basic Books.

Baubérot, J. (2007). *Histoire de la laïcité en France*, Paris: PUF.

Beyer, P. (1994). *Religion and Globalization*, London: Sage.

Beyer, P. (2006). *Religions in Global Society*, London: Routledge.

Bruce, S. (1988). *The Rise and Fall of the New Christian Right: Conservative Protestant Politics in America 1978–1988*, Oxford: Clarendon.

Casanova, J. (1994). *Public Religions in the Modern World*, Chicago, IL: University of Chicago.

Dawkins, R. (2006). *The God Delusion*, London: Bantam.

Durham, M. (2000). *The Christian Right, the Far Right, and the Boundaries of American Conservatism*, Manchester: Manchester University Press.

Gilkyson, E. (2005). 'Man of God', Red House Records, Inc.

Haines, B.L. (1979). 'Islamic Fundamentalism and Christian Responsibility', *Christian Century*, 96, pp. 365–6.

Harris, S. (2004). *The End of Faith: Religion, Terror and the Future of Reason*, New York: Norton.

Hitchens, C. (2007). *God is Not Great: How Religion Poisons Everything*, Toronto: McClelland and Stewart.

Jaffrelot, C. (1996). *The Hindu Nationalist Movement in India*, New York: Columbia University Press.
Keddie, N.R. (2003). *Modern Iran: Roots and Results of Revolution*, New Haven, CT: Yale University Press.
Khosrokhavar, F, and O. Roy. (1999). *Iran: Comment sortir d'une révolution religieuse*, Paris: Seuil.
Liebman, R.C., and R. Wuthnow (eds). (1983) *The New Christian Right: Mobilization and Legitimation*, New York: Aldine.
Marty, M.E., and R.S. Appleby (eds) (1991–95). *The Fundamentalism Project*, 5 vols, Chicago, IL: Chicago University Press.
Mehden, Fred R. von der. (1980). 'Religion and Development in Southeast Asia: A Comparative Study', *World Development*, 8, pp. 545–53.
Qutb, Sayyid. [n.d]. *Milestones*, Cedar Rapids, IA: Unity Publishing.
Rashid, A. (2000). *Taliban: Militant Islam, Oil and Fundamentalism in Central Asia*, New Haven, CT: Yale University Press.
Veer, P. van der (1994). *Religious Nationalism: Hindus and Muslims in India*, Berkeley, CA: University of California Press.
Weil, P. (ed.) (2007). *Politiques de la laîcité au XXe siècle*, Paris: Presses de l'Université de France.
Wilcox, C. (2000). *Onward Christian Soldiers: The Religious Right in American Politics*, 2nd edn, Boulder, CO: Westview.
Yavuz, M.H. (ed.) (2006). *The Emergence of a New Turkey: Democracy and the AK Party*, Salt Lake City, UT: University of Utah Press.

Chapter 3
Intellectual Challenges from Religion

Sven-Eric Liedman

Some time ago I was talking to a friend about religion. We agreed that we were both atheists. But he added, 'I am a Jewish atheist.' And I had to clarify myself in a similar way. I am a Lutheran atheist.

That is the immediate limitation imposed by atheism. The word 'atheism' is a negation – the belief that God does not exist. Furthermore, an atheist has escaped from the dominant faith of the culture that shaped his or her childhood. Atheism is the negative of the photograph with which believers describe the world.

It goes without saying that non-believers have the same attitude towards the deities of all religions. I do not believe any more in Allah or Vishnu than the God of Christianity. But I have never had to confront the challenge of finding my faith in the Koran or the Bhagavad-Gita.

Being defined as a negation poses a constant challenge to atheism. It says what someone doesn't believe in, but not what he or she embodies in a positive sense. As a result, atheism often appears to be tedious and monotonous. Whereas religion paints the world in bright colours, seeks meaning in magnificent tales and derives the distinction between right and wrong from an extraterrestrial sphere, an atheist may reflexively answer that the truth is fairly trivial, that the Scriptures are simply good literature, and that morality is a wholly human affair.

At the end of this presentation, I shall sketch the outlines of an atheism that does not come across as gloomy, while avoiding insensitivity and lack of tolerance for the great aesthetic and cultural values that religion represents. Several impassioned confessions of atheism, including *The God Delusion* (2006) by English biologist Richard Dawkins, and *Traité d'athéologie* (2006) by French philosopher Michel Onfray, have been published in recent years. I shall conclude with some comments about them as well.

The precipitating factor for the books by Dawkins and Onfray is the religious resurgence that has been so conspicuous in virtually the entire world over the past few decades. Politics is now suffused with religious attitudes and convictions to an extent that would have been wholly alien to my generation. Former president Bush is a born-again Christian who never missed an opportunity to justify his decisions by referring to God. Islam has become a political force on the world stage. Religion is an increasing problem for the Chinese government, given that it does not fit into the official ideology's mix of capitalism and communism.

The growing prominence of religion in political discourse is matched by popular fervour for various religious movements. Islam and Christianity are the two main faiths that are winning new converts. A number of Muslim movements are gaining ground around the world – I shall focus mostly on Sunni *Salafism*. Meanwhile, Christian Pentecostalism is scoring the greatest triumphs. It is growing even faster in Latin America and Africa than in the United States. If the trend were to continue, three-quarters of humanity would embrace some brand of Christianity by 2050 (Chelini-Pont 2007). While Pentecostalism is spearheading these developments, the apparently stalwart Catholic Church and other denominations are actually losing adherents.

The expanding Christian and Muslim movements of the past few decades have much in common, including a clearly fundamentalist orientation and a good measure of anti-intellectualism as manifested in an aversion to traditional religious ideology (*kalam*) and science. Television, the Internet and other contemporary media are instrumental to their progress. But both cases illustrate a tendency of modern secular society by which religion increasingly dissociates itself from the culture that spawned it and recruits its adherents among those who live under completely different cultural conditions than it had confronted earlier.

Faced with the forward march of certain religious movements in recent decades, some scholars have claimed that the accelerating secularisation of modern society is in the process of coming undone. The most famous tract that takes such an approach is *The Desecularization of the World* (1999) by American sociologist and theologian Peter L. Berger. According to the opposite interpretation, the world is going through a new, even more powerful phase of secularisation in which educational and political institutions – which remained strong in the modern age – are losing their privileged status, thereby leaving religion as the only refuge for the individual when all other norms have evaporated. Olivier Roy, a French expert on Islam, advances that thesis in his book *La laïcité face à l'Islam* (2005)[1] and elsewhere.

Berger and Roy clearly ascribe different connotations to the troublesome word 'secularisation'. I shall not explore more deeply the best way to define the word. However, I shall discuss the highly complementary perspectives that Berger and Roy have on the current situation. The opposites of 'disenchantment' and 're-enchantment'[2] are two other words that are central to the discourse about modernity. Disenchantment, which comes from Max Weber's *Entzauberung* – and in another way from Franz Rosenzweig – has played a key role in discussions about modern society ever since World War II. The idea that enchantment, at least as Weber understands the word, is inherent to modernity emerged at an early stage. I shall maintain that the idea is largely justified. But I shall argue just as forcefully that enchantment has more limited application today, so that it conflicts less with

---

[1] Particularly p. 14. Jean-Paul Willaime regards that wave of secularisation as typical of what he calls ultramodernity; see his article 'Reconfigurations ultramodernes', *Esprit*, 3–4, mars–avril (2007: 149 and *passim*). See also Roy (2007: 242–52).

[2] It is an interesting fact that the French translation has the title *Le réenchantement du monde* (Paris: Bayard, 2002).

the re-enchantment of the world that followers of resurgent Pentecostalism and Islam apparently experience.

The notion that the world is heading towards a deeper and deeper religious re-enchantment has one major exception – Europe. De-Christianisation appears to be proceeding unabated in most European countries, particularly the members of the European Union. Pentecostalism is showing only negligible gains in most of Europe. And while Islam is making headway, that is mostly due to immigration from countries where it is the predominant religion. Even though Christianity and Islam are spreading according to the same pattern as on other continents, what is most noticeable from a global perspective is how limited their progress has been in Europe. The *European Values Survey* and *World Values Survey*, the major international studies of religious attitudes and practices, make one thing clear – Europe is far more de-Christianised than other parts of the world in which Christianity has been widespread, while other religions are not filling the vacuum that de-Christianisation has left in its wake.

However, the past 10 to 15 years have witnessed a remarkable renewed interest in traditional theological questions among many leading European intellectuals who are normally associated with irreligious or areligious currents. I don't mean Onfray and Dawkins, whose atheistic treatises would appear to be typical. The people I'm referring to are Alain Badiou, Jürgen Habermas, Slavoj Žižek, Giorgio Agamben and a number of others who have written important works about religion in general and Christianity in particular. Several of them have openly declared that they are atheists, or at least agnostics. Following in Weber's footsteps, Habermas refers to himself as *religiös unmusikalisch*.[3] But all of them are clearly interested in how religion has manifested, both in our times and in the past. Their intention is not to oppose religious faith, but to understand it and its inherent power – particularly its political potential. Their primary focus is not Pentecostalism or Salafism, but a more moderate, intellectually and ethically balanced faith. Žižek assumes an extreme position in maintaining that Christianity and Marxism are the only serious challenges to the militant neo-liberalism that predominates in our times (Žižek 2005).

It would be an exaggeration to claim that European intellectuals are caught up in the same re-enchantment that is so palpable in the religious movements that are gaining the most ground these days. But they nevertheless exhibit a kind of fascination that stems from the same historical situation, which is typically referred to as postmodern, post-secular, post-Christian, and so on.

---

[3] Habermas used the expression when he received the 2001 German Book Trade peace prize. For its origin and significance, see Michael Meyer-Blanck, "'… religiös unmusikalisch?" Zum Nutzen theologischer Bildung in Wissenschaft und Beruf', at www.uni-bonn.de/www/Evangelische_Theologie/Dekanat/Dekanatsrede_WS_2004_2005.html, accessed 20 July 2007.

That is also the context within which the conclusion of this presentation strives to outline a positive form of atheism, spurred by a kind of enchantment when encountering the richness of life and the world.

Disenchantment and Re-enchantment

Poetic narratives of the 18th and 19th centuries used the word *Entzauberung* to refer to people who had been released from a curse or a spell. You might say that Sleeping Beauty was *entzaubert* when a prince's kiss awoke her after a hundred years. That was the word that Weber turned into a technical term to describe the transformation that society and thought had undergone in modern times. Actually, he defined the term more narrowly than that, relating it to the legitimisation of social actions. According to Weber, people can justify their behaviour in two main ways. One justification is magical and one is rational. In line with the magical justification, people avoid certain actions because they are commonly viewed as leading to unhappiness or a curse, while choosing other actions that bring luck and the favour of the gods. A rational justification does not appeal to any superhuman or non-human powers, but examines only the observable consequences that an action may be expected to have, its advantages vis-à-vis the disadvantages of the alternatives. According to Weber, the magical and rational justifications are opposite poles on a continuous scale along which actual justifications can be located. His thesis is that Europe has experienced a constant shift towards the rational pole in recent centuries.[4]

Weber's concept has had great resonance and is now part of the standard intellectual repertoire for describing how modern reality differs from more traditional perceptions. The concept, which is linked to the Weberian theses of rationalisation, implies that the processes previously assumed to be subject to the caprice of unpredictable powers can now be mastered by rational knowledge. The advantage of the change is that fear of the unknown abates, while the disadvantage is that mythical and imaginative notions give way to dreary calculation and spiritually numbing routine.

A glance at our times reveals that its disenchantment is far from complete, even on a superficial level. Horoscopes, crystals and Tarot cards still have a flourishing market. Even leading politicians may have superstitions about good and bad luck. But it is easy to see that nearly everyone ultimately submits to modern rationality. People may be relieved to know that an aeroplane doesn't have a row 13. But when they finally board it, they put their faith in calculating, rational technology more than anything else.

---

[4] Weber discusses the concept of *Entzauberung* in *Wirtschaft und Gesellschaft* (1956 [1920]). W.M. Sprondel provides a short overview of the concept's evolution in the article 'Entzauberung' in *Historisches Wörterbuch der Philosophie* (bd 2, Darmstadt 1972), column 564f.

It is far from obvious that science and technology, or modern life in general, should be characterised by words like 'cold' and 'dreary'. On the contrary, they can fill both their practitioners and observers with enthusiasm and joy, stimulating an unquenchable thirst for knowledge. More generally, they can instil a sense of confidence in constant progress that will improve people's lives.

Martin Heidegger talked about the enchantment of modern times as early as the 1930s. Contemporary humanity is spellbound by the forward march of technology, obsessed by the conviction that everything can be calculated, utilised and managed (Heidegger 1989: 124f). Heidegger's line of thought appears to be largely reflexive and unexamined, stemming from his typical aversion to exact science and technical calculations. A more reasonable, neutral approach would be to associate the enchantment of modernity with the very concept of progress. Many people, particularly leaders, of the 18th, 19th and 20th centuries, were driven by the belief that life would become better in every respect. The most outspoken concept of progress, as articulated by thinkers such as Jean Antoine Condorcet in the late 18th century, foresaw interrelated improvements everywhere, including art and morality.

The enchantment inherent to such thinking is the conviction that all problems will be resolved in the future thanks to unstoppable progress. That attitude has led to striking nonchalance when it comes to both technological developments and various kinds of social experimentation. Its proponents have counted too much on the future to remove any and all barriers that stand in the way of human fulfilment.

Recent decades have brought about a change in that respect. Fewer people subscribe to promises of a future that is better in every imaginable way. Instead, storm clouds are gathering. Of course, there have always been prophets of doom. But not only have their numbers become greater, but their predictions are now based on the solid evidence of environmental deterioration, psychological dysfunction, and the like.

Unruffled faith in progress assumed that every essential aspect of life and society was part of a common process. As it turned out, that notion didn't pass the test of reality. Both Nazi Germany and the Soviet Union reconciled cruel dictatorships with economic, technological and scientific progress. The People's Republic of China of today is an even more dramatic example.

Thus, the doctrine of progress launched by the Enlightenment project is not cast in a single mould. However, modernity contains a solid component, which includes the interrelated disciplines of exact science, technology, economics and modern rational administration. Progress has continued unchecked in these areas. We never question that the computers of today are better than those of yesterday but not as good as those of tomorrow. Every contribution to research, no matter how modest, is intended to promote scientific progress. It is axiomatic for economists that a country's GDP will grow every year. If it doesn't, something must be seriously wrong.

If we look at these areas in isolation, the enchantment of modernity is alive and well. What can't be solved today will be solved tomorrow.

But modernity also has softer components. The classical believers in progress strike us as naïve when they assert that the human race is improving on the moral plane. Even stranger is the notion that art is always rising to new levels – who has surpassed Dante or Shakespeare? Some political thinkers still argue that democracy will inevitably triumph. But signs are amassing that, even where it appears to be secure, democracy is facing daunting challenges that suggest growing uncertainty about the future.

Most remarkable is the new view of religion. A longstanding intellectual construct was that modernity and religion are irreconcilable. Religious faith would die out as society became more and more modern. The religious worldview would be replaced by that of science, while art would come to satisfy the need for devotion, passion and meaning.

That idea seems to be obsolete these days. In many parts of the world, religion's hold is stronger than it has been for a long time. Religion often goes hand in hand with the solid components of modernity – it is spread in the new media, many of its enthusiastic adherents are technologically or scientifically knowledgeable, and it is closely linked to the global economy.

There is good reason to speak of a re-enchantment of the modern world. That re-enchantment does not collide in the least with the enchantment of modernity's solid components. On the contrary, they can join forces in what appears to be a harmonious way. George W. Bush may have been a typical example of that alliance. His faith in the ability of business and technology to meet the challenges of the present and future appeared no less unshakeable than his faith in God.

Religion clearly satisfies vital needs in a world that is often referred to as postmodern or late modern. Personally, I prefer the expression late modern. But what needs are we talking about? The needs often referred to are connectedness and meaning, as well as finding or encountering something that is greater than we are.

It is natural to see the fascination with religion among European intellectuals in that light. Religion has become a challenge for them as well. Although they do not sacrifice themselves or their convictions to religion, they regard it as a phenomenon that must be seriously examined.

Religious Anti-intellectualism

The resurgence of religiosity and its political consequences have been the subject of a steady stream of books. Probably the most comprehensive is *Political Theologies*, which contains almost 800 pages of studies dealing with both historical and contemporary problems (Vries and Sullivan 2006). The interface between politics and religion was in the spotlight earlier today. But I shall focus on religion's intellectual, not its political, challenges. We can distinguish between two challenges that are partially in conflict with each other. One challenge is characterised by anti-intellectualism to one extent or another. The other challenge involves a serious, intellectually responsible discussion about how religion relates to secular philosophy, contemporary science and late modern society.

Zwischen Naturalismus und Religion, an extensive series of articles by Habermas – who has assumed a central position in the philosophically oriented debate about religion – identifies two contradictory tendencies in modern society. The first tendency involves major advances by religious orthodoxies. The other tendency is towards unapologetic naturalism, according to which mental life is reduced to brain physiology and behaviour to a simple manifestation of genetic makeup (Habermas 2005: 7). From all appearances, the tendency towards naturalism – to which I shall return at the end of this presentation – appeals to a considerably narrower stratum of society than religious orthodoxies. But it is important to keep naturalism's position in mind when observing anti-intellectual strains, particularly within Pentecostalism and Salafism.

Whether 'orthodoxy' is the ideal term to describe the movements that are now challenging reliance on science can be called into question. The most successful movements are far from 17th-century Christian orthodoxies and their strict intellectualism. While striving for doctrinal purity, they use very different tools than the Aristotelianism that Jesuits, Calvinists and Lutherans developed several hundred years ago. The term 'fundamentalism' is certainly more appropriate, assuming that it is used in a broad, flexible sense to refer to the desire to establish an unassailable, timeless foundation for religious faith.[5]

That desire is common to Salafism and Pentecostalism, no matter how different they may be in other respects.

The Salafists look back to the dawn of Islam. Based on a *hadith* of Mohammed, they assert that Islam reached its apex as a doctrine and norm during its first three generations, the first of which consisted of Mohammed and his contemporaries. All later additions must be regarded as distortions and blind alleys. That is one of the reasons for their rejection of *kalam*, the Muslim theology that injects foreign, Platonic and Aristotelian elements. Another, more all-encompassing reason is aversion to anything that smacks of intellectual hair-splitting. Islam must be simple, resolute and resistant to dialectic ambiguities.

I hardly need to point out that today's Salafism plays a key political role, both in most traditionally Muslim countries and around the world. The role isn't unequivocal – Salafism comes in many shapes and forms other than the one that Osama bin Laden and al-Qaeda represent. The Salafists are ideologically anti-modernists, but use today's technology to disseminate their message. They rely on television and the Internet just as unabashedly as do the Pentecostalists. Those two media have permitted both movements to expand worldwide.

---

[5] The literature on contemporary fundamentalism is growing exponentially. The most comprehensive effort is still *The Fundamentalism Project* led by Martin E. Marty and R. Scott Appleby and described in a series of volumes by the same name. See the first volume, *Fundamentalisms Observed*, ed. M.E. Marty and R.S. Appleby (1991).

But the Muslim approach differs from the Christian in one essential respect – its attitude towards capitalism. While the Salafists regard capitalism as a manifestation of Western sinfulness and spiritual sterility, almost all of the international Pentecostal movement is thoroughly imbued with capitalist thinking. Its many churches are ordinarily run as businesses based on the maximisation of profit, and private wealth is viewed as a sign of God's favour. A person who remains poor either lacks faith or belongs to the wrong church. Particularly in Africa, the Pentecostal churches proliferate through a kind of mitosis – they are always in pursuit of even greater devotion and more ecstatic worship.[6]

Neo-evangelicalism and its thinking reached the pinnacles of power and worldly success under the Bush Administration. Fundamentalist constructs have been used to justify not only the bloody war in Iraq but decisions concerning, among others, stem cell research.

The name 'Darwin' has acquired a special significance in American public discourse. Bush once said in an interview that students should learn not only the Theory of Evolution but Intelligent Design, the Christian Right's version of biblical creation.[7] The Intelligent Design theory is a concession to the Theory of Evolution insofar as it accepts that life on earth emerged during a period of time considerably longer than one week. But its advocates maintain that life processes are so complex that they must be traced back to an intelligent creator.

Intellectually speaking, the argument in favour of intelligent design is extraordinarily weak. Not even the defenders of Intelligent Design who have scientific training can get their articles published in scholarly journals. Their contributions are too encumbered by dubious deductions or abstruse mathematical reasoning. Advocates of intelligent design are clearly more interested in influencing public opinion than in scientific discourse. They know that the broad swath of American society that supports the political right has a major influence, particularly on schools, libraries and the mass media.

Thus, the Intelligent Design theory has not garnered any scientific or intellectual credibility.[8] Only in an entirely different sense does resurgent Christianity, particularly in the guise of the new wave of Pentecostalism, pose a challenge

---

[6] An authoritative presentation of such trends is by A. Carten and R. Marshall-Fratani (eds), *Between Babel and Pentecost: Transnational Pentecostalism in Africa and Latin America* (2001). See also the excellent, rich and varied section 'La vague évangélique et pentecôtiste', in *Esprit* (mars–avril, 2007), pp. 156–230, including articles by both Corten and Marshall(-Fratani).

[7] For the interview and reactions to it, see P. Baker and P. Slevin, 'Bush Remarks on "Intelligent Design" Theory Fuel Debate', *Washington Post*, 3:8 (2005). The Bush Administration's cavalier treatment of science is described in C. Mooney, *The Republican War on Science* (2005; rev. edn 2007).

[8] A number of devastating critiques have been levelled against Intelligent Design theory. One outstanding example is found in M. Young and T. Edis (eds), *Why Intelligent Design Fails: A Scientific Critique of the New Creationism* (2004).

to scientific thinking in the narrow sense of the term, as well as to a worldview that proceeds from what reason can deduce on its own merits. The critique that cries for an answer does not concern the content of intellectual argumentation but the danger that it will eviscerate the very experience of life. In opposition to the magnificence of biblical narrative, science posits a world that may appear to be cold and calculating. It offers no safe sanctuary for *joie de vivre*, much less for the ecstasy that is so central to the Pentecostal movement. Whether science can provide moral guidance is doubtful, and it relegates issues of good and evil, right and wrong to discussions that can never lead to a definitive conclusion. It often dismisses questions concerning the meaning of life as incorrectly formulated without sufficiently acknowledging their existential significance. And what does science have to say about suffering, grief and mortality?

Salafism does not pose exactly the same challenge given that ecstasy is not among its ideals, but its critique of strict intellectualism is similar. In place of endless reasoning, it offers strict guidelines and unwavering faith.

Egyptian writer Sayyid Qutb has become a classic source of inspiration for the Salafism of today. Qutb, who was executed in 1966 under Gamal Abdel Nasser's regime, was an articulate opponent of both capitalism and communism. He wrote in 1949 that the world was divided between an Eastern and Western bloc only superficially. Both blocs struggled over worldly influence and a competitive edge in the market, not over ideas and convictions. The real dividing line lay between the materialistic view of life epitomised by each of the blocs, and the teachings of Islam.

Qutb found Islam to be compatible with modern technology. The only threat came from Western value systems. The goal of life must never be material gain, but fidelity to Islam's original teachings. One of those teachings is concern for the welfare of others. The Muslim brotherhood to which Qutb belonged and remains the most important thinker has a social programme.[9]

Qutb's line of thought resonates in Salafism, if often in a more militant form. Belief in the power of reason to generate sustainable results is rejected with the same avidity as in fundamentalist Christianity.

The Capacity and Limits of Reason

The wave of fundamentalism provides an immediate backdrop to the renewed interest in theological questions that has been so conspicuous among Westerners, particularly European thinkers of the last few decades. But criticism of secular reason also comes from various religious adherents who by no means doubt the

---

[9] A careful, almost nearsighted review of Qutb's political thought and relationship to Islam appears in S. Khatab's *The Political Thought of Sayyid Qutb: The Theory of jahiliyyah* (2006). The 1949 quote is the motto of the entire book. It comes from the period when Qutb was in the United States; see pp. 138–46.

capacity of reason in itself. Their point is rather that reason is insufficient and must be enriched with a religious perspective.

The leading theological traditions of Islam, Christianity and Judaism interpret their religious teachings with tools originating in Greek philosophy. Secular reason provides guidance but is always regarded as inadequate. Knowledge of the complete truth about the world requires revelation or, more broadly, the guidelines offered by the Scriptures.

Demonstrating almost paradigmatic clarity, theologian Joseph Ratzinger – now Pope Benedict XVI – took that position in a conversation with Habermas of 19 January 2004 (Habermas and Ratzinger 2005). A typical exponent of the learned Catholic tradition, particularly Thomistic philosophy, Ratzinger discusses whether the natural law that has historically been so central to both Catholic and secular thought has lost its appeal today. The word 'nature' no longer stands for that which is indisputably rational – evolutionary biology has dispelled that notion. Only human rights, which Ratzinger believes should be supplemented by corresponding 'human obligations,' still linger on from the original idea. But reason alone cannot guarantee the protection of either rights or obligations in the long run. Left alone, reason can be misused in many different ways. Ratzinger's conclusion is that reason needs religion if it is not to go astray. By the same token, religion needs reason, without which it can degenerate into unbridled fanaticism (ibid.: 50–57).

For his part, Habermas trusts that both rights and obligations will grow out of human intercourse, that is, communicative action. But he admits that what he calls 'post-metaphysical thinking' is strikingly at a loss when it comes to concepts of the good or exemplary life. Such concepts must be lucid in order to provide human beings with concrete guidelines for their actions and visions of the future.

This is where philosophy has something to learn from religious thought that is free of dogmatism and moralising. The secular thinking of today offers insufficient avenues for expression and is insensitive to the problem of wayward lives, unreasonable aspirations and perverted social conditions. Religion is better equipped for the challenge. At the time that Christianity and Greek philosophy joined forces, the latter was enriched by crucial concepts from the former – Habermas gives the examples of incarnation, alienation and fulfilment. Post-metaphysical thinking has disinherited itself, and Habermas foresees the need of concepts translated from the language of religion. He mentions only one example – how the Judaeo-Christian notion that man was created in God's image has been translated into the secular concept of the value of the individual. While that is an old case of a translated concept, Habermas argues that its power must be rejuvenated, perhaps such that people are treated as if they had been created in God's image even if God doesn't actually exist (ibid.: 31ff.).

That isn't particularly clarifying – lucidity isn't the German philosopher's strong point. However, Habermas alludes to Walter Benjamin, another master of that tradition. Benjamin was able to translate the entire power of religious thought into secular concepts. Another text by Habermas mentions what he calls Benjamin's 'anamnetic solidarity'. That solidarity becomes the equivalent of the concept of the final judgement, when all injustices will be revealed and punished. But as soon as the idea of that ultimate administration of justice loses sway, a vacuum emerges. That is when collective memory takes over – people must be able to feel deep solidarity with past victims of injury and suffering (Habermas 2005: 250).[10]

More generally, we might assume that Habermas has Benjamin's messianism in mind. That messianism, which loomed large during Benjamin's final years, when his faith in a communist utopia had been shaken and Nazism posed a direct threat to his life, may be regarded as a belief or faith despite – or in defiance of – the dictates of reason.

Habermas is in a much calmer mood when he provides examples of how Benjamin secularises religious language. His allusions to Benjamin can readily be compared to those that Jacques Derrida, his former opponent, made in some of his later writings. Particularly relevant is *Spectres de Marx* (1993), Derrida's book about the various ways that Marx's thinking remained indispensable even after his great programme had collapsed. The messianic motif emerges there as a kind of utopia in a world brimming with injustices. But the remarkable thing is that Marx's theses of human liberation are infused with a kind of post-Marxist significance – instead of the appearance of a new world, the old one will be illuminated by the hope for justice (Derrida 1993: 124–55).

Benjamin, Habermas and Derrida are all close to a tradition that can be traced to Marx himself and even further back, in which religious narratives, symbols and covenants are imbued with worldly meaning. For instance, that imperative is central to Marx's entire ideological project and its desire to translate 'heavenly' content into concrete reality. The tradition's modern master is Ernst Bloch, whom Habermas also mentions (Habermas 2005: 240). Bloch's thinking makes use of central components of Judaeo-Christian conceptual structures, but only to shed light on human conditions in the visible, material world. For instance, that is the way in which his magnum opus *Das Prinzip Hoffnung* assigns such a decisive secular role to hope, which is central to both Jewish messianism and Christian faith.

Habermas mentions both Benjamin and Adorno in the same breath as Bloch. But I would argue that there is an important difference between Bloch and the other two, as well as between Bloch and Derrida. The difference may be expressed in terms of the enchantment of modernity. Bloch remains entirely in the embrace of that enchantment and is convinced that scientific, technological and economic progress will be accompanied by the emergence of a world without injustice or exploitation. The others are disillusioned in that respect. The world will always be an arena that features overwhelming problems, as well as actual or impending injustices that must be fought as best we can. Even though religious symbols and narratives are ultimately human constructions, they can help spearhead that battle.

---

[10] Habermas's introduction to his discussion with Ratzinger is also included in *Zwischen Naturalismus und Religion*; the reference to Benjamin and the need for translation, p. 116.

Žižek is one of the most prominent philosophers of recent years who have been fascinated by the ability of religion, particularly Christianity, to inspire people to monumental projects. He claims to be an unflinching atheist, even alleging that atheism is implicit to the cry of Jesus on the cross, 'My God, my God, why hast thou forsaken me?' God has abandoned humanity, but the concept of God lives on. The concept fills people with *Geist*, a word that Žižek uses in a rich, many-faceted Hegelian sense that includes both conceivable transcendental perspectives and a worldly *spirit* that can inhabit a group of people, a congregation or a joint project. He seems to see Christianity's primary and immediate significance in terms of that worldly spirit. In a time of unbridled capitalism, Christianity is able to assemble devout multitudes that have their sights set on something other than consumption or rapacity. Thus, Žižek regards Christianity and Marxism–Leninism as the only effective counterweights to capitalism (Žižek 2005).

The fascination that the Apostle Paul has held for a number of European philosophers, including Žižek, in recent years is a chapter in itself.[11] That interest manifests in many ways – from Giorgio Agamben's close reading of the Epistle to the Romans in *Il tempo che resta* (2000) to Alain Badiou's considerably looser discussion in *Saint Paul* (1997). Common to them all is a fascination with Paul as the founder of something new – a church, a community that transcends borders, a project with all the power of eschatology. Above all, Badiou is captivated by the ability of Paul, who never met Jesus, to establish the doctrine that Jesus was the Messiah for the heathens as well as for the Jews. In Badiou's eyes, that makes Paul the first universalist. For his part, Agamben is most concerned with Paul's messianism, and he goes on to ask what kind of messianism is possible today. He compares messianism with apocalyptic thinking. A believer in the apocalypse is certain of the future – the end times are near. With his messianic approach, Paul speaks of an unknown future – the time that remains. Agamben draws a parallel to the distinction between the revolutionary and the rebel. The revolutionary knows what will happen after the revolution. The rebel sees only far enough to conclude that current conditions must be changed.

The fascination with Paul is a kind of focal point for the renewed interest among secularised European intellectuals in the worldly potential of religion, particularly Christianity.

Devotion, Distance and the Enchantment of Reality

The attitude assumed by Žižek, Agamben, Badiou and others is light years away from the militant atheism of Onfray and Dawkins. While the former write against

---

[11] An excellent overview of that interest appears in *Ésprit*'s theme issue 'L'événement saint Paul: juif, grec, romain, chrétien' (février 2003), including articles by Stanislas Breton, Paul Ricœur and Jean-Claude Monod. See also Ola Sigurdson's article, 'Paulus - filosofernas apostel? Badiou, Agamben, Žižek', in *Glänta*, 4 (2005).

the backdrop of secularised European society, the latter have contemporary religious mass movements and their fundamentalist intolerance in view. As a biologist, Dawkins feels threatened by the anti-Darwinist currents among the many self-proclaimed experts on the origin of life. As a philosopher, Onfray is fiercely opposed to the anti-intellectualism that he finds in the three great monotheistic religions.

Personally, I am highly sceptical of belligerent atheism. Is that really a productive attitude; doesn't it only compound the problem? It is easy to understand Dawkins's dismay with the attacks on evolutionary biology. That sublime theory, which has acquired additional explanatory power and inner cogency over the past few decades, is being threatened not by a scientific rival but by what appears to be pure ignorance. But is not Dawkins being overly strident? Is he not parrying religious intolerance with another kind of intolerance? Meanwhile, Onfray is occupied with an ill-natured interpretation of the Bible and Koran that hardly contributes to a deeper understanding of religion's significance today.

Habermas takes a much more fruitful approach. He subscribes to what he calls a 'soft naturalism,' (Habermas 2005: 157ff., 171f., 215) by which he means that the human world originates from nature but cannot be reduced to natural occurrences. Consciousness is not simply an insignificant by-product of various brain processes as a 'hard' naturalism would allege. While consciousness stems from biological evolution, it becomes a precondition for all of human civilisation once it begins to function. Religion also plays a vital role in that civilisation, not only through cognitive confusion and intolerance as Onfray and Dawkins maintain, but as the source of indispensable cultural values.

I find 'naturalism' to be a dubious term and prefer the older word 'materialism', even though it also carries multiple meanings. But the expression 'non-reductive materialism' is fairly unambiguous. It is the notion that reality consists of a number of levels, each of which originates from the level directly below it but with new qualities and contexts that cannot be explained with reference to lower levels. The levels that may be discerned are ultimately dependent on human knowledge. For the time being, it appears reasonable to differentiate between organic and inorganic matter. And it goes without saying that we perceive the human world to be a level of its own. But the number of levels also reflects how closely we observe an object under study. The evolution of biological species or the human race may be regarded as a large number of levels in which new constellations constantly emerge. When all is said and done, non-reductive materialism is a theory of evolution characterised by temporal continuity back to a relatively simple beginning (currently thought to be the Big Bang) but amenable to the steady appearance of new contexts (Liedman 1986: 162–6). These are normally referred to as emergent properties.

It is also possible to equip this worldview with emotional power greater than what the arid term 'non-reductive materialism' can generate. Dénis Diderot, the great French Enlightenment thinker, speaks of *le matérialisme enchanté* (Fontenay 1981). That is an appropriate alternative name for the same concept. The adjective 'enchanted' hints at the bewildering and wondrous aspect of that grand process of reality.

A possible objection is that Diderot lived at a time when the findings of research really could lead to wonder. Are we not inevitably more blasé these days? We know that the universe is vast. We know that its building blocks are inconceivably small. We know that biological evolution has been going on for billions of years – our genealogies disappear across savannas, into the sea, all the way back to life's primordial soup. Information about all that is just as available on the Internet as my neighbour's blog. We can watch television programmes about it whenever we like. It has become trivial.

But that trivialisation is exactly what we must overcome. Aristotle says in his *Metaphysics* that all knowledge begins with wonder. We might add that knowledge also remains dynamic and vital thanks to wonder. Swedish biologist Stefan Edman just published a book entitled *Förundran* (2006) (the Swedish word for wonder) that seeks to instil in us a renewed fascination for the remarkable interconnections between the universe and all living beings. As a Christian, Edman sees the glory of the universe as the ultimate evidence of an intelligent creator.

For me, Edman's fascination is contagious, but not his faith. To imagine a creator behind all this is to rely on a simple explanation for something much greater. The claim that someone has created the universe is a far-flung analogy to what human beings can accomplish with their tools and machinery. Does that not reduce and anthropomorphise the universe?

When we say that the universe arouses wonder, we have nothing to compare it with other than its components, particularly human inventions. The whole is greater than the sum of its parts. So what? Does that mean that there is another whole called God that is even greater?

One of the most important missions of religious faith is to confront human beings with something that is bigger than they are. Overestimating ourselves is one of the greatest pitfalls we face, imprisoned as we are in ourselves, our times, our countries and our civilisations.

But the concept of God's greatness can only be visualised through the greatness of the universe. Do we need God then?

The biggest challenge resides on another level – what norms might there be for human beings in a world without God? That brings us back to the debate between Ratzinger and Habermas. While Ratzinger believes in a divinely sanctioned morality, Habermas sees morality as – at best – the result of free communicative action.

But if we don't believe in God, why should we believe in a divinely sanctioned morality? Furthermore, it turns out that morality based on religious grounds is far from unambiguous.

We have to accept the fact that human society is an enterprise that offers no guarantees. The same is true of the life of the individual. In one sense, we are all consigned to ourselves, both as individuals and as a collective, in a world filled with cruelty, suffering and sorrow as well as joy and pleasure.

One image of God is that of a being who is not the master of the universe but who struggles against evil alongside human beings. That image holds great allure for me – it is very beautiful. But what reason do we have to believe in that kind of God? Have we not merely created an idealised version of ourselves?

Homo sapiens emerged very late in the evolutionary process – in terms of geological time, it was just an instant ago. The species has accomplished a great deal in such a brief period. The first thing that might occur to us is all the suffering we have caused each other through war, cruelty and oppression. But human development is also a fantastic tale of constant achievements – from cave paintings to agriculture, the potter's wheel, writing, the Internet and biotechnology. People have created a civilisation whose art, religion and science constitute a huge symbolic universe, just as remarkable in its way as the visible universe.

All of that is worthy of wonder as well. So much has been wrested from so little.

That wonder is always accompanied by a sense of terror - the whole thing can be annihilated at any moment. Human beings are just as much destroyers as they are creators.

Civilisation has an inexhaustible supply of ways to express both wonder and horror. Many of them come in the guise of religion. That doesn't make them any less useful. Just as the Song of Songs (a worldly love poem) could evoke religious sensibilities, the Book of Revelation, Bach's Christmas Oratorio and the great Sufi poets can convey thoughts, feelings and sensations that lack the religious association of God for us but that nevertheless retain their full cogency and power.

References

Agamben, G. (2000). *Il tempo che resta: Un commento alla lettera ai romani*, Torino: Bollati Boringhieri.

Badiou, A. (1997). *Saint Paul. La fondation de l'universalisme*, Paris: Presses Universitaires de France.

Baker, P., and P. Slevin (2005). 'Bush Remarks on "Intelligent Design" Theory Fuel Debate', Washington Post, 3 August.

Berger, P.L. (ed.) (1999). *The Desecularization of the World: Resurgent Religion and World Politics*, Washington, DC: Ethics and Public Policy Center.

Carten, A., and R. Marshall-Fratani (eds) (2001). *Between Babel and Pentecost: Transnational Pentecostalism in Africa and Latin America*, London: Hurst

Chelini-Pont, B. (2007). 'Le réenchantement discret des mondialisations religieuses', *Esprit* 3–4 (mars–avril), pp. 161–8.

Dawkins, R. (2006). *The God Delusion*, London: Bantam.

Derrida, J. (1993). *Spectres de Marx. L'État dela dette, le travail du deuil et la nouvelle Internationale*, Paris: Éditions Galilée.

Edman, S. (2006). *Förundran. Tankar om vår stund på jorden*, Örebro: Cordia.

Ésprits (2003) (theme issue). 'L'événement saint Paul: juif, grec, romain, chrétien', février.
Fontenay, É. De (1981). *Diderot ou le matérialisme enchanté*, Paris: Grasset.
Habermas, J. (2005). *Zwischen Naturalismus und Religion. Philosophische Aufsätze*, Frankfurt a.M.: Suhrkamp Verlag.
Habermas, J., and J. Ratzinger (2005). *Dialektik der Säkularisierung. Über Vernunft und Religion*, Freiburg–Basel–Wien: Herder.
Heidegger, M. (1989). 'Beiträge zur Philosophie', *Gesammtausgabe*, 65.
Khatab, S. (2006). *The Political Thought of Sayyid Qutb: The Theory of jahiliyyah*, London and New York: Routledge.
Liedman, S.-E. (1986). *Das Spiel der Gegensätze: Friedrich Engels' Philosophie und die Wissenschaften des 19. Jahrhunderts*, Frankfurt: Campus.
Marty, M.E., and R.S. Appleby (eds) (1991). *Fundamentalisms Observed*, vol. 1 of *The Fundamentalism Project*, Chicago, IL: University of Chicago Press.
Mooney, C. (2005). *The Republican War on Science*, New York: Basic Books.
Onfray, M. (2006). *Traité d'athéologie: Physique de la métaphysique*, Paris: Bernard Grasset.
Roy, O. (2005). *La laïcité face à l'Islam*, Paris: Stock.
Roy. O. (2007). 'Le découplage de la réligion et de la culture: une exception musulmane?', *Ésprit* 3–4 (mars–avril): 242–52.
Sigurdson, O. (2006). 'Paulus - filosofernas apostel? Badiou, Agamben, Žižek', *Glänta*, 4, pp. 61–72.
Sprondel, W.M. (1972). 'Entzauberung', in J. Ritter and K. Gründer (eds), *Historisches Wörterbuch der Philosophie*, Darmstadt: Schwarbe, vol. 2: 564f.
Vries, H. de, and L.E. Sullivan (eds) (2006). *Political Theologies: Public Religions in a Post-Secular World*, New York: Fordham University Press.
Weber, M. (1956 [1920]). *Wirtschaft und Gesellschaft*, Tübingen: J.C.B. Mohr.
Willaime, J.-P. (2007). 'Reconfigurations ultramodernes', *Esprit*, 3–4 (mars–avril), pp. 146–55.
Young, M., and T. Edis (eds) (2004). *Why Intelligent Design Fails: A Scientific Critique of the New Creationism*, New Brunswick, NJ, and London: Rutgers University Press.
Žižek, S. (2005). 'The Thrilling Romance of Orthodoxy', in C. Davis, J. Milbank and S. Žižek (eds), *Theology and the Political*, Durham, NC, and London: Duke University Press, pp. 143–96.

Chapter 4
Political and Intellectual Challenges: A Sociological Response

Grace Davie

My response to the three stimulating and very different contributions above will be threefold. I want first to emphasize the importance of language, ensuring that words that are used casually in popular parlance are employed with due care in a field in which pejorative overtones all too often creep into the agenda. The second task is to underline the significance of context in understanding the relationship between religion and the modern world. Religion does not simply encounter or challenge modernity. Particular forms of religion encounter/challenge particular forms of modernity in different, and specified, places. Here the notion of *multiple* modernities, already introduced by José Casanova, will be central. Thirdly I would like to engage *sociologically* the eternal question, 'Does God exist?' Philosophically, there is no answer; we need nonetheless to deal with the consequences of individual, group and societal convictions – either one way or the other. How, in other words, should the social scientist respond to the truth claims of many millions of people and the communities of which they are part?

Both Peter Beyer and Sven-Eric Liedman draw heavily on the concept of fundamentalism in their papers. Both recognize the pitfalls of this approach and both are careful to protect themselves from accusations about the misuse of this term. The problem, however, needs to be pursued further if we are to understand more fully the place of religion in the 21st century. Central to this debate are the categories in which we think, many of which imply value judgments. These are best expressed in a series of questions. For example, do the principal lines of division lie between or within religions; between the religious and the secular; between 'fundamentalist' religion and other forms of religion; between 'fundamentalist' ideology (both religious and secular) and other forms of ideology; between 'good' and 'bad' fundamentalists; between 'good' and 'bad' secularists; between religious organizations and religious people/constituencies; and so on?

Not all of these questions can be engaged in this relatively short response. Two, however, can be taken as illustrations. The first concerns the distinction between 'good' and 'bad' fundamentalists – a point nicely captured by the contrasting ways in which two former American Presidents from roughly the same faith community are currently regarded. Why is Jimmy Carter (a Democrat) considered – admittedly more in retrospect than during his presidency – as a man of principle, whereas George W. Bush (a Republican) invites a very different reaction? The same point can be made in general rather than particular terms. A faith commitment that enables an individual to live an effective and coherent life, directed by firm boundaries and a supportive community, is one thing; quite another is an excluding and exclusive religious organization that encourages shocking and at times violent behavior. But where one merges into the other is not entirely clear. Indeed, discerning this point and the circumstances that are likely to bring this about (a tipping point if ever there was one) should become a major preoccupation of the social sciences. Preventing the slide from one into the other could have major social benefits, but is not achieved simply by decrying all conservative (or indeed 'fundamentalist') forms of religion.

My second example develops the nuances within what has become known as the New Christian Right (NCR) in the United States and its engagement in the foreign affairs of the nation. Recent material from the Pew Research Center provides a good picture of what is going on;[1] so too does the work of Christian Smith and colleagues (1998, 2000). It is important first to distinguish the general attitudes of the Evangelical population from the activities of Evangelical organizations (such as the National Association of Evangelicals and the Southern Baptist Convention, the largest Evangelical denomination). Interestingly, Evangelicals as a whole do not differ from the wider population in their views on foreign policy (including the invasion of Iraq), with one crucial exception – they are more pro-Israel than any other non-Jewish group. That said, American policy in the Middle East has always been strongly pro-Israel under every post-war administration, Republican or Democratic. With this in mind, one must be skeptical about the degree to which Evangelical sentiments were an important factor in the policies of the Bush (junior) Administration.

But when it comes to the activities of Evangelical *organizations*, there has been significant influence in three areas, but – and here is the crucial point – each of these leads to different and at times surprising ad hoc alliances. With respect to human rights, for instance, Evangelicals have quite clearly played an important role in the debate about religious freedom in different parts of the world, leading to tactical alliances with the broader (and generally liberal) human rights constituency. Both groups want freedom of speech, but for different reasons – the former to proselytize, the latter to satirize. The second issue, the international traffic in women for sexual purposes, has also led to political activity, in which Evangelicals found rather different allies – this time in the feminist movement. Thirdly, on the issue of the civil wars in Sudan, allies were found in the Congressional Black Caucus. With respect to the last example, it is important to grasp that interest in Sudan was first stimulated by the civil war in southern Sudan, where the rebels were mostly Christians, but the commitment was then extended to Darfur, where the dividing line was racial rather than religious.

---

[1] See, for example, 'God's Country? Evangelicals & U.S. Foreign Policy', at http://pewresearch.org/pubs/73/gods-country, a Pew Forum discussion following the publication of Walter Mead's *Foreign Affairs* article entitled 'God's Country' (2006).

One final point concludes this section. What, in our scheme of things, are we to do with clearly conservative religious constituencies that have little to do with fundamentalism. Two examples come to mind, both of which introduce a further complicating element: that of gender. The first is a fascinating study of Polish nuns (Trzebiatowska 2008), which reveals that religious sisters in a clearly conservative context are in fact independent and, in their own way, feminist thinkers – though they might not use this term; they are not simply the downtrodden victims of the Catholic Church. The second comes from the growing body of material on Pentecostalism, which exposes the crucial role of women and their capacities for creativity within a seemingly patriarchal form of religion (Martin 2000). Close scrutiny of both cases reveals in fact the real problem; this lies not so much in the cases examined, but in the stereotypical expectations of Western theorizing. Neither Polish nuns, nor Pentecostal women from the global South fulfill the expectations of Western feminists. They are, however, strong and independent women acting out of their own convictions and finding innovative ways of confronting the challenges of modernity.

It is here that we need to pick up the second point in this discussion – that is, the nature of modernity itself. Is this one thing or several? The final section of José Casanova's contribution to this book engages this idea very directly. It is time, Casanova insists, 'to revise our teleological conceptions of a global cosmopolitan secular modernity against which we can characterize the religious "other" as "fundamentalist."' Conversely, it is also time 'to make room for more complex, nuanced and reflexive categories that will help us to understand better the already-emerging global system of multiple modernities' (p. 34). What, then, is this concept of multiple modernities, and how might it help our understanding? The following paragraphs draw directly on the work of Shmuel Eisenstadt, the leading figure in this increasingly important debate.

Eisenstadt starts by setting out the *negative* aspects of this idea:

> The notion of 'multiple modernities' denotes a certain view of the contemporary world – indeed of the history and characteristics of the modern era – that goes against the views long prevalent in scholarly and general discourse. It goes against the view of the 'classical' theories of modernization and of the convergence of industrial societies prevalent in the 1950s, and indeed against the classical sociological analyses of Marx, Durkheim, and (to a large extent) even of Weber, at least in one reading of his work. They all assumed, even only implicitly, that the cultural program of modernity as it developed in modern Europe and the basic institutional constellations that emerged there would ultimately take over in all modernizing and modern societies; with the expansion of modernity, they would prevail throughout the world. (Eisenstadt 2000: 1)

Right from the start, therefore, Eisenstadt challenges both the assumption that modernizing societies are convergent, and the notion of Europe (or indeed anywhere else) as the lead society in the modernizing process.

How, then, does the multiple modernities approach develop from a *positive* point of view? In the introductory essay to an interesting set of comparative cases, Eisenstadt suggests that the best way to understand the modern world (in other words, to grasp the history and nature of modernity) is to see this as 'a story of continual constitution and reconstitution of a multiplicity of cultural programs' (2000: 2). A second point follows from this. These ongoing reconstitutions do not drop from the sky; they emerge as the result of endless encounters on the part of both individuals and groups, all of whom engage in the creation (and re-creation) of both cultural and institutional formations, but within *different* economic and cultural contexts. Once this way of thinking is firmly in place, it becomes easier to appreciate one of the fundamental paradoxes of Eisenstadt's writing: namely, that to engage with the Western understanding of modernity, or even to oppose it, is as indisputably modern as to embrace it. It is equally clear that the form of modernity that has emerged in Europe is only one among many; it is not necessarily the global prototype.

Such a statement is crucial with respect to religion, and goes straight to the core of an increasingly urgent question: is secularization intrinsic or extrinsic to the modernization process? The answer, moreover, must be sought empirically as well as theoretically. What does the evidence discovered in the modern world lead us to conclude? Whatever we may *think* about the facts that increasingly assert themselves in public as well as academic agendas, it is difficult to maintain that the modern world as a whole is secular and systematically becoming more so; indeed much of it is, following Peter Berger's graphic phrase, 'as furiously religious as ever' (Berger 1993: 34).

Exactly the same point can be put in a different way, framing the question as follows: is Europe secular because it is modern (or at least more modern than other parts of the world), or is it secular because it is European, and has developed along a distinctive pathway unlikely to be repeated elsewhere? Saying 'yes' to the first of these options is effectively a restatement of the secularization thesis. Saying 'yes' – however cautiously – to the second opens up new and much more creative ways of thinking, including a significant reappraisal of academic priorities. The latter point derives from the evident connection between the norms of social science, including those that relate to religion, and the European context from which they emerge. Social science is, without doubt, the child of the European – most notably, the French – Enlightenment. It is this Enlightenment, moreover, that is premised on an anti-religious epistemology. Deeply embedded in this way of thinking is the notion of Enlightenment as a 'freedom from belief'; it is very different indeed from the version that made its way across the Atlantic and took root in the United States. Here the Enlightenment expressed itself as a 'freedom to believe', which – together with a very different and distinctive set of economic, political and cultural circumstances – produced in the fullness of time a modern, industrial society, in which vibrant and effective religious economy forms a crucial part. The corollary is clear: if the European case turns out to be the exceptional rather than typical case, and Europe gave us social science, where should we look for conceptual tools to understand better what is happening in the rest of the world?

Economic, political and social scientists – whether interested in religion or not – should ponder carefully the implications of the previous paragraph. They can be summarized as follows: what are the consequences of taking seriously the fact that, for the great majority of the world's populations in the 21st century, it is not only possible, but entirely 'normal', to be both fully modern and fully religious? Might this make a difference to the paradigms that we construct in order to understand better what is happening around us? The answer must surely be 'yes'. Indeed, to follow this through would eliminate at a stroke what the British sociologist, James Beckford, has termed the insulation and isolation of the sociology of religion (1989). Putting the same point more positively, it would once and for all restore religion to its rightful place in the social scientific agenda.

There are signs that this is happening. I shall conclude by citing two of these, the first of which has already been mentioned by Sven-Eric Liedman. Jürgen Habermas, perhaps the most prominent philosopher in modern Europe, argues as follows. Secular citizens – he insists – must learn, sooner rather than later, to live in a post-secular society. In so doing, they will be following the example of religious citizens, who have already come to terms with the ethical expectations of democratic citizenship, in the sense that they have adopted appropriate epistemic attitudes towards their secular environment. So far secular citizens have not been expected to make a similar effort – a situation that leads to the current 'asymmetric distribution of cognitive burdens', an imbalance that needs to be rectified sooner rather than later (Habermas 2005: 17).

The argument can be amplified as follows. Habermas addresses the debate in terms of John Rawls's celebrated concept, the 'public use of reason', using this to invite of secular citizens, including Europeans, 'a self-reflective transcending of the secularist self-understanding of Modernity' (Habermas 2006: 15) – an attitude that quite clearly goes beyond 'mere tolerance' in that it necessarily engenders feelings of respect for the worldview of the religious person. Hence the need not only for a growing reciprocity in the debate (the point already made), but for an additional question. Are religious issues simply to be regarded as relics of a pre-modern era, or is it the duty of the more secular citizen to overcome his or her narrowly secularist consciousness in order to engage with religion in terms of *reasonably expected disagreement*' (2006: 15), assuming in other words a degree of rationality on both sides? The latter appears to be the case.

In other words, we must act *as if* the religious response is reasonable, whether we agree with this or not. Religion is, and must remain, a central factor in economic, political, social and cultural analysis – this is the core theme of my second example, an important essay published in *The Economist* (2 November 2007). The turn-around is dramatic. As the author of the *Economist* essay points out, religion does not appear once in the index of *Diplomacy*, Henry Kissinger's 900-page masterpiece on statesmanship (1994). Such an omission – however disconcerting this may be for the secular liberals of the West – is no longer admissible. The remainder of the essay follows the point through, examining the implications of seriously held religion for the major diplomatic debates of the 21st century. It has become required reading for my students in the sociology of religion.[2]

References

Berger, P. (1993). *A Far Glory: The Quest for Faith in an Age of Credulity*, New York: Doubleday.

Beckford, J. (1989). *Religion and Advanced Industrial Society*, London: Routledge.

Eisenstadt, S. (2000). 'Multiple modernities', *Daedalus: Journal of the American Academy of Arts and Sciences*, 129, pp. 1–30.

Habermas, J. (2005). 'Religion in the Public Sphere', lecture presented at the Holberg Prize Seminar, 29 November, at http://www.holbergprisen.no/images/materiell/2005_symposium_habermas.pdf#nameddest=habermas, accessed 8 February 2010.

Habermas, J. (2006). 'Religion in the Public Sphere', *European Journal of Philosophy*, 14:1, pp. 1–25.

Kissinger, H. (1994). *Diplomacy: The History of Diplomacy and the Balance of Power*, New York: Simon and Schuster.

Martin, B. (2000). 'The Pentecostal Gender Paradox: A Cautionary Tale for the Sociology of Religion', in R. Fenn (ed.), *The Blackwell Companion to the Sociology of Religion*, Oxford: Blackwell, pp. 52–66.

Micklethwait, J., and A. Wooldridge (2009). *God is Back: How the Global Rise of Faith is Changing the World*, London: Allen Lane

Smith, C. (2000). *Christian America? What Evangelicals Really Want*, Berkeley, CA: University of California Press.

Smith, C., M. Emerson, S. Gallagher, P. Kennedy and D. Sikkink (1998). *American Evangelicalism: Embattled and Thriving*, Chicago, IL: University of Chicago Press.

Trzebiatoska, M. (2008). 'Gender, Religion and Identity: Catholic Nuns in Twenty-First Century Poland', unpublished Ph D thesis, University of Exeter, UK.

---

[2] This essay has been expanded into a book: Micklethwait and Wooldridge 2009.

Chapter 5
Political and Intellectual Challenges: A Theological Response

Niels Henrik Gregersen

It is a privilege for me to respond to the contributions of José Casanova, Peter Beyer and Sven-Eric Liedman. Each in his own way illustrates how religion is resiliently present in public life – sometimes as an invisible cultural background condition; sometimes in such robustness that the persistence of religion also affords its negation. Indeed, both the co-presence of a new public visibility of religious life-forms and a transformation of formative religious ideas into the guise of more or less shared 'values' indicate why the significance and transformation of religion cannot easily be accommodated into a single scheme of explanation.

In what follows I first address the difficulties in using general analytical labels such as 'fundamentalism' and 'liberalism' in social scientific descriptions of religion. I argue that these terms tend to be used too indiscriminately, and I propose alternatives such as 'foundationalism' and 'communitarian ideals'. My main focus, however, will be on the many faces of 'secularization' that come to the fore in the three chapters: Do theories of modernity imply a notion of a general process of secularization, or do we need to be more historically sensitive in order to see what our terms are able to catch, and fail to catch, in the religious situation? To what extent do we live in clean rooms of separation between religious and public life; to what extent are the domains intertwined or entangled; and to what extent does religion even saturate the 'tone' of social life beyond the religious or anti-religious commitments of individuals?

The Politics of Analytical Labels

Grace Davie, in her sociological response, has already offered reasons for caution concerning labelling groups and persons as 'fundamentalist'. Let me here distinguish between three different uses of the term 'fundamentalism'.

Used as *historical term*, 'fundamentalism' may best be reserved for persons and groups who (1) promote certain 'sacred texts' as divinely inspired, (2) assume a religious as well as a historical inerrancy of these sacred texts, and (3) use them as final arbiters on contemporary ethical or political issues. As such, the term 'fundamentalism' has rightly been used to refer to counter-modern Protestant groups, who since the 1870s have argued against historical–critical studies of the

Bible (with respect to criteria 1 and 2). But only in the 20th century, and especially after World War I, did self-declared Protestant 'fundamentalists' engage in a more thorough critique of modernity (in line with criterion 3) (Marsden 1980). One could meaningfully extend the label to other groups, for example to Muslims that take a similar stance towards the Quran (including criterion 3). On such textual definition of 'fundamentalism', however, it would be difficult to extend the term to, say, Pentecostals whose 'living testimonies' of the Spirit abound, or to Roman-Catholic Christians, who appeal to the fine balance between fixed Scripture and living tradition, and who point to the Pope as having the right, in principle, to make shared spiritual experiences explicit in new communal teachings. As is the case with Hindus, the relevant texts for the Catholic are so many that it is highly difficult to be a Roman-Catholic fundamentalist, though the obedience towards the authority of the Church may be interpreted as such by outsiders.

This historical designation of the term 'fundamentalism' should be distinguished from the *pejorative use* about persons or groups who take their religious, ideological or scientific views somehow 'too seriously', and commit to them in a 'one-eyed' manner. This is how the term has come to be used in the media as well as in more contentious public debates on religion, politics and science.

The question is now, whether 'fundamentalism' can be rescued as an *analytical term*, to be used from a more generalized social science perspective in order to study functional equivalents among diverse religious or ideological groups – groups who may differ in terms of religious content and liturgical orientation yet who are supposed to exemplify the same 'fundamentalist' mindset. From a functionalist perspective, a Leninist may be termed a Marxist fundamentalist, just as a 'militant' atheist such as Richard Dawkins may be said to succumb to the fundamentalism of scientism (meaning that science is the only reliable source of information about fundamental reality).

I remain sceptical about the gains of such broad-scale analytical notion of 'fundamentalism'. Peter Beyer uses it throughout his chapter, though he, in a footnote, carefully explains that he 'continue[s] to use the word "fundamentalist" to refer to this sort of religious challenge [that is, from the contents of religion to the realm of politics]', though 'it should be understood that the word always appears in scare-quotes because of the pejorative connotations that it usually carries and the arbitrary way in which it is often used'. But then, why not look for less arbitrary concepts?

In his conference presentation, Sven-Eric Liedman used the label 'fundamentalism' without further apologies when speaking about Pentecostalism. 'The term "fundamentalism"', he said, 'is certainly more appropriate [than orthodoxy], assuming that it is used in a broad, flexible sense to refer to the desire to establish an unassailable, timeless foundation for religious faith'. In the revised version of his paper printed here there are only a few references left to fundamentalism, which I find wise. Liedman, though, still speaks about the 'fundamentalist constructs' that have been 'used to justify not only the bloody war in Iraq but decisions concerning, among others, stem cell research' (p. xx).

I would agree with Liedman that arguments in favour of going to war and arguments forbidding stem cell research are contrived and 'constructed', as all public statements are. But as far as I'm aware, not many (if any) pro-war contenders referred to biblical prophecies about Saddam Hussein. Here as elsewhere, concrete ethical stances were mediated by values and norms (that is, preferential rules) based in the lifestyles and ideals of already-established communities. If this analysis is basically correct, it seems more precise to refer to 'communitarian ideals' of American conservatism. Or take another example, the emphasis on 'family values' in the American so-called *Moral Majority Movement*. After all, the Jewish Bible prefers polygamy to monogamy, and neither Jesus nor Paul was particularly fond of marriage. According to central New Testament texts, celibacy is clearly to be preferred to middle-of-the road family life. Such facts, however, have not disturbed proponents of Moral Majority to remain eager to maintain their lifestyles, but more so perhaps they are Texans (or whatever) than because they are Christians. It would indeed be a hard job to justify high marriage values with Scripture. What people normally do is to make an argument building on several resources, while stating some values to be the 'core values' for the community. In the case of the Iraq war and stem cell research, the core values may be 'the right of self-defence' (concretized in the new construct of 'pre-emptive strike') and a 'pro life-attitude' (concretized in relation to the new technological possibilities of stem cell research).

Especially when addressing intellectual ideas (the topic given to Liedman), I would prefer to use the term 'foundationalism' for the kind of thinking that Liedman wants to critique. Foundationalism encompasses a view about how to justify beliefs and ethical stances. The foundationalist assumption is, in short, that knowledge and ethics ultimately rest on a foundation made up of previously established beliefs, usually stemming from non-inferential resources. Religious arguments of many sorts (first-hand evidence, communal values, tradition, biblical references) can thus be used to justify forays into the political realm.

Observe, however, that the foundationalist search for a safe haven for religious practices may also characterize other kinds of arguments. On the above definition Richard Dawkins may be termed a foundationalist, insofar as he wants to derive all knowledge about reality from science, in particular from Darwinian resources. A curious example can be found in his atheist manifest *The God Delusion*, from 2006. Arguing against the so-called Anthropic Principle (the idea that the physical laws of nature are fine-tuned for the purpose of life), he sides with physicist Lee Smolin, who has argued that laws of nature come and go, and hence are the result of a cosmic selection process, analogous to Darwin's principle of natural selection in biology. Dawkins here wonders 'whether some other physicists are in need of Darwinian consciousness-raising' (Dawkins 2006: 146). What is strange about this argument is the suggestion that biology can explain the world of physics rather than the other way around. This is obviously an irrational move. By comparison, Dawkins's assumption that evolution might explain religion is a stronger candidate for truth. In both cases, however, Dawkins argues as a foundationalist (though hardly as a 'fundamentalist'). Marxist–Leninists (in so far as they still exist) may also be aptly described as foundationalists, but not necessarily as fundamentalists (though the special caste of the school of *Kapital-Logiker* may suit the term). In short, all fundamentalists are foundationalists, but not all foundationalists are fundamentalists. Neither are proponents of Intelligent Design necessarily fundamentalists (most of them are not), but they argue within a foundationalist framework.

The same caution may be relevant concerning the distinction between 'liberalism' and 'conservatism'. Peter Beyer helpfully points to the different sorts of religious forays into politics, including the 'liberal' ones from Mahatma Gandhi of India and Desmond Tutu of South Africa. This distinction between liberals and conservatives is a category from the political sciences. But I wonder whether they are apt in relation to religiously motivated challenges to politics such as Gandhi and Tutu. One could well argue that both represent fairly orthodox versions of the Hindu and Christian traditions respectively.

More important to my argument below is that a Desmond Tutu would hardly be able to sort out exactly what is religious ('Christian') and what is political ('anti-Apartheid') about his views. From an 'orthodox' Christian perspective, poor people are not just citizens of South Africa, or other countries, with democratic 'rights'; they are first and foremost 'neighbours'. In the concept of being 'brothers and sisters' to one another, one cannot separate the secular and the religious aspects, the 'political' and the 'Christian' meanings. For as Judge of the World says according to the Gospel of Matthew, 'Truly I tell you: anything you did for one of my brothers there, however insignificant, you did for me' (25:40; REB). And so the other way around: 'Anything you failed to do for one of these, however insignificant, you failed to do for me' (25:45). The 'secular' realm is here saturated with religious significance. From Tutu's point of view the two realms can hardly be taken apart. This raises the general question, in what sense can secular notions of religion-free domains be imagined from a religious perspective?

The European Process of Governmentalization and the Emergence of Secular Mentalities

In his magnum opus *A Secular Age*, philosopher Charles Taylor has helpfully distinguished between various meanings of secularity. *Secularity1* means the retreat of religion from public life, *secularity2* the decline in religious belief and practice, and *secularity3* the change in the conditions for having religious beliefs (Taylor 2007: 423). Taylor insists that something new has taken place in our attitudes to religion. But he agrees with the analysis of José Casanova that the differentiation of society, which is part of modernity, does not necessarily lead to a privatization of belief (ibid.: 426). On the contrary, the cases for a de-privatization of belief are many, not only in the Muslim world, but also in Hinduism, Buddhism and Christianity (Gandhi, Dalai Lama, Tutu and Bush, just to mention a few).

Peter Beyer's chapter explores in detail such intersections in a cross-cultural perspective.

Casanova, in particular, points to the historical difficulties of maintaining the secular meta-narrative of how we all became secular in the public realm, while religion is steadily receding into a private religiosity for those who – allegedly for opaque psychological reasons – still happen to have religious sentiments. This myth is not sustainable, shows Casanova. Not only have we witnessed persistent trends towards de-secularization and de-privatization over the last forty years, but a longer historical perspective suggests a continuous entanglement of religion and society. As Casanova reminds us, the end of the Thirty Years' War (1618–48) did not result in an elimination of religion from public significance. On the contrary, the Augsburg Interim of 1548 led to a stark confessionalization of Christian traditions, a confessionalization accompanied by an 'ethno-religious cleansing' of those not belonging to the religion of the sovereigns.

Casanova's analysis could be supplemented with the historical material offered by Michel Foucault in his 'Lectures at Collège de France' 1977–78 (especially from 15 February 1978). Here Foucault formed the concept of 'governmentality' for a fundamental change of a government influencing everyday mentalities, hence also changing the conditions for having religious belief (secularity3, in Taylor's terms). The term 'governmentality' links the idea of government to the mentality of the citizens by referring to 'the conduct of conduct'. Based on mostly Catholic material, Foucault saw this development in the 17th and 18th centuries, but he was well aware that this development had already taken place in the 16th century in Protestant countries: 'There is a double movement, then, of state centralization, on the one hand, and of the dispersion and religious dissidence, on the other. It is, I believe, at the intersection of these two tendencies that the problem [of governmentality] comes to pose itself with this particular intensity, of how to be ruled, how strictly, by whom, to what end, by what methods, and so on. There is a problem of government in general' (Foucault 1991: 202). The point is the government's seeking control, not by controlling what the citizens should do, but by teaching them how to think. The intensive use of catechism is a major case pointing in the direction of a religious self-control that later on turned into a mindset of gaining institutional help for moral and religious self-help (Gregersen 2008). The resulting self-control, however, usually remains linked up with the social expectations of society at large, including expectations of some measure of orthodoxy in religious beliefs, moral common sense, and ideas of what constitutes a healthy lifestyle. And yet, by articulating doctrinal beliefs, it was now also possible to stand back from religious beliefs. From this context, it makes sense to say, 'I am a Lutheran atheist', as Liedman describes himself. Thus the very process of governmentalization (secularity3, in Taylor's terms) created the possibility for taking distance to beliefs (secularity2, in Taylor's terms).

During the late 18th and 19th centuries, religion retreated from the public sphere in the wake of the new distinction between state and society. With the principle of freedom of belief also the possibility of a freedom from belief was offered. Gradually it was understood that citizens could be morally reliable and fully trustworthy without consenting to the majority religion, indeed without having any religious engagement at all. For some time, however, the state-based school system continued to back religious education by virtue of morning hymns, school prayer, and so on. The strong state-regulated institutions in Europe thereby continued to provide a cultural matrix for social bonding effects. Governmentality was still at rule, though its reign was contested.

An example is so-called Golden Age Denmark, 1800–1870. With influential figures such as fairy-tale writer Hans Christian Andersen, philosophers such as F.C. Sibbern and Søren Kierkegaard, theologians such as H.L. Martensen and N.F.S. Grundtvig, and scientists such as H.C. Ørsted (the discoverer of electromagnetism), we had a hegemonic knowledge regime of Christian ideas and values, though with room for dissenting voices. Kierkegaard wanted Danes to be more Christian (or at least to acknowledge that they were not genuinely Christians), whereas H.C. Ørsted translated Christian ideas into a *Naturphilosophie* that openly negated central aspects of Christian orthodoxy, such as the divinity of Jesus. There was space for dissent in consensus Denmark. To a wide extent, this is still the case. It is more upsetting to most Danes if one expresses overly strong religious sentiments than if one disavows religion altogether. This is a clear case of secularity3 (a change in the conditions of belief), which indeed makes belief less natural, which may (or may not) lead to secularity2 (a decline in belief and practices).

Separation, Intertwinement or Saturation?

Now, how should we interpret this situation? The 'orthodox' secularization theory started out from a separation between state and religion, while presupposing a continuous sidelining of the latter until we reach a virtual elimination of it. However, no empirical indications in terms of religious practices and belief warrant such conclusion. New statistics for Denmark (presented and discussed in Højsgaard and Iversen 2005) suggests a country not divided into naturalists versus theists, but rather with a general acceptance of science coupled with a widespread 'belief in God thinly spread', as aptly formulated by Ingvild Sælid Gilhus (2005). All follow more or less the available religious resources, while also claiming to 'believe in one's own way', as put by Hans Raun Iversen (2005). It's like with furniture: people opt for a personal style, but still go to IKEA to buy their armchairs. There is help for self-help, while also freedom from help to self-help.

For more than a hundred years, Denmark has not hosted cultural collisions between an aggressive atheistic naturalism and a self-assertive classic theism. One indication is the curious fact that Denmark, according to a survey in *Science* 2005, scores the second highest (next to Iceland) worldwide adherence to Darwinian evolution (82 per cent), exactly the same percentage of contributing members of the Evangelical–Lutheran Church (the so-called 'People's Church') in 2008. It can be argued that Lutheranism (which does not harbour any expectation of natural theology) is a factor in explaining why Darwinism was so relatively easily accommodated in Denmark (Gregersen and Kjærgaard, 2009). But even without suggesting a too-strong connection between Darwinism and Lutheranism, there obviously exists, even on the most critical interpretation, some significant overlap.

Law school professor Lisbet Christoffersen (2006) has proposed the notion of a historically based *intertwinement* of religious and cultural institutions, especially between legal and religious institutions. Similar concepts play a central role in the study *At the Heart of Denmark*, where Peter Gundelach, Hans Raun Iversen and Margit Warburg (2007: 136–53) count 'religion' as one of the seven relatively shared 'sister institutions' in Denmark alongside family, school, the welfare state, the work sphere, civil society and the nation. This concept of intertwinement seems consonant with José Casanova's reference to the 'very "unsecular" entanglements' that we observe empirically as well as legally across Europe.

Whereas 'separation' suggests clear walls between religion and society, 'intertwinement' points in the direction of distinct treads being woven together through a historical process. However, the case made above concerning Desmond Tutu even points in the direction of more fundamental undercurrents, a sense of a stream of togetherness so deep-seated that the 'secular' and the 'religious' elements of contemporary society cannot be taken apart. I do not claim this as an alternative sociological theory. But I do at least want to indicate that this is how society may be perceived from a religious perspective. Insofar as the religious perspective is a fact of life, it is also part of the *fait social total* (to speak in the vein of Marcel Mauss).

In his posthumous work *Die Religion der Gesellschaft*, from 2000, social philosopher Niklas Luhmann argued that the concept of secularization need be defined relative to the observers. As part of the secular meta-narrative exposed by Casanova, reference to secularization was part of the expectation of religion's extermination in a foreseeable future. The so-called 'new atheism' of Dawkins, Christopher Hitchens or Daniel Dennett may in part stem from a deep frustration that religions after all haven't gone away, but rather gained new momentum. Similarly, 'secularization' may be part of an 'observation of the observation' of the relation between religion and its environment, seen from the religious viewpoint (Luhmann 2000: 282). Secularization here expresses the blind spot of secular sociologists who don't understand that 'sleeping late on Sunday' doesn't mean 'refusing the sacrament' (ibid.: 283). I would suggest, however, that modern religions also continue to host a sense of *attunement* with wider reality, a sense of being in accord with an undivided realm of nature–society–individuality. Casanova points in a similar direction when he, in *Public Religions in the Modern World*, writes as follows: 'Religion always transcends any privatistic, autistic reality, serving to integrate the individual into an intersubjective, public and communal "world". Simultaneously, however, religion always transcends any particular community cult, serving to free the individual from any particular "world", and to integrate the same individual into a transsocial, cosmic reality' (1994: 216).

Let me take this quotation as a pointer to the ways in which religion today can perceive the 'secular' world. My point here also is that a modernized form of religion (such as Protestantism and most forms of practised Catholicism in the West) can feel quite relaxed about distinctions between the ecclesial and the political realm, while nonetheless being predisposed, as it were, to make the kind of forays into the general social field as suggested by both Beyer and Casanova. At least monotheistic religions see 'world' as 'creation', that is, they perceive the nexus of nature, society and individual existence as a playing field of God's continuous, yet always variegated, creativity. God is here not 'a being' to be believed (or not to be believed) to 'exist' on the top of the world, apart from worldly realities. Rather God is assumed to 'saturate' reality as the very Being-in-being at the core of reality, as well as the Becoming-coming-into-being in new possibilities afforded by reality. There are deep-seated biblical expressions of such a view. 'Do I not fill heaven and earth?', came the Word of the LORD according to the prophet Jeremiah (23:23; REB). Likewise according to the New Testament, Paul said to his contemporary Greek audience: 'Indeed he [God] is not far from each of us, for in him we live and move, in him we exist' (Acts 17:28; REB).

We here arrive at a perspective that is also seen by Charles Taylor: religion 'saturates' reality rather than being 'sidelined' (Taylor 2007: 816). This view, however, relates not necessarily to institutionalized religion, as it is about what religion is (or can be) about. Protestantism (and many strands of Catholicism) live quite comfortably with the secular fact that the Church cannot, and should not, fill out the world, but in a sense *must* be sidelined to exist alongside other social institutions. However, streams of worldly reality may still be 'full of God'. As Friedrich Schleiermacher once intimated in *On Religion: Speeches to its Cultural Despisers* (1799): 'To present all events in the world as actions of a god is religion; it expresses its connection to an infinite totality' (Schleiermacher 1996: 25). Or expressed more modestly: in spite of all secularity, the world still affords the presence of events and processes that continue to trigger a religious sensibility. The sun still rises, the air in the lungs still feels refreshing, birds continue to sing and cats to move, children are born and grow up, people mourn for their lost friends, family life still goes on, and the neighbour remains a source of both surprise and irritation.

Religion may no longer be necessary from the perspective of the other functions of society. But religion deals with experiences in the midst of social life that are more than necessary, experiences filled with cognitive complexity, with moral demands, and with the aesthetic excess of reality.

References

Casanova, José (1994). *Public Religions in the Modern World*, Chicago, IL: University of Chicago Press.
Christoffersen, Lisbet (2006). 'Intertwinement: A New Concept for Understanding Religion–Law Relations', *Nordic Journal of Religion and Society*, 19:2, pp. 93–106.
Dawkins, Richard (2006). *The God Delusion*, Boston: Houghton Mifflin Company.
Foucault, Michel (1991; [1978]). 'Governmentality', in Graham Burchell, Colin Gordon and Peter Miller (eds), *The Foucault Effect: Studies in Governmentality*, Chicago, IL: University of Chicago Press, pp. 87–104.
Gilhus, Ingvild Sælid (2005). 'Gudstro smurt tyndt udover' ['Belief in God, Thinly Smeared'], in Morten Thomsen Højsgaard and Hans Raun Iversen (eds), *Gudstro i Danmark* [*Belief in God in Denmark*], Copenhagen: Anis, pp. 83–100.
Gregersen, Niels Henrik (2008). 'Religion in der Öffentlichkeit. Die Zwei-Regimente-Lehre zwischen Privatisierung und Gouvernementalisierung', *Forum historiae iuris. Europäische Internetzeitschrift für Rechtsgeschichte*, 1–40, at www.forhistiur.de/zitat/0808gregersen.htm, accessed 5 February 2010.
Gregersen, Niels Henrik, and Peter C. Kjærgaard (2009). 'Darwin and the Divine Experiment : Religious Responses to Darwin 1859–1909', *Studia Theologica – Nordic Journal of Theology*, 63:2, pp. 140–61.
Gundelach, Peter, Hans Raun Iversen and Margit Warburg (2007). *I hjertet af Danmark. Institutioner og mentaliteter* [*At the Heart of Denmark: Institutions and Mentalities*], Copenhagen: Reitzel.
Højsgaard, Morten Thomsen, and Hans Raun Iversen (eds) (2005). *Gudstro i Danmark* [*Belief in God in Denmark*], Copenhagen: Anis.
Iversen, Hans Raun (2005). 'Gudstro i den danske religionspark' ['Belief in God in the Danish Park of Religion'], in Morten Thomsen Højsgaard and Hans Raun Iversen (eds), *Gudstro i Danmark* [*Belief in God in Denmark*], Copenhagen: Anis, pp. 103–23.
Kjærgaard, Peter C., Niels Henrik Gregersen and Hans Henrik Hjermitslev (2008). 'Darwinizing the Danes, 1859–1909', in Eve-Marie Engels and Thomas F. Glick (eds), *The Reception of Charles Darwin in Europe. Volume I*, London and New York: Continuum Press, pp. 146–55.
Luhmann, Niklas (2000). *Die Religion der Gesellschaft*, Frankfurt a.M.: Suhrkamp.
Marsden, George M. (1980). *Fundamentalism and American Culture*, Oxford: Oxford University Press.
Schleiermacher, Friedrich (1996). *On Religion: Speeches to its Cultural Despisers*, ed. and trans. Richard Crouter, Cambridge: Cambridge University Press.
Taylor, Charles (2007). *A Secular Age*, Cambridge, MA: Belknap Press of Harvard University Press.

The Religion and Science Debate

Chapter 6
Challenges in the 21st Century: Religion and Science

Philip Clayton

The heritage of Denmark, and for that matter the heritage of most of Europe, is deeply religious. As early as the early 11th century Denmark was considered to be a Christian state. The national Church of Denmark quickly grew out of the Protestant Reformation, which was introduced into Denmark in 1536. According to the *Encyclopedia Britannica*, about 90 per cent of Danes are, at least nominally, members of the state Evangelical Lutheran church ('Denmark' 2007).[1] Today, however, the number of Danes who characterize themselves as religious or who participate regularly in religious activities is among the lowest in Europe. With the exception of the Christian Democrats and the Ministry for Ecclesiastical Affairs, there is little appeal to belief in God in Danish politics today. Contrast this with the United States, where belief in God plays a major political role and politicians regularly appeal to their religious motivations.

According to an English dictionary, a legacy is 'something transmitted by or received from an ancestor or predecessor or from the past' (Merriam–Webster Collegiate Dictionary 1999: 664). Like a church building long since become inactive and now visited only as a historical curiosity, religion no longer determines the daily moral, ethical or political decisions of most residents in northern Europe; the same is increasingly true in southern Europe as well.

Thus scholars study the Danish religious 'legacy', and people visit old churches to observe it. By contrast, it would be absurd to speak of the 'scientific legacy' of Denmark, as if the scientific quest were a thing of the past. If you want to know about science in Denmark today, you don't visit the museum of Tycho Brahe. Denmark ranks fourth in the world on scientific publications per million inhabitants, and fourth in the world on how frequently its scientific publications are cited. Denmark spent 11.4 billion kroner on research in 2004, or 0.72 per cent of the gross domestic product. In the same year Danish *companies* spent 26.2 billion kroner on research, or almost 1.8 per cent of the GDP. This is the third best result in the EU, surpassed only by Sweden and Finland. The government has promised to allocate a further 10 billion kroner to research above this level in the years 2005–2010 ('Factsheet on Denmark: Public Research' 2007). The scientific mind is alive and well in Denmark.

---

[1] Church leaders tell me that 83 per cent would be a more accurate figure.

Thus, in the Danish context today, as in most of Europe, it's the *disanalogies* between science and religion of which we are most aware. This is one reason that one might approach a talk on religion and science with a certain degree of skepticism. Of course, there are also *other* reasons to be skeptical. First of all, what passes as science–religion discussion in the popular media, both in Europe and in America, has become famous for denying things that seem obviously true on the one hand, and for affirming things that appear to be obviously false on the other. (This is not a good sign for *any* academic discussion!) Affirming the obviously false, one finds thinkers who maintain that science has already disproven religion, and others who allege that religion disproves the core assumptions of science. On the other hand, denying the obviously true, one encounters various thinkers who maintain that there simply can be no complementarity in any respect between these two different sets of practices.

In contrast to such simplistic conclusions, I wish to make a plea for a more complex exploration of science–religion relations. This task is not easy; influential purveyors of simple answers exist on both sides. Thus, for example, a movement called 'Young Earth Creationism' maintains that the earth is 'on the order of 6,000–10,000 years old, rather than the commonly accepted age of approximately 4.5 billion years old.' How would one reach such a conclusion? 'This figure is arrived at using complicated dating procedures based upon biblical records', writes Austin Cline (2007). Apparently geology and astrophysics are not required!

Now one might think that a literal reading of the Bible would have to be anti-scientific and would have to acknowledge itself as such. Not so, according to Robert A. Herrmann, an American evangelical Christian. Herrmann complains that liberals (he cites the John Templeton Foundation in particular) believe

> ... that various 'scientific' findings require a vast reinterpretation of the Scriptures, at the very least. This is especially so when the 'scientific' findings require acceptance of either cosmological or biological evolution as defined by the atheistic community. As I have shown in my research, this reinterpretation requirement is utterly false. No interpretive modifications are needed; *no changes whatsoever from the most literal Scriptural meanings are necessary* when a particular interpretation of the scientific model I term the General Grand Unification model (GGU-model) is applied. (Herrmann 2002, italics added)

In short, holding a literal interpretation of the Bible does not need to stand in any tension whatsoever with science.

But simple answers are not the provenance of religious believers alone. Consider the string of certainties penned by the British physical chemist Peter Atkins:

> Science is the only path to understanding. It would be contaminated rather than enriched by any alliance with religion ... Atheism, and its justification through science, is the apotheosis of the Enlightenment. Religion implicitly

scorns humanity by asserting that it is intellectually simply too puny ... [A] religious view is that God is the universal proctor of behavior, ceaselessly and ubiquitously ensuring that laws are obeyed, except where a flamboyant miracle is required. Once again, this busybody notion of God is shown by quiet scientific reflection to be wholly unnecessary, and perceived by an atheist as a fantasy of busybody minds anxious to find a cosmic role for their invention. (Atkins 2006: 124, 136, 127)

According to Atkins, *everything* related to religion is simplistic – and just simply wrong. Nothing complicated about it. No exceptions.

Perhaps the world's best known advocate of the simple refutation of religion is Richard Dawkins. It's interesting to consider just a few passages from his recent *The God Delusion* (2006), which provide a fair snapshot of his interactions with religious perspectives and of the sort of arguments that he provides:

- 'I am not attacking any particular version of God or gods. I am attacking God, all gods, anything and everything supernatural, wherever and whenever they have been or will be invented.' (36)
- 'God, in the sense defined, is a delusion; and, as later chapters will show, a pernicious delusion.' (31)
- 'The God of the Old Testament is arguably the most unpleasant character in all fiction: jealous and proud of it; a petty, unjust, unforgiving control-freak; a vindictive, bloodthirsty ethnic cleanser; a misogynistic, homophobic, racist, infanticidal, genocidal, filicidal, pestilential, megalomaniacal, sadomasochistic, capriciously malevolent bully.' (31)
- 'Fundamentalist religion is hell-bent on ruining the scientific education of countless thousands of innocent, well-meaning, eager young minds. Non-fundamentalist, "sensible" religion may not be doing that. But it is making the world safe for fundamentalism by teaching children, from their earliest years, that unquestioning faith is a virtue.' (286)
- 'Faith is an evil precisely because it requires no justification and brooks no argument ... Faith can be very dangerous, and deliberately to implant it into the vulnerable mind of an innocent child is a grievous wrong.' (308)

One has to search hard in Dawkins's writings to find a passage that is positive about religion – or even one that acknowledges some level of complexity to the debate. The best I could find appears in an extremely short section in the book entitled 'Direct Advantages of Religion,' where Dawkins writes, 'There is a little evidence that religious belief protects people from stress-related diseases' (166). Hardly a roaring endorsement.

Is Productive Religion–Science Dialogue Possible?

Many signs would suggest that productive dialogue between religion and science is *not* possible. No simple 'fix' will remove the difficulties, and I will offer no easy 'fixes' here. Instead, I wish to begin with a rather more humble question: why might real dialogue between these two great social forces – a dialogue whose very possibility is deeply disputed today – even be valuable in the first place? *If* real dialogue is possible, what conditions would have to be met for it to take place? *If* it could occur, what might society gain from such a partnership? We know that attempts at real dialogue may be doomed to fail. But the possibility remains intriguing nonetheless.

I ask these questions as a philosopher, not as an empirical social scientist. Philosophers share the interest of social scientists in how beliefs (religious or otherwise) function. But they are also concerned about the *content* of various kinds of beliefs, and about when, if ever, they can count as knowledge. Philosophers express their own kind of bewilderment about what religious belief means in the 21st century.[2] Deep philosophical issues are raised by the question of whether genuine dialogue between science and religion is possible. The question gives rise to a speculative inquiry in the spirit of Kant: what are the conditions of the possibility of such a dialogue? What would have to be fulfilled for it to occur? Note that persons might come to agree on the conditions for the dialogue even when they continue to disagree on whether these conditions are, or even can be, fulfilled in practice.

Ultimately, the theoretical questions about religion–science dialogue are the most interesting topic. I begin, however, with the pragmatic dimension. What might scholarship have to gain from such a dialogue, and how (if at all) might it be helpful to the broader society?

Regarding the first question: as with all other interdisciplinary dialogues, we shall only know what kind of scholarship this dialogue will produce once we have attempted it. We do know, however, what makes interdisciplinary dialogue *impossible*. A profitable dialogue presupposes that each side brings some unique features and strengths to the table. This is the condition, one now recognizes, that is not met by the scholars we have considered so far. Instead, they emphasize the virtues of their particular perspectives – either the merit of science or the value of religion – and then attempt to score as many rhetorical points against the opposing side as possible.

The second pragmatic argument for seeking partnership between religious motivations and scientific study is ethical and political. We owe its thesis statement to Albert Einstein and his famous aphorism: 'Science without religion is lame; religion without science is blind.' It is not the place of science qua science to

---

[2] A similar 'bewilderment' (his term) was expressed by the 'Lutheran atheist' Professor Sven-Eric Liedman, in his deeply probing 'Intellectual Challenges from Religion', Chapter 3 of this book.

make proclamations about what ought to be. Scientists can and should be involved as ethical and political advocates, but when they are, they do not act purely as scientists. When scientists as individuals speak out against the nuclear arms race or global warming, or when they band together to form organizations such as the Union of Concerned Scientists, they draw on deeper values – from whatever sources – that go beyond the parameters of science as such.[3] By contrast, the impressive successes of the sciences in recording data and in explaining observed phenomena in the simplest and most law-like terms is due to science's first methodological commitment: to state *what is* apart from *what ought to be*.

Yet the very value-neutrality that is the secret to scientific success can also be its liability. It is not the place of science qua science to determine the values by which policymakers should decide between competing options; for that, values-based discourses are necessary. One of the places where such values are codified and elaborated – though certainly not the only place – is in the world's various 'wisdom traditions,' which serve as repositories for human values and for their justifying stories and arguments. These 'wisdom traditions' belong to a stratum of inherited beliefs and values that is broader than the ideology of a nation-state, yet in most cases more narrow than humanity as a whole. These traditions are not infallible; indeed, many of them contain justifications of racism, sexism, xenophobia, and ethnocentrism, which modern culture is still struggling to overcome. Still, the obvious fallibility of the world's religious and wisdom traditions does not invalidate them as useful discussion partners. Suitably updated and interpreted, they can offer guidance at least in formulating the ecological and bioethical dilemmas of contemporary science; and they can help place these in the context of (often implicit) views of human nature and human flourishing.

According to advocates of science–religion dialogue, humanity has a better chance of dealing successfully with the immense challenges that it faces in the present century – challenges such as nationalism, terrorism, the environmental crisis, and economic disparity – if it can find a way to draw on the conceptual and axiological resources of these traditions. The complex questions being raised today in genetics, bioengineering and medical nanotechnology call for resources that the sciences do not possess. Moreover, religious myths, stories and practices sometimes have the power to motivate altruistic behavior on the part of individuals and groups, for example in reducing their levels of consumption and waste.

Religion may be able to play some positive role as humanity puzzles its way through the challenges that now beset it; but religion by itself is certainly not sufficient. Without the facts and data provided by the sciences, without a scientific understanding of nature's regularities, and without the technological know-how that science provides, no amount of wisdom will suffice. One thinks of the beautiful

---

[3] This does not mean that I disagree with Jacob Bronowski in his *Science and Human Values*, rev. edn (New York: Harper & Row, [1956], 1975). The scientific method *does* entail certain values of its own. But these values are not sufficient to ground the sorts of ethical and political action that are necessary in light of today's challenges.

stories told by the Native American peoples of the harmony between man, animal and nature. Thus in the 19th century the native woman 'Eyes of Fire' from the Cree tribe called all people back to the Great Spirit, who is the source of all life. When we live in harmony with this Spirit, 'The rivers will again run clear, the forests will be abundant and beautiful, the animals and birds will be replenished. The powers of the plants and animals will again be respected and conservation of all that is beautiful will become a way of life' (Rakkandee 2007). This is a moving vision. And yet only science can detect the patterns of global warming; only science can ascertain its chief causes; and – on the assumption that humanity will never voluntarily return to a pre-technological world of simple subsistence within nature – only science can develop the alternate means by which industry, transportation and utilities can serve their functions without destroying the planet and virtually all life on it.

This possible partnership of scientific knowledge and religiously supported values has its limits. There is no place for a Rousseau-like return to a pre-scientific state; nor is there any prospect for a theocracy in which the 'rule of God' replaces the quest for knowledge. Jürgen Habermas (1998) correctly identifies the free and open exchange of ideas within democratic states as the best framework for adjudicating human differences and fostering public dialogues of all kinds, including this one. He argues that:

> ... the public sphere is a warning system with sensors that, through unspecialized, are sensitive throughout society. From the perspective of democratic theory, the public sphere must, in addition, amplify the pressure of problems, that is, not only thematize them, furnish them with possible solutions, and dramatize them in such a way that they are taken up and dealt with by parliamentary complexes. Besides the 'signal' function, there must be an effective problematization. The capacity of the public sphere to solve problems *on its own* is limited. But this capacity must be utilized to oversee the further treatment of problems that takes place inside the political system. (Habermas 1998: 359)[4]

The question before us is whether one must give up on religious belief, and the forms of theology and *Naturphilosophie* with which it is associated, in order to participate fully in the life of today's democratic states. It has been a widespread belief in European intellectual history since the Enlightenment that some fundamental opposition exists between religion and what has been called 'the project of modernity'. Does this judgment stand up to careful study? Here careful empirical work is necessary. For example, it could be that participation of

---

[4] See also his *Zwischen Naturalismus und Religion: Philosophische Aufsätze* (Frankfurt a.M.: Suhrkamp, 2005); *Religion and Rationality: Essays on Reason, God, and Modernity*, ed. Eduardo Mendieta (Cambridge, MA: MIT Press, 2002); and Habermas with Joseph Cardinal Ratzinger (Pope Benedict XVI), *Dialectics of Secularization: On Reason and Religion* (San Francisco: Ignatius Press, 2006).

religious persons in the public sphere requires an approach to their own tradition that is more open-minded in spirit (cf. the Danish *frisind*), more ready to question and revise beliefs inherited from their tradition. Or perhaps it's not revision but only a certain degree of tolerance that's required of religious believers in the public sphere – a willingness to participate in democratic processes or to accept 'the rule of law', but with no more fundamental changes. I shall ague that a more *frisind* approach to religion is required, even on the part of believers; we return to this question in a moment.

The religion–science dialogue is *already* confronting religious believers with these questions in Europe, in America, and across Asia as well. Study is urgently needed of the new forms of religiosity that are resulting, as well as of the impact that religious traditions are having on scientists and public policies. There was a time when the idea of a serious dialogue between scientists and religious persons would have been unthinkable. Today, such interactions are no longer unthinkable; as this volume shows, they are becoming a social and political necessity.[5]

Religious Studies and the Voice of Religion

The emerging dialogue between science and the religions raises interesting questions at both empirical and speculative levels. We cannot presuppose that a real 'partnership of equals' is possible; indeed, the very appearance of dialogue may be illusory. But, I am arguing, we *can* ask: what are the conditions under which real dialogue becomes possible? It turns out that some of these conditions concern the social scientific study of religion, and others pertain to religious believers who wish to participate in the discussion. So let's be more specific about how the dialogue will affect the two sides. What would it mean, even as a theoretical exercise, to reconceive religion for an age of science? And what will social scientific practice look like when science begins to acknowledge a realm of values and beliefs that are not resolvable through scientific study alone?

Consider first the social sciences, and *Religionswissenschaft* in particular. We are clearly past the stage when people doubted whether the study of religion was significant. The contributions of religion to the 20th century, both positive and negative – its social, political, legal, cultural and artistic impacts – were of undeniable importance; and all signs indicate that religion's role will only increase in the 21st century. *Not* to study the wide variety of manifestations of religion would be unwise, if not outright irresponsible.

---

[5] I write these words on the day that the United States, which is not the world's most secular nation, observes the sixth anniversary of the World Trade Center bombings. As I write on 9/11 in 2007, the newspapers and radio shows manifest the struggles of at least some Americans who are attempting to evolve a more liberal form of religious belief and practice. Of course, media broadcasts in the US today also show signs of apathy, hatred and xenophobia.

Yet as religion–science dialogue advances, it will introduce a further standard for the social scientific study of religion. Many scholars of religion retain a careful critical distance from the phenomena and persons that they study – some because they believe that 'scientific objectivity' requires this critical distance, and others because they feel superior to religious persons and to the irrationality of their beliefs and practices. How should one evaluate these two reasons: the argument from scientific objectivity, and the perceived superiority of scholarship over religious belief?

A religion–science partnership will question the traditional claim that detachment is the precondition for any adequate empirical study of religion. It raises the heretical-sounding possibility that the 'insider's' perspective on the religious life is compatible with good social science. Of course, this possibility is not without antecedents in the history of social scientific theory. Its advocates go back at least to Wilhelm Dilthey in the 19th century, who argued that there is no comprehension of the other without *Verstehen*, the sort of 'empathetic understanding' that intuits its way into the mindsets and worldviews that motivate human action. Likewise, such a methodology is connected to the standard of *depth interpretation* made famous by Clifford Geertz. Geertz writes:

> Believing, with Max Weber, that man is an animal suspended in webs of significance he himself has spun, I take culture to be those webs, and the analysis of it to be therefore not an experimental science in search of law but an interpretive one in search of meaning ... It is explication I am after, construing social expressions on their surface enigmatical. (1973: 5).

Human cultural constructs, Geertz writes, are built up out of 'a multiplicity of complex conceptual structures, many of them superimposed upon or knotted into one another, which are at once strange, irregular, and inexplicit, and which [the ethnographer] must contrive somehow first to grasp and then to render' (ibid.: 10). This fact leads Geertz to emphasize the analogy between anthropology and art: 'the line between mode of representation and substantive content is as undrawable in cultural analysis as it is in painting' (ibid.: 16). He concludes: 'the whole point of a semiotic approach to culture is ... to aid us in gaining access to the conceptual world in which our subjects live so that we can, in some extended sense of the term, converse with them' (ibid.: 24). *Verstehen* and depth interpretation are certainly no less urgent in comprehending the worlds of religious belief and practice.

What, then, of the second major point, the question of the innate inferiority of religious cognition? Some who appeal to the theoretical resources of psychology, sociology, cultural studies, biology, and other disciplines are openly motivated by the goal of showing how misinformed, misguided, and even immoral are the religious beliefs and practices that they study. Their writings aim to show that religious persons are fundamentally deluded about the reasons for their own actions; that they act irrationally (or with a sort of infantile rationality); and that their actions are best explained not by the viability of any of their beliefs, but by motivations and functions to which they are blind. When 'religion explained' – to cite the well-know title from Pascal Boyer – is taken to mean 'religion explained away', then genuine religion–science dialogue becomes impossible from the start.

Can Belief and Critical Questioning Be Combined?

Many of the papers in this volume are exploring new approaches to religious studies. Inspired by their innovations, I have asked a philosophical question: what would be the preconditions within the study of religion for real religion–science dialogue? Now we must move to our second, and somewhat more speculative, question: what changes in mindset, if any, will be required *on the part of religious believers* if there is to be genuine, bi-directional dialogue with the results of the natural and social sciences? Will it require a different kind of religious reflection, a different relationship to the inherited beliefs of one's own religious tradition? Leading scholars in religious studies are seeking to innovate how religion is studied scientifically, from the outside; let me, in closing, speculate on what will be required of those who work from *within* a religious perspective.

Any reflection that remains distinctively religious will still presuppose the life of faith; it will thus remain, in some sense, believing reflection. But the question is, in what sense? A continuum of answers is possible, ranging from 'No changes at all are required on the part of religious believers' to 'Radical changes are required'. Because the latter response is the most controversial, it may be valuable to explore it in some detail. Suppose, then, that being involved in deep and open dialogue with scientific results and methods requires a new openness on the part of a religious person. Suppose that the nature of her 'faith' and her religious reflection will inevitably be affected by the dialogue. What might these changes be?

This question raises the possibility of a life of faith that does not exclude doubt, but *includes* it – includes doubt and radical questioning, and sometimes even despair – within the normative, everyday experience of faith. The phenomenology of this sort of faith has been worked out in some detail by modern religious thinkers such as Karl Jaspers, Paul Tillich and Louis Dupré.[6] According to them, faith is not defined by some pre-existing realm of the sacred, nor is it radically set off from the 'profane' (hence corrupt, 'fallen' and morally suspect) world. Rather, faith of this sort exists in, with and through the world's ambiguities and uncertainties. It is deeply troubled by the problem of evil, though perhaps not completely destroyed by it; it is humbled before other religious traditions, though not ready therefore to

---

[6] See, among many publications, Louis K. Dupré, *The Other Dimension: A Search for the Meaning of Religious Attitudes* (Garden City, NY: Doubleday, 1972). I owe to Prof. Dupré my introduction to the great Dutch phenomenologist G. van der Leeuw, and through him to the phenomenology of religion. A fascinating interview with Dupré, 'Seeking Christian Interiority,' is available at http://www.religion-online.org/showarticle.asp?title=214, verified 28 July 2005.

accept the meaninglessness of all religious distinctions; it is respectful of the power of scientific achievements, though not prepared to reduce the spiritual dimension to what science can grasp of it.

A few years ago I used the term *secular believer* to describe this new mode of belief:

> The secular believer may address skepticism using the formulations of his religious tradition. But, because doubts are no longer external to his religious belief, the effort to answer them in a generally acceptable manner becomes an intrinsic part of the life of faith ... The point here is that this effort does not need to be external or reductionistic to religious belief, but *it can instead be internal to the dynamic of belief.* Secular believers might take the well-known quote from Diderot as their motto: 'Doubts in the matter of religion, far from being acts of impiety, ought to be seen as good works, when they belong to a man who humbly recognizes his ignorance and is motivated by the fear of displeasing God by the abuse of reason.' (Clayton 1989: 138, italics added)

A reciprocal relationship exists between one's picture of faith and the manner in which one pursues religious reflection. When religious practices depend on possessing absolute truth or certainty, they produce theologies that see themselves as repositories of unchanging dogmas and completed revelations. By contrast, a religious life that embraces doubt and ambiguity correlates with a theology that exists with humility in the midst of the sciences, one laborer among many. This is theology as a partner in liberal democracy, not theology as queen of the sciences.

A key step in this direction was taken by the German theologian Wolfhart Pannenberg. Pannenberg (1991–98) begins his major systematic work by insisting that theology must thematize the question of its own truth:

> *If* the dogmas of Christians are true, they are no longer the opinions of a human school. They are divine revelation. Nevertheless, they are still formulated and proclaimed by humans, by the church and its ministers. Hence the question can and must be raised whether they are more than human opinions, whether they are not merely human inventions and traditions but an expression of divine revelation. Thus there arises once again, this time with respect to the concept of dogma, the truth question that is linked more generally to the concept to theology .... (Pannenberg 1991: 9f., italics added)

On this new approach, old appeals to authority are abandoned. Scriptures are now viewed as historical records of the origins of a religion and repositories of its myths and stories, hence as (at most) *indirect* authorities. Nor does an individual's experience become an absolute authority in questions of truth:

> Individual experience can never mediate absolute, unconditional certainty. At best it can offer no more than a certainty which needs clarification and

confirmation in an ongoing process of experience. This subjective certainty does indeed experience the presence of truth and its unconditionality, but only in an ongoing process. (Pannenberg 1991: 47)

Here the controversial nature of religious belief is embraced and allowed to determine one's mode of religious belief and practice. Imagine, for example, discussing with Christians, Jews or Muslims who do not despair at or seek to evade the scientific results – physics or biology or archeology or historical–critical scholarship – but who are ready to take charge in exploring where it leads.

Some will object that the essence of religious faith is to hold to the truth of certain non-scientific beliefs with absolute conviction. It's not clear, however, that comparative religious studies actually support this contention. Jewish rabbinical disputations, medieval Islamic theology, and disputations within the Hindu traditions are just a few of the cases where belief does not stand opposed to study and debate. Even the history of Christian thought reveals a much more subtle confluence of belief and doubt, doctrine and hypothesis, than the proclamations of the magesteria would suggest.

Could Religious Reflection be Critical? Could There Be a Hypothetical Theology?

The idea of a self-critical religious faith gives rise immediately to a variety of serious objections. One wonders first whether this sort of religious stance can actually serve the central functions that religions have traditionally fulfilled; can it impart meaning to believers, and can it manifest sufficient stability that it can constitute a religious form of life? The theologian Paul Tillich has proposed that religious reflection begin with the *question* of meaning rather than with religious answers.[7] In our day, for example, one might begin with the questions of whether the cosmos possesses any inherent or ultimate meaning (whether we are 'at home' in the universe), or whether contemporary biology allows for religious construals of the purpose and goals of human existence, or whether historical–critical scholarship really supports the historical claims that religious traditions, and especially Christians, have made. These issues are infused with such a level of urgency in late-modern literature, philosophy and theology that one can imagine that the entire passion of the religious quest – what Kierkegaard in *Concluding Unscientific Postscript* calls 'the infinite passion of inwardness' (Kierkegaard 1992: 204) – might, in principle, be linked to their study and debate.

Of course, even if wrestling with questions such as these can represent a mode of religious existence, it is one without any advance guarantee of success.

---

[7] One example is the famous 'method of correlation' in the theology of Paul Tillich; see for example his *Systematic Theology*, 3 vols (Chicago, IL: University of Chicago Press, 1951–63), esp. vol. 1.

At any time, historical–critical scholarship, or new cosmological models such as the multiverse theory, or new reflections on the problem of evil, could lead the 'secular believer' to abandon her quest. On the other hand, this impermanence does not mean that the religious stance becomes less authentic in the meantime. Indeed, advocates of 'existential' theories of religion – one thinks of the very different descriptions by Kierkegaard, Heidegger, Jaspers and Rahner – will insist that vulnerability and authenticity are central features of the religious life.

Still there are further difficulties. Even if a questioning or self-critical faith constitutes a viable form of religious practice, it may still fail as religious reflection. For example, the tensions between this cognitive style and traditional theologies may simply be too great. Or it may be impossible to find a middle place between the Scylla of dogmatic certainty and the Charybdis of a religious life bereft of all content and conviction. Addressing these worries brings us to the heated debates about the epistemic status of theological assertions within the various religious traditions.

The challenge – and perhaps the hint of a possible solution – has been effectively posed by the American pragmatist Charles Sanders Peirce. Peirce's philosophy combines a sophisticated theory of critical inquiry with an underlying commitment to realism. Peirce famously argued that 'truth is the character which … we may *justifiably hope* will be enjoyed by beliefs that survive however long or far inquiry is pursued or prolonged' (Wiggins 2004: 114). This led him, despite (or perhaps because of) his own deep religious convictions, to sharply challenge theology, which he claimed 'masqueraded as a science while it was, in essence, antithetical to the spirit of science' (Anderson 2004: 181). As Douglas Anderson comments,

> Theology thus embodies all that Peirce resisted: tenacity, authority, closure of inquiry, and absence of growth. It has repeatedly proved itself a danger to humanity, and, as Parker aptly states, theologians are 'to be chastised as much for muddying the waters of religion as they are for obstructing the scientific spirit'. (Ibid.: 182)[8]

Peirce believed that theology was *essentially* exclusivistic in this sense, and that its primary task 'was to demand adherence to a specific doctrine and to reject, usually in an articulate fashion, any deviation from this doctrine' (ibid.). Elsewhere, Peirce claimed that 'religious truth having been once defined [theologically] is never to be altered in the most minute particular' (Hartshorne and Weiss 1931–58: vol. 1: 40).

But does Peirce show that theology is beyond all reform, or does he merely presuppose it? Why is it not possible to theologize in a manner that corresponds

---

[8] The reference is to Kelly A. Parker, 'C.S. Peirce and the Philosophy of Religion', *Southern Journal of Philosophy*, 28 (1990), pp. 193–212. See also Parker, *The Continuity of Peirce's Thought* (Nashville, TN, and London: Vanderbilt University Press, 1998).

to his own more open model of the religious life? Peirce beautifully described the open spirit that religion *can* manifest:

> ... if religious life is to ameliorate the world, it must ... hold an abiding respect for truth. Such respect involves an openness to growth, to development. Thus, as ideas develop through the community of inquirers, they will have a gradual effect on religious belief and subsequently on religious practices. (Hartshorne and Weiss 1931–58: vol. 1:184)

Peirce thus thought it completely reasonable, as Michael Raposa (1989: 13) puts it, 'that certain religious beliefs should be revised or even discarded as a result of new scientific discoveries.'

Why couldn't religious reflection also find a place within this same ongoing, open-ended process? Why not model theology on the passage just quoted? Assume for the moment that Peirce is right in insisting that respect for truth can lie at the heart of faith, that religious beliefs can be revised, and sometimes discarded, in light of new scientific discoveries. Might not theologians in the various traditions work in the same spirit? Instead of functioning as the guards of traditional beliefs in their inherited form, theologians might become intellectual guides to assist those in their tradition as they struggle to know when to revise and when to discard beliefs inherited from the past.

In the end, we must credit Peirce with recognizing two of the most basic assumptions of inquiry in any field – including theology. First, private claims to knowledge are not enough; validity claims must be 'redeemed' through critical discourse. (Habermas, following Peirce, refers to these as *einlösbare Geltungsansprüche*.) The goal of the truth-seeker, as Hilary Putnam (1990: 221) nicely puts it, is to find 'a coherent system of beliefs which will ultimately be accepted by the widest possible community of inquirers as a result of strenuous inquiry.' Second, the inquirer must presuppose that inquiry is moving towards a final hoped-for consensus, even while she may be rather skeptical concerning the current results of inquiry. Peirce puts the point concisely: 'Undoubtedly, we hope that this, *or something approximating to this*, is so, or we should not trouble ourselves to make much inquiry. But we do not necessarily have much confidence that it *is* so' (Hartshorne and Weiss 1931–58: vol. 5: 432).[9] Theology, and with

---

[9] This notion of inquiry as self-correcting is linked to Peirce's equally important work on semiotics. Signs are never exhaustive of meaning, and meaning is always self-corrected by those constructing and receiving signs. As Peter Skagestad notes in *The Road of Inquiry: Charles Peirce's Pragmatic Realism* (New York: Columbia University Press, 1981), 'The sign user's understanding, namely, is modified by further experience and is not complete until there is nothing left to experience. Hence the precise meaning of a sign is something which we can ascertain only when we have attained omniscience; indeed, only then will the sign have a precise meaning' (165).

it all other disciplines, might just be able to exist, and even to prosper, in this ongoing *Spannungsfeld* of hope, faith, doubt and skepticism.

The Cognitive Contribution of Religion

Of course, it might be *desirable* for religious persons and religious scholars to make these sorts of contributions, and yet still not possible. Certainly in most Enlightenment-based theories of modernity, religion and science have been taken to express two completely different orders of knowledge – if these theorists are ready to grant that religion could express an order of knowledge at all.

This challenge remains the starting point. But various developments in the theory of knowledge (epistemology and philosophy of science or *Wissenschaftstheorie*) in the 20th century have challenged the strict separation that underlies positivist and neo-Enlightenment thinking. Consider just a few of the recent developments that may open the door to genuine dialogue between the sciences, the humanities, and religious traditions:

1. the demise of those empiricisms, whether of Humean or Kantian origins, that claim to ground all knowledge on the indubitable foundation of sensory inputs;
2. a widespread disillusionment with 'unity of science' claims that, similarly, promise that we shall some day be able to build all acceptable knowledge upward from the most fundamental science (presumably microphysics) by means of exhaustive 'bridge laws' between all the sciences in one unbroken hierarchy of objective knowledge;
3. the equally clear demise of rationalisms that proclaim absolute truths known a priori (or by invincible authority) on which the edifice of knowledge should be constructed;
4. complementary to the previous point, the increasingly problematic status of hegemonic truth claims advanced by the fundamentalist religious traditions, often based on a foundationalist appeal to an 'inerrant' revelation in one particular set of holy scriptures, especially when these are taken as an infallible source of scientific and historical knowledge;
5. a growing skepticism about 'anything goes' relativisms, according to which religious traditions don't make any claims at all, or according to which *all* knowledge claims exist in separate air-tight containers, that is, incommensurable language games (L. Wittgenstein);
6. an undercutting of alleged fact–value distinctions, at least when they are drawn so sharply that the two sides have nothing to say to one another; hence,
7. an awareness of the interpretive or 'hermeneutical' nature of all dialogue between competing views of the world (cf. the defense of 'situated knowledges' by feminist thinkers such as Donna Haraway).

Each of these seven theses requires deeper analysis and further study. Still, whatever controversy one or the other formulation may raise, they do evoke our changed epistemic and intellectual context, which is being hotly debated across the spectrum of contemporary philosophy (see Chapter 3 by Professor Sven-Eric Liedman). Any serious attempt to conceive a possible partnership between the sciences and the religions must reflect deeply on this more nuanced understanding of the hermeneutical nature of *all* human knowledge claims.

Conclusion

In these few pages I have explored a possibility, not delivered a proof. The tentative bridges I have built may of course collapse; all of them may be 'too little too late'. In the 21st century we may discover that religion is inherently pre-scientific, so that all dreams of an intellectually credible religious stance in an age of science constitute mere wishful thinking. If so, the risky speculations hesitantly put forward here are all doomed to failure, and in this century science will replace the religious convictions of former centuries.

When an author engages in risky speculations, as I have done, one may justifiably wonder what has motivated him to do so. I close with an attempt to answer that question.

The loss of certainty and the hypothetical attitude that I have endorsed here would undoubtedly be a serious transformation of religious belief and of every form of theology, indeed a radical one. But, I suggest, the alternative is worse: that theologies continue to be based on outdated scientific cosmologies and empirically false claims about the world. Surely it's better for the scriptures of the various religious traditions not to function as dikes to protect religious persons against advances in human knowledge. Therein lie the Dark Ages indeed!

Few pictures of the damaging, anti-scientific role of religion are more evocative, and more painful, than Bertold Brecht's famous scene with the telescope in *The Life of Galileo*. In this memorable scene, Galileo is standing on the roof of his house in Florence under the starry sky. With him are two papal astronomers. He points his telescope at the moons of Jupiter and bids the two astronomers simply to look. The evidence is right before them; they could easily observe what their theology denies: that some heavenly bodies orbit objects other than the sun. Yet, with the evidence only inches away, the astronomers launch into a long diatribe, in which they use Aristotle and the Scriptures to prove a priori that no heavenly body *could* orbit any other object than the sun. Since they know with certainty that their theology is true, they have no need to look through the telescope. Indeed, they also know a priori that this instrument must be a tool of the devil.

Even today one can find theological treatises that contain analogous arguments, albeit more subtly expressed. But the open pursuit of knowledge has a way of winning in the end. It is far better for religious persons to accept the risks of aligning themselves with the best human efforts at knowledge than to remain 'suckled in a creed outworn' (Wordsworth). Recall this time a later moment from Brecht's play. Galileo is condemned for his heresies and sentenced to house arrest. After the verdict is read, the representatives of the papal inquisition depart. Alone on a darkening stage, condemned for his heretical claim that the earth moves around the sun, Galileo stands for a moment in silence. Finally, just before departing, he shakes his fist in the direction of the authorities who have just condemned him, and yells triumphantly, 'aber sie bewegt sich doch!' ('but it moves nonetheless!').

The urgency of revisions on *both* sides of the religion–science dialogue stems not (just) from the quest for better explanations. The call for religious believers to engage in a serious, intense and sustained wrestling with science is in the end just as much political and ethical as anything else. Simply put: without cooperation between scientific knowledge and know-how on the one hand, and the immense ethical and motivational power of religion on the other, the human species is unlikely to solve the severe challenges before us. This is no vague concern, for there is a very real prospect that we shall not survive the present century – or, more carefully put, that in the lifetime of many in this room humans will manage so to cripple the earth and so to decimate its other inhabitants that it will take the planet hundreds or even thousands of years to recover.

In light of this very real prospect, I suggest, it becomes more urgent that we explore the possibility of some partnership between the sciences, the 'magisteria' of knowledge (Stephen J. Gould), and the religious traditions as repositories of values. Politically, it may prove to be vital to enlist these two very different expressions of the human spirit as allies. If this is true, we have pragmatic grounds for eschewing both scientific and religious triumphalism; grounds for avoiding the temptation to dismiss the other side as 'not really serious'; grounds for engaging in some good Swedish diplomacy. For this reason I have here defended the possibility of radically new forms of dialogue between science and religion: dialogues that do not remake religion in science's image or science in the image of religion; dialogues that let natural scientists say what science is and religionists describe what religions are; dialogues that allow for cooperation without identification or subordination. Scholars in various countries are now extending this dialogue to cosmology, fundamental physics, theoretical biology, ecology, neuroscience, cognitive science and the social sciences. Given the urgency of the crises we face, it is undoubtedly a project worthy of our attention.

References

Anderson, D. (2004). 'Peirce's Common Sense Marriage of Religion and Science', in Cheryl Misak (ed.), *The Cambridge Companion to Pierce*, Cambridge: Cambridge University Press, pp. 175–92.

Atkins, P. (2006). 'Atheism and Science', in P. Clayton (ed.), *Oxford Handbook of Religion and Science*, Oxford: Oxford University Press, pp. 124–36.

Clayton, P. (1989). *Explanation from Physics to Theology: An Essay in Rationality and Religion*, New Haven, CT: Yale University Press.
Cline, A. (2007). 'Young Earth Creationism: Creationists Who Believe that the Earth is Young', at http://atheism.about.com/od/creationismcreationists/p/yec.htm, accessed 10 September 2007.
Dawkins, R. (2006). *The God Delusion*, London: Bantam Books.
Denmark. (2007). 'Denmark', in *Encyclopædia Britannica*, at www.britannica.com/eb/article-33914, accessed 4 November 2007.
'Factsheet on Denmark: Public Research' (2007), at www.globalisering.dk/multimedia/Factsheet_public_research1.pdf, accessed 7 September 2007.
Geertz, C. (1973). *The Interpretation of Cultures*, New York: Basic Books.
Habermas, J. (1998). *Between Facts and Norms*, Cambridge, MA: MIT Press.
Hartshorne, C., and P. Weiss (eds) (1931–58). *The Collected Papers of Charles Sanders Peirce*, 8 vols, Cambridge, MA: Harvard University Press.
Herrmann, R.A. (2002). 'The Theological Foundations of the John Templeton Foundation', at www.serve.com/herrmann/tphilo.htm, accessed 10 September 2007.
Kierkegaard, Søren (1992). *Concluding Unscientific Postscript*, trans. Howard V. Hong and Edna H. Hong, Princeton, NJ: Princeton University Press.
Merriam-Webster's Collegiate Dictionary (1999). *Merriam-Webster's Collegiate Dictionary*, 10th edn, Springfield, MA: Merriam-Webster.
Pannenberg, W. (1991–98). *Systematic Theology*, 3 vols, vol. 1 [1991], trans. Geoffrey Bromiley, Grand Rapids, MI: Eerdmans.
Putnam, H. (1990). *Realism with a Human Face*, Cambridge, MA: Harvard University Press.
Rakkandee, W. (2007). 'The Great Spirit and Hiers Warriors of the Rainbows', at www.godsdirectcontact.org.tw/eng/news/161/os1.htm, accessed 10 September 2007.
Raposa, M.L. (1989). *Peirce's Philosophy of Religion*, Bloomington, IN: Indiana University Press.
Wiggins, D. (2004). 'Reflections on Inquiry and Truth Arising from Peirce's Method for the Fixation of Belief', in Cheryl Misak (ed.), *The Cambridge Companion to Peirce*, Cambridge: Cambridge University Press, pp. 87–126.

Chapter 7
Religions and the Natural Sciences: Appeals to Science as Religious Advocacy?

Willem B. Drees

'Religion in the 21st Century' is a most relevant theme, both socially and academically. The cooperation of legal scholars, sociologists of religion, scholars in the history of religions, theologians and philosophers, and so on, in this volume sets an outstanding example. My only concern with the title of this book is the use of the word 'religion' in the singular, as if 'religion' is a coherent matter, as if one can argue 'for religion' or 'against religion', without considering *which* religion one argues for or against. Using the plural occasionally is important, because it may make us alert to the possibility that the main point about 'religion in the 21st century' is not that one understands 'religion' or that one argues for or against 'religion', but that one might become involved in struggles between *different particular* religious and secular positions.

This struggle is not to be seen as a struggle between different traditions as wholes, say Christianity versus Islam; the main struggle takes place *within* traditions, over authority. Who speaks for the Church? Evangelicals, Catholics, mainline Protestants? Who represents 'genuine' Islam: radical salafi's, moderates or mystics?

An example of this intra-religious role of arguments about 'religion and science' is provided by the interesting essay on 'religion and science' by Philip Clayton in this volume. His contribution is a plea for a particular, liberal attitude in religion, in contrast with certain orthodox ones. The vocabulary of his essay speaks of the dialogue between science and religion, but the main drive seems to be the advocacy of a particular religious self-understanding, 'the secular believer'.

Let me quickly summarize the main thrust of my essay in relation to Clayton's reflections. I share the respect for the natural sciences, and the conviction that these cannot be neglected in theological reflection. Personally, as a believer I also share the preference for liberal religion, accepting cognitive and existential doubt as part of our existential situation. Though I share the religious perspective and the attitude with respect to science, I disagree with most of the arguments and ideas presented by Clayton, and with the morale of his essay. As academics we need not just argue for our preferred position; we need to understand orthodoxy. And as liberal believers, it is part of our responsibility to allow more traditionalist religious voices to exist alongside others in modern societies. Tolerance does not come from modernization of beliefs. I don't see tolerance as a cognitive matter, a responsibility to bring others closer to the truth, but as a social virtue to accept those we consider mistaken.

My own thesis in this essay is that 'religion and science' is not about building a bridge between two given entities, the one labelled 'religion' and the other labelled 'science'. Rather, that which is presented as 'religion and science' serves at least three other purposes: apologetics for science, apologetics for religion, and apologetics for religious studies and theology in the modern research university.

'Religion and Science' as Apologetics for Science in Modern Society

After the shooting at the high school in Columbine, April 1999, there was on 16 June a debate in the US House of Representatives on a law regarding juvenile offenders. Tom DeLay, leading Republican, read a letter of someone who argued that this shooting was due not to the availability of guns, but to broken families; day care centers; TV and computer games; small families due to sterilization and contraception; abortions; and 'because our school systems teach the children that they are nothing but glorified apes who have evolutionized out of some primordial soup of mud.'[1] As this exemplifies, the real struggle over evolution is not about biology; the fear is that with the acceptance of evolution a whole cluster of social values would be put at stake. Controversies over evolution are controversies over social issues, reflecting different theological responses to modernity.

In such a context, 'religion and science' supplements science education as *apologetics for science*, especially in religious cultures such as the United States where distrust in science is widespread. By emphasizing that science need not be in conflict with religious beliefs, science is presented as acceptable. This is an age-old project; in the 18th century natural theology also served to inform people on new scientific insights and to convey to them the message that science is an ally rather than an enemy. This role of 'religion and science' as apologetics for science makes intelligible why so many communications presented as 'religion and science', whether via websites or popular books, are almost indistinguishable from science popularization. As apologetics for science, elaborate arguments are not needed; the purpose may be served by popular science with a pious gloss at the end or by a presentation of apparent parallels between religious convictions and scientific insights. If the parallels are convincing, science cannot be perceived as a threat to these religious convictions. As a bonus, one may even conclude that a religious tradition has been there first, a matter of priority that makes science even less threatening.

Compatibility may also be argued by suggesting that the domain of science is limited. Quite a few appeal to Thomas Kuhn (1970) and other philosophers

---

[1] Debate on the 'Consequences for Juvenile Offenders Act, of 1999', *Congressional Record – House*, 16 June 1999, p. H4366; at http://thomas.loc.gov, accessed 21 October 2008.

of science to argue that science is tied to paradigms, perspectives and personal preferences, and hence is not as objective and universal as it seems. However, reconciliatory goals can also be served by ontological arguments, indicating that there might be 'room for God' in the context of scientific insights. There are many different strategies, but as examples of 'religion and science' they all serve as apologetics for science.

Advocacy for science thus may take the form of natural theology or of a separation of religion and science, since these strategies serve well as apologetics for descriptive and explanatory dimensions of science. However, apologetics for science may also take the form of a plea for social responsibility and engagement, as apologetics for technology. There are major theological differences involved, emphasizing creation as given rather than a call for conversion and transformation. When 'playing God' serves as an accusation, theology tends to emphasize the given character of reality, whereas the same expression may also serve as an appeal for liberation, for taking our moral responsibility and using our capacities to transform the world, to make this world better. How the expression will be used is not just 'religion and science', but part of a wider struggle between different theologies. Apologetics for cosmology or evolutionary biology is theologically different from apologetics for nanotechnology or genetic engineering. In my opinion, the active, transformative side of science is neglected too often in favor of the more passive role of science in understanding reality. However, the choice between an emphasis on 'understanding creation' and 'transforming reality' is a religious and moral one. To this decision is connected a major choice regarding the role of religion in public conversation on technology, to serve as a source of motivation for science and for technology or to serve again and again as a brake on technological developments.

'Religion and Science' in the Academy

The academic world offers a particular context for 'religion and science'. In the modern university, a recurrent issue of academic politics is whether theology deserves a place in a secularized institution. In this context it may be useful to argue that the structure of theology resembles that of respected scientific disciplines. One strategy could be, to reformulate theology in terms derived from Imre Lakatos, 'methodology of scientific research programmes' (Murphy 1990). What are norms for being scientific (or academic)? Can theology live up to those standards? Are the standards for the humanities lower than those for the natural sciences? If so, does that help theology? Are the standards for the sciences lower than we thought? Would that help theology, or is a *tu quoque* argument, suggesting that science is also perspectival and dogmatic, not enough? Alongside such debates on academic norms and the nature of science comes the important question of whether theology should seek to live up to such norms. Thus, the question also concerns the nature of religious belief – is it propositional like scientific theories, or is it an existential judgement on meaningfulness, or otherwise? In this context, controversies are not just about the nature of science but as much about the nature of faith.

There is another side to 'religion and science' in the academy, and that is the avoidance, by and large, of engagement with the secular study of religion, for example the history of religions, and anthropological and social studies of religions. Such studies are often methodologically agnostic and functional in orientation. Some voices in the study of religion are perceived as reductionist and challenging, setting up such studies of religion in competition to a religious understanding of religion; for instance, 'God is not, like pain, a reality to be explained, but it is rather, like atoms, an explanation of reality' (Segal 1999: 158).

The secular study of religion with its immanent, social and naturalistic vocabulary conflicts with the religious interest of 'religion and science' even if 'methodologically agnostic', as the success of a secular understanding of religious history seems to make the theological 'insiders' narrative superfluous. In my opinion, however, such a challenge is to be accepted. Avoidance of the social scientific perspective, self-limiting 'religion and science' to engagement with the natural sciences, threatens the credibility of 'religion and science', and thus in the long run its relevance.

The dislike of social studies of religion is, it seems to me, also exemplified by the contribution by Philip Clayton (see pp. 85–101). He argues that the student of religion needs to take the insiders perspective more seriously. Clayton quotes the anthropologist Clifford Geertz as opting for an approach to culture that gains us 'access to the conceptual world in which our subjects live'. I agree that one has to understand the conceptual world of the believer, but this does not entail that the scholar of a religious culture has to accept the beliefs as possibly true; he only needs to see them as the beliefs considered true by the people studied. Geertz's anthropological research is premised on the opposite of what he is used for by Clayton. The anthropologist can engage in thick description, combining concepts that are experience-near and experience-distant, and thereby understand what drives those people *without* sharing their beliefs. This can be described as methodological agnosticism or as a symbolic–cultural understanding of religious practices and beliefs. Clayton is suspicious of those who study religion 'from the outside' as 'motivated by the goal of showing how misinformed, misguided, and even immoral are the religious beliefs and practices that they study' (idem.). This has not been my experience with such academic colleagues. But more important, why would it not be legitimate to see how far you get by understanding religious beliefs as delusions? If the argument carries, so be it; we have learned a painful lesson. We understand why people perceive the earth as flat and the universe as turning around ourselves, and quite a few think that our folk psychology with a soul is at substantial odds with the genuine processes within our selves. The point is not to forbid such studies, but to engage the arguments and see whether they can be shown to fall short – and if so, where.

'Science and Religion' as Using Science in Intra-Religious Controversies

Not only the acceptance of science in society and the role of theology in the academy provide contexts for 'religion and science'. Most significant, I would say, is the role of 'religion and science' in intra-religious disagreements. Even if people have the same beliefs, they need not mean the same by 'believing'. Within traditions there is a range of views. What is most important to some is totally uninteresting to others. Some focus on a tradition that provides a worldview. Others emphasize tradition too, but more as the source of our practical identity, in food, clothing and feasts. Others see their faith mainly in normative, moral terms. When it comes to worldviews, book stores do not present us only with the philosophically respectable abstract ones such as theism, panentheism, pantheism or naturalism. Books and TV deal also with witches and vampires, while for many the most important issue is life after death, rather than God. Many options, many preferences. What are we after when we advocate religion: myth, mystery, metaphysics, morality, magic?

Which understanding of religion is dominant in 'religion and science'? Those involved, myself included, tend to be on the intellectual side, avoiding the wide range of popular beliefs. But still within the academic setting, there is enough disagreement to invite an explanation. The diversity of approaches and positions may be due to the difficulty of the questions. But the diversity may also reflect a struggle for power. 'Religion and science' is about the truth of ideas, but as much about authority *within* religious traditions. 'Religion and science' is a major battle ground between revisionists and traditionalists in each tradition. Let me support this thesis with brief reflections on some major cases in 'religion and science'.

The controversies surrounding Galileo began with a dispute within the scholarly community, between advocates of scholastic approaches and those who favored the use of new instruments. Religious accusations were used by adherents of the scholastic science, thereby using religion within scientific disputes. However, the conflict shifted from within the scientific community to within the Church. There it was not so much a dispute between religion and science, but rather between different religious factions, such as the different religious orders (Jesuits, Dominicans) and the representatives of different nationalities (Italians, Spanish). Most importantly, the Galileo affair provided the context of a struggle over authority in exegetical matters, the outcome affirming the authority of the Pope and Church officials over lay reading of Scripture, in the aftermath of the Protestant Reformation and the Council of Trent (Pedersen 1983; Drees 1996: 60–62).

In the reception of Darwin's ideas during the 19th century, the issue was not just evolution. Even the exchange between Bishop Wilberforce and Thomas Huxley in Oxford in 1860 was not just about the implications of evolution. Tension arose also due to the changing nature of the scientific profession, the replacement of an elite of gentleman-naturalists by scientific professionals doing science for a living (Turner 1978). Alongside this intra-scientific dimension to the controversy, an even more important intra-religious disagreement was involved, which might be summarized all too briefly as one between liberals and orthodox believers. Science was just a minor issue in the debate, which raged more deeply over the acceptability of a historical understanding of one's own tradition and its sources, Scripture (Welch 1972 and 1985; Drees 1996: 64-7).

Even the most well-known title suggesting a conflict between science and theology, Andrew White's *History of the Warfare of Science with Theology in Christendom* is itself misunderstood if the intra-religious dimension is neglected. White was the first president of Cornell University, a non-denominational institution. Cornell was set up as a Christian university, with compulsory attendance at chapel (Altschuler 1979: 68, 81). Frustration about the ecclesiastical opposition he met from those in charge of denominational colleges probably influenced White's articulation of a warfare of science with theology. White took religion seriously, but quarreled with sectarianism and theological dogmatism. He envisaged a religion that would be in harmony with science. 'Religion, as seen in the recognition of "a Power in the Universe, not ourselves, which makes for righteousness", and in the love of God and of our neighbour, will steadily grow stronger and stronger' (White 1896, vol. I, xii; see also Drees 1996: 67-8).

The reception of White's book as anti-religious might be seen as an example of a more general trend, described in Jeffrey Stout's *Democracy and Tradition* (2004). Stout signals how orthodox believers and outspoken secular authors use each other for contrast, as if these two approaches are the only ones available. Stout comes out in favor of a more nuanced landscape, distinguishing alongside the 'Augustianian' form of religion also an 'Emersonian' one, which is less institutionalized and not anti-modern. What is often perceived as the secular voice of liberal democracy might in many cases, according to Stout, be better understood as a different religious voice, the Emersonian one.

Let me emphasize that 'religion and science' is not just an intra-religious issue within Christianity. To give an example from a different cultural context: the Mind and Life Conferences and the project 'science for monks', initiated by the Dalai Lama, are in part also about the modernization of Buddhism. In the quest for modernization we have a contest for authority, as some Tibetan monasteries are not participating; Buddhism is not a unified whole. The engagement is not just with science for science's sake, but with science as an instrument in a struggle over the reform of Tibetan Buddhism.

I shall now consider one more example, this time from the world of Islam. Even though the popular understanding, especially since September 11 2001, is that Islamist groups oppose Western culture, their main opponents are not Westerners. The more fundamental issue is a struggle for authority *within* Islam. Who speaks for the true faith? There are quite a few contributions to 'religion and science' by Islamic authors who seek to affirm traditional readings of the Qur'an. However, here too there is an alternative attitude towards the interpretation of the Qur'an, acknowledging the role of hermeneutical processes and human interpretation, concentrating the significance in a moral or metaphysical core. 'Islam and science' cannot but be a part of the wider struggle as to which type of Islam will acquire the upper hand – a traditional and mainly anti-modern version, or a more liberal one. Controversies in Christianity in the 19th century, over Scripture, science and history, have close parallels in current controversies among Muslims (Taji-Farouki 2004).

To conclude: 'religion and science' is about the truth of ideas, but it is as much about *authority* within religious traditions. It is a major battleground between revisionists and traditionalists within each tradition. Thus, in speaking of 'religion and science' we need to be aware that there should be a plural – 'religions'. Not as Christianity versus Buddhism, and so on, but as a reminder that appeals to science serve in a competition between multiple ways of understanding the substance and nature of faith within each tradition. Clayton's essay may well be understood as another example of such an engagement with science that is not primarily a dialogue *with science* but rather a plea for a particular stance in religious life: 'the secular believer'. By using a singular, 'religion', we may lose sight of the fact that different religious positions are competing for public and academic recognition.

Acknowledgments

The core of the response has been published previously (Drees 2005) and is developed in greater detail elsewhere (Drees 2010). The example of Buddhism and science is inspired by the research of a PhD student of mine, R.M. Hogendoorn.

References

Altschuler, G.C. (1979). *Andrew D. White – Educator, Historian, Diplomat*, Ithaca, NY: Cornell University Press.
Philip Clayton (2010). 'Challenges in the 21st Century: Religion and Science', in Lisbet Christoffersen, Hans Raun Iversen, Hanne Petersen and Margit Warburg (eds), *Religion in the 21st Century* (pp. 85–102). Farnham: Ashgate.
Drees, W.B. (1996). *Religion, Science and Naturalism*, Cambridge: Cambridge University Press.
Drees, W.B. (2005). '"Religion and Science" as Advocacy of Science and as Religion versus Religion', *Zygon: Journal of Religion and Science*, 40 (3 September), pp. 545–53.
Drees, W.B. (2009). *Religion and Science in Context: A Guide to the Debates*, London: Routledge.
Kuhn, T. (1970). *The Structure of Scientific Revolutions*, 2nd edn, Chicago, IL: University of Chicago Press.
Lakatos, I. (1970). 'Falsification and the methodology of scientific research programmes', in I. Lakatos and A. Musgrave (eds), *Criticism and the Growth of Knowledge* (pp. 91–196). Cambridge: Cambridge University Press.

Murphy, N. (1990). *Theology in the Age of Scientific Reasoning*. Ithaca, NY: Cornell University Press.

Pedersen, O. (1983). 'Galileo and the Council of Trent', *Journal for the History of Astronomy*, 14, pp. 1–29. Rev. edn reprinted as O. Pedersen, *Galileo and the Council of Trent*. Vatican City State: Vatican Observatory, 1991.

Segal, R. (1999). 'In defense of reductionism', in Russell T. McCutcheon (ed.), *The Insider/Outsider Problem in the Study of Religion: A Reader* (pp. 139–63). London: Cassell. Reprint from *Journal of the American Academy of Religion*, 51 (1983), pp. 97–124.

Stout, J. (2004). *Democracy and Tradition*. Princeton, NJ: Princeton University Press.

Taji-Farouki, S. (ed.) (2004). *Modern Muslim Intellectuals and the Qur'an*. Oxford: Oxford University Press.

Turner, F.M. (1978). 'The Victorian Conflict between Science and Religion: A Professional Dimension', *Isis*, 69, pp. 356–76.

Welch, C. (1972, 1985). *Protestant Thought in the Nineteenth Century*, 2 vols. New Haven, CT: Yale University Press.

White, A.D. (1986). *A History of the Warfare of Science with Theology in Christendom*, vol. I. New York: Appleton & Co.

Chapter 8
The Need of Real Doubt in Religion and Science

Jesper Hoffmeyer

There is hardly a major point made in Philip Clayton's contribution that I cannot embrace myself. And yet I do not consider myself a religious person, whereas Clayton obviously considers himself what he calls a *secular believer*. I could not object even to the wonderful quote from Diderot that Clayton suggests is the motto of a *secular believer*:

> Doubts in the matter of religion, far from being acts of impiety, ought to be seen as good works, when they belong to a man who humbly recognizes his ignorance and is motivated by the fear of displeasing God by the abuse of reason. (Diderot 1875, in Clayton 1989: 138)

As a scientist, I am not used to accommodating God in my ideas, but I agree with what Diderot said, because doubt is certainly the very crux of thinking. You never think about the things you know well, only about the things you are not so sure about, or, in other words, you only think when you are in doubt. Indeed, it seems slightly blasphemic to suppose that God (or evolution for that matter) created our ability to think, with the strange ulterior motive that it would be a sin (or dangerous for the survival) to make use of it in the form in which it comes to mind, that is, doubting whatever is not known for sure. In fact, the whole business of university life in principle is supposed to be built upon the value of a systematic process of doubting. Unfortunately, however, it is my experience that real doubt is perhaps as rare in university life as it is among religious believers.

By now I have already hinted at the far-reaching simplification of equating God with evolution and I am sure Clayton would not be willing to support such a flat notion of God. However, this is perhaps also the point where my own heresy comes into play (a heresy, I am afraid, as significant in the eyes of mainstream scientists as is the *secular believer*'s heresy in traditional parts of the Church society), when I suggest that *the prevailing scientific conceptions of evolution are unnecessarily flat*. I am well aware that this is a risky proposition these days, considering the heavy attacks on evolution from a diversity of religious positions, as Clayton has already pointed out. It therefore may be necessary to specify the exact sense in which I think that 'prevailing conceptions of evolution are unnecessarily flat'. So let me emphasize the following three points:

1. If you deny that the human animal is a product of billions of years of evolution you can as well claim that the earth is flat.
2. I am sure Darwin himself got it essentially right. Natural selection is indeed one very important component in the explanatory matrix needed to make evolution understandable
3. My heretical claim is not directed against Darwinism as such, but only against *the modern fusion of Darwin's theory with molecular genetics*. For this fusion leaves behind the human experiential world as either an illusion or, worse I think, a phenomenon to be explained only through supernatural intervention.[1]

Charles Darwin did break the hold of the Cartesian mischief by establishing indirectly a cosmology that allowed humans to belong in the world without having to invoke any supernatural causes or beings. And since Darwin had no trouble in accepting the idea that animals possess feelings and exhibit 'strivings' (his word) – and that therefore, in a very elementary sense of the term, animals are *subjects* – his conception of the human situation, vis-à-vis nature, was not very far from the biosemiotic conception that I am presenting in an upcoming book, *Biosemiotics: An Examination into the Signs of Life and the Life of Signs* (Hoffmeyer 2008). However, when Darwin's theory in the 20th century was fused with molecular genetics, a burden was placed upon the shoulders of 'natural selection' that slowly annihilated Darwin's original vision. For now, even thoughts and feelings had to be understood as genetically based components in the behaviour of an animal – a kind of behavioural spasm or, at least, involuntary reflexes, like the movements of a compass needle – and lost with this new perspective was the possibility of conceptualizing animals as autonomous intentional agents or *subjects* in some modest sense of this word. So, although Darwin himself placed the human being safely and understandably within the masterpiece of nature, the neo-Darwinist so much less safely and understandably threw us out again, telling us that, while our *genes* may well belong to the reality of nature, our *thoughts* and *feelings* were now well outside the reach of science. Consequently, those previously least deniable aspects of our own biological experience – because they could not be reduced to a molecular explanation – came to be viewed with increasing suspicion, as if they were *Fata Morganas*, or epiphenomena without proper autonomous ontological reality.

What went wrong in the fusion of Darwinism with molecular genetics was the uncritical appropriation by evolutionary theory of a gene concept that may have worked well in genetics but that was now put to work in a much broader context, where the autonomy of the gene could no longer be upheld. As Philip Clayton well knows, biosemiotics – the field in which I have worked for the last ten years or more – denies this construction of living creatures as gene-

---

[1] This is actually why creationists and so-called Intelligent Design theoreticians love to stick with the good old Newtonian paradigm for science.

determined robots (or 'survival machines') in the hard-hitting terminology of Dawkins (1976). Biosemiotics thereby re-establishes the conception of living beings as *intentional creatures* whose activities are governed by internal models of their surroundings.

Thus, the point I am trying to make by emphasizing these connections is that, in science itself, a current movement is also taking place that in many ways seems symmetrical to the one taken in theology by the proponents of the position of the secular believer. This movement is also built upon a fundamental doubt that is far from always welcomed by mainstream scientists, a doubt that concerns what we might call *the ontology of natural law*. With this expression I refer to the belief that the laws of physics *describe all possible things and behaviours in this world*. That natural laws do indeed seem to characterize many aspects of the world we inhabit of course cannot be denied. But the deeper question is another one, namely this: *Was the universe an orderly place from the very beginning? Or is the lawful behaviour of things in the world, that now seems so pronounced, instead the result of an emergent process?*

Or, in other words, is the world as such lawful, or rather, is the lawfulness of the world the very problem that science should explain?

The key term here, of course, is *emergence*. Mainstream science regards emergence theories with great scepticism, fearing, I am afraid to say, that such theories are smuggling supernatural intervention through the back door. I find this to be very unfair, for the ontology of natural law is certainly no less metaphysical than is the ontology of emergence. In all truth, the idea that God in His benevolence would not have created nature as an unruly and lawless place seemed obvious to most Christian thinkers and stems as far back, I assume, at least to Thomas Aquinas. And this of course is the one idea that originally made natural science possible in the first place, for without an orderly universe there would be no natural laws for science to study. The heresy of emergence theories, in other words, is to reject the Christian metaphysics that justifies the ontology of natural law.

Let me here confess outright that I do not believe that the world is fundamentally a lawful place. Instead, I find it to be more consonant with modern scientific conceptions building on non-equilibrium thermodynamics or non-linear systems dynamics, complexity theory and biosemiotics that the world in the beginning was indeterminate, an unruly mess, and that the orderliness we find in this world is indeed the result of an ongoing process of emergence that has so far been operative through several billions of years.

These are not matters for discussion here. But the fact that, in recent years, increasing segments of scientific society are approaching the stance of emergence theories does as such have consequences for the conciliatory processes between science and religion that Phil Clayton so eloquently outlined in his talk. For it lends very forceful support to a negation of the kind of totalitarian thinking that is so widespread in science and easily freezes to the kind of dogmatic statements of belief we know so well from Richard Dawkins and, unfortunately, from many other prominent scientists.

One of the important consequences of a scientific movement in the direction of emergentist conceptions is that the sharp fact–value distinction separating science and humanities or theology cannot be upheld. Science may not directly tell us what human beings *ought* to do, but neither can it deny with any certainty that something like 'ought-ness' might exist in the world. Adopting an emergentist conception of the world also opens automatically for the study of non-deterministic processes, and this implies that there is no longer any logical need for an outright rejection of the reality of human experiential worlds or free will. Again, science may not be a good tool for analysing the content of human experiential worlds, but it does allow such worlds to exist. And biology, furthermore, should feel compelled to produce theories to explain what would be the evolutionary advantages of possessing this – scientifically seen – strange capacity for experiencing the world and not just behaving in it (an attempt to do this was made in Hoffmeyer 2008).

In ending this comment, I would also – like Philip Clayton – draw attention to the time of Galileo, though to Galileo's predecessor, a professor of mathematics in Padova, Giordano Bruno, rather than to Galileo himself. Bruno not only claimed that there was an infinity of worlds like ours, but he also had the audacity to claim – and this was his real heresy in the eyes of the scholastics – that this infinity of emerging new worlds exemplified God's true greatness. By claiming this, charged the Church, Bruno had identified the creativity of nature with the creativity of God, making God inherent to or immanent in the world.

Maybe it is now time that science and religion give up the old alliance they formed with each other back in Galileo's century on the conception of Nature as an irreparably passive realm to be ruled by God or by natural laws (given by Him). Bruno's emergent universe rather than Galileo's mathematical lawfulness would then set the tone for future negotiations between science and belief.

I am sure this would make for much more fruitful debates on how to solve the great problems of our world. And Clayton is right, of course, in claiming that we cannot safely do without the old wise traditions of humankind. Neither science nor historically acquired cultural wisdom is given. Each is in need of constant doubt and reinterpretation.

References

Clayton, P. (1989). *Explanation from Physics to Theology: An Essay in Rationality and Religion*, New Haven, CT: Yale University Press.

Dawkins, R. (1976). *The Selfish Gene*, Oxford: Oxford University Press.

Hoffmeyer, J. (2008). *Biosemiotics: An Examination into the Signs of Life and the Life of Signs*, Scranton, PA, and London: University of Scranton Press.

PART II:
TRANSFORMATIONS

Islam and State Politics

Chapter 9

'Systemically closed, cognitively open'?[1]
A Critical Analysis of Transformative Processes in Islamic Law and Muslim State Practice

Shaheen Sardar Ali

Introduction

This contribution sets out to engage in a critical analysis of the transformative processes within Islamic law and its articulation in Muslim state practice as well as individual and collective articulations of Muslims. It suggests that, despite consistent proclamations to the contrary, the Islamic legal tradition has and always had an in-built dynamism and evolutionary process as one of its ingredients and strengths; further, that this persistent state of denial of the evolutionary nature of the Islamic legal tradition by some (Muslims and non-Muslims) results from an inability to separate belief in the unchanging status of the *Qur'anic* text as the word of God, from its human formulation described as 'Islamic law' or more appropriately, the Islamic legal tradition. The existence of transformative processes in no way contradicts the fact that the cardinal principles of the Islamic religion per se remain the same; what evolves, or is modified, is the perception and response of succeeding generations of Muslims to the requirements of Islam as they perceive it.

The present contribution advances the argument that the Islamic legal tradition is systemically closed, that is, it operates within the boundaries of a divinely prescribed framework and endeavors to jealously guard those systemic origins. Simultaneously, and in keeping with the overarching principle of *'adl* or justice as enunciated within the *Qur'an*, the application of these systemically closed channels of legal rules is cognitively open to the imperatives of evolving norms, the 'living law', and changing needs of people and time.

Last, but not least, the present contribution comprises an attempt to understand and share the complex and nuanced nature of the Islamic legal tradition, raising some issues affecting our lives in a globalised world. It is also an endeavor to make a case for abandoning the orientalist (or indeed, occidentalist) approach to

---

[1] This phrase is inspired by the line of argument in Balz 1995–96: 37–53.

scholarship on Islam and the Islamic legal tradition by creating deeper linkages and ongoing dialogue between the Islamic legal tradition and its Western counterpart emanating mainly from the liberal tradition.

The Islamic Legal Tradition: A Brief Analytical Overview

This section presents a brief analytical overview of what constitutes the Islamic legal tradition, that is, its sources and techniques insofar as these have a bearing on our exploration of the extent to which there is evidence of transformative processes within this tradition and Muslim state practice.

To place our discussion in context, it is important to clarify the core concepts and terminology employed in this contribution. *Shari'a* is the overarching umbrella of rules, regulations, values and normative framework covering all aspects and spheres of life for Muslims. It constitutes the divine injunctions of God (the *Qur'an*), divinely-inspired *sunna* (words and deeds of the Prophet Muhammad), as well as the human articulation and understanding of these sources (see Rahim 1995; Kamali 2003; Ramadan 1999; Doi 1984; and Fyzee 1974). An-Naim states:

> The term Shari'a refers to the general normative system of Islam as historically understood and developed by Muslim jurists, especially during the first three centuries of Islam – the eighth to tenth centuries CE. In this commonly used sense, Shari'a includes a much broader set of principles and norms than legal subject matter as such. (An-Naim 2002: 1–2)

As I have quoted elsewhere, Parwez brings out the true essence of the breadth and reach of *Shari'a* when he describes it thus:

> The Shari'a refers to a straight and clear path and also a watering place where both humans and animals come to drink water, provided the source of water is a flowing stream or spring .... (Parwez 1960: 941)

Stagnant, standing water is not and cannot be *Shari'a,* and it is therefore

> ... no slight irony and tragedy that the Sharia, which has the idea of mobility built into its very meaning, should have become a symbol of rigidity for so many in the Muslim world. (Hassan 1980: 4)

Emerging from the foregoing description of *Shari'a*, is the inference that the concept is more than black letter law and legal principles, and encompasses social, moral and ethical normativities affecting human lives (Rehman 1979: 68; Allot 1980; Fyzee 1974; Pearl and Menski 1998). I suggest elsewhere that the phrase 'principles of Islamic law' more appropriately captures the true breadth of this concept as opposed to terming it immutable, unchangeable and divine law. This definition, I submit, lays the foundation of my argument that, as the human interpretation of the divine will, *Shari'a* is the embodiment of a rich, dynamic, responsive living organism of norms, legal and non-legal; hence transformative over time and place.[2] I define the legal component of *Shari'a* as the 'Islamic legal tradition' and consciously use this term rather than 'Islamic law' to avoid creating a restrictive fence around an evolving tradition. This description is especially important in a discussion within Western scholarship that defines law largely as formal, black letter, written law.[3] By the same token, and following Hallaq and others, I distance myself from writers on the subject who believe that 'Islamic law'

> ... was the result of a speculative attempt by pious scholars working during the first three centuries of Islam, to define the will of Allah. In self-imposed isolation from practical needs and circumstances they produced a comprehensive system of rules, largely in opposition to existing legal practice which expressed the religious ideal. (Coulson 1957, in Hallaq 1994: 29)

Coulson's notion of the 'isolationist development' of what he describes as Islamic law does not reflect the entire landscape of the development; and as a later section of this contribution will describe, throughout Muslim history, *muftis* and other scholars have been influenced and have influenced the existing practices of Muslims, feeding these into the transformative and evolutionary processes of the Islamic legal tradition.

Sources of the Islamic legal tradition have been categorised as primary, that is, the *Qur'an*[4] *and sunna*;[5] others secondary, including *Ijma* (consensus of opinion)[6]

---

[2] I have developed the idea of the 'operative' Islamic law as opposed to *Shari'a* in my *Gender and Human Rights in Islam and International Law Equal Before Allah, Unequal Before Man?*, The Hague: Kluwer Law International (2000).

[3] I am conscious of the fact that some scholars and students believe that the term 'Islamic law' is more appropriate and that by defining it as the 'Islamic legal tradition' we are somehow taking away its authoritative status. My reason for choosing this manner of description is to widen the remit and reach of the concept.

[4] The *Qur'an* is believed by Muslims to be the word of God, and was revealed to the Prophet Muhammad through the Angel Gabriel over a period of 22 years, 2 months and 22 days. It is divided into 114 chapters and has a total of 6666 verses and 30 sections.

[5] *Sunna* means the words and deeds of the Prophet Muhammad, also known as traditions and compiled as *Hadith* (singular) and *Ahadith* (plural). A tradition or *Hadith* is composed of the *matn* (text) of the tradition and the *isnad* (chain of transmitters).

[6] This is defined by A. Rahim as 'agreement among the Muslim jurists in a particular age on a question of law' (Rahim 1995: 97); '*Ijma* is defined as the unanimous agreement of the mujtahidun of the Muslim community of any period following the demise of the Prophet Muhammad on any matter' (Kamali 2003: 230).

and *Qiyas* (analogical deduction).[7] In addition to these sources of law there exists a range of juristic techniques, some of which are presented here: *ijtihad*, the literal meaning of which is striving hard and strenuousness, denotes exercising independent juristic reasoning to provide answers when the *Qur'an* and *sunna* are silent on a particular issue.[8] *Taqlid*, or duty to follow, is considered by most students of Islamic law as mere 'imitation' – to emulate or copy. As a term of jurisprudence, *taqlid* may be used in the context of accepting someone's intellectual authority (Rahim 1995: 144–5; Coulson 1994: 80–81). The reality of the Islamic legal tradition, however, shows that *taqlid* was employed by Muslim jurists to engage in juristic methods and processes that were anything but blind emulation. While inhibiting independent legal formulations, *taqlid* allowed latter-day jurists a choice from among variant views recorded in authoritative texts. Coulson describes the much-maligned *Taqlid* in a positive light, as a vehicle of evolution and transformation of the Islamic legal tradition, in the following words:

> It is the principle that *taqlid* allows a choice from among variant views recorded in the authoritative texts which has permitted extensive modification of the law as traditionally applied in Middle Eastern countries and which, as exploited by modern reformers, has lent an added significance to the alleged statement of the prophet that 'Difference of opinion among my people is a sign of the bounty of God'. (Coulson 1994: 182)

Similarly, by applying the process or technique of *ikhtilaf* or the 'unity in diversity' doctrine, jurists of the various schools of thought, as well as practitioners, arrived at positions that were as varied as the colours of the rainbow (ibid.: 86). However, the beauty of this divergence of opinion was that it was not hidden from view in an attempt to look uniform but, in the words of Gerber, 'paraded with relish'.

But by far the most dynamic concept in Islamic jurisprudence is *Takhayyur*, meaning the process of selection. As a term of jurisprudence, it has been used to consider possible alternatives from a range of juristic opinions on a particular point of law and with the intention to seek less restrictive legal principles in application to issues that arise. *Takhayyur* has been of enormous significance in developing a number of women-friendly codes of family laws in Muslim jurisdictions. For example, regarding circumstances where a married Muslim woman may seek dissolution of her marriage, the Hanafi School is restrictive whereas the Maliki is flexible and allows a wife to seek dissolution on the grounds of cruelty of her husband. This was incorporated in a number of personal status laws in the Muslim world. Likewise, the Hambali doctrine of abiding by stipulations (based on the

---

[7] As a source of law, *qiyas* comes into operation in matters not covered by an express text of the *Qur'an* and *sunna* nor dealt with by *ijma*. The law deduced by application of what has already been laid down by the three sources is *Qiyas* (Rahim 1995: 117).

[8] A person qualified to undertake *ijtihad* is known as a *mujtahid*, and there are specific qualifications for a person to be so acknowledged.

hadith of the Prophet Muhammad) led this school of thought to declare that the marriage contract could stipulate monogamy of the husband, the wife could choose the place of residence, and so on. Examples of *takhayyur* include the Dissolution of Muslim Marriages Act 1939, the Moroccan Code of Personal Status 1858, the Jordanian Law of Family Rights 1951, the Syrian Law of Personal Rights 1953, the Ottoman Law of Family Rights 1917, and the latest, the Moroccan Family Code (*Moudawana*) 2004 and others.

Talfiq, translated literally as 'a patchwork', implies the process whereby Muslim jurists constructed legal rules by the combination and fusion of opinions derived from different schools of thought on a particular issue. An interesting example of *talfiq* is the landmark case of Muhammad Ibrahim v. Gulam Ahmed (1864), where a girl brought up as a *shafi'i* married without her father's consent. When the case came up in court, she declared that she had chosen to change her school of juristic thought to the Hanafi School because Hanafi law allows an adult Muslim woman to marry without the consent of her guardian.

Maslaha (the public good or in the public interest), or *masalihu'l-mursala wa'listislah*, is a doctrine propounded by Imam Malik, who allowed 'a deduction of law to be based on general considerations of the public good' (Rahim 1995: 140; Coulson 1994: 144). There is evidence that *qadis* and jurists in Muslim history have employed this concept to override problems arising from adherence to strict doctrine enshrined in the classical legal texts. *Darura* (necessity/duress) is a technique applied where it becomes imperative to make permissible previously prohibited things and situations. Last, but certainly not least, is custom or *'urf* as a source of law, also termed *ta'amul* or *'adat*. At times controversial, this source of law and juristic technique plays an important role in the growth of the Islamic legal tradition as it speaks to the commonly held beliefs and convictions of communities. Thus some communities of South Asia relied upon *'urf* to interpret Muslim laws of inheritance.[9]

The above discussion has outlined some of the mechanisms employed by Muslim jurists to explore avenues of legal expression within an environment more tolerant of divergence and difference. Muslim jurisprudence at this stage was inclusive and afforded multiple spaces for divergent opinions without appropriating a 'superior location' for any single school of thought and belief. Jurists and judges alike struggled to seek out the most favorable legal position for litigants appearing before them. Inherent in this struggle were seeds of transformation, nuanced and implicit and not always apparent to the undiscerning eye (Moors 1995; Mernissi 1991; Sonbol 1996; Tucker 1997; Welchman 2000).

---

[9] For example, in the Pakistan province of Punjab and among the Khojas of Bombay, some Pukhtun tribes of the North-West Frontier Province of Pakistan. For application of customary norms intertwined with Islamic concepts of inheritance and other family law matters, the Indonesian *adat* is a fascinating example. See Bowen's excellent work in this area (Bowen 2003).

The above-mentioned juristic techniques and mechanisms developed within the Islamic legal tradition point to the reality of the complex transformative processes inherent within it. A number of factors set off this process: for instance, interpretative diversity of the Islamic legal tradition due to the various schools of juristic thought; the fact that the *Qur'an* was revealed in Arabic; and that the primary sources are in that language and the vast majority of Muslims are not native Arab speakers relying on translations. But the most definitive step towards transformation of the Islamic legal tradition began early in Islamic history when the *fuqaha* (jurists) receded from lawmaking and political authority/-ies appropriated this space. As the state, and its political power and institutions, stabilised and consolidated itself, they legitimated the role of lawmaking in the public sphere to themselves without much protest from the jurists. The state thus appropriated lawmaking into the public and political domain. Human endeavor at legislating had the effect of distancing it from *Shari'a* perceived as divine. A neutral, secular, non-religious arena was thus created where religion played a less pronounced role (Ali 2007c: 69). The gap between the theory and practice of *Shari'a* became apparent, a space that was continually filled by state-sponsored lawmaking (including codification during the Ottoman Empire). This process of lawmaking or *siyasa sharia* resulted in law known as *qanun*. The effect of this method of lawmaking was dissipation of the flexibility of juristic techniques applied by jurists and practitioners of the classical period (Baderin 2003: 52–3).

A second factor supporting transformative processes within the Islamic legal tradition was the language of the *Qur'an* being Arabic. Following the spread of Islam, non-Arab Muslims (except for the few who learned the language) relied on translations of the *Qur'an* and *Ahadith*. This automatically resulted in variations in the understandings of the finer and more complex aspects of the law based upon *Qur'anic* text and/or *Ahadith*. It also led to an ongoing debate among scholars and the laity alike as to whether a hierarchy of knowledge had been created, the more 'Islamic' one based upon (Arabic, original) readings of the *Qur'an* and *Hadith*, with non-Arab-speaking scholars, students and researchers, indeed, all other Muslims, possessing inferior knowledge due to the secondary source material used. Thus some Arab-speaking Muslim scholars applauded the contemporariness of the *Qur'an* and Arabic

> ... because the categories of grammar, lexicography, syntax and redaction of the Qur'anic text, and those of Arabic consciousness embedded in the Arabic language have not changed through the centuries. This phenomenon is indeed unique .... (Al-Faruqi 1978: 85)

Others, including An-Naim, remind us that 'The Qur'an was revealed in Arabic, which is a human language that evolved in its own specific historical context, and many verses of the Qur'an were addressing specific situations in the daily lives of early Muslims at that time (610–32 CE) in their local context of western

Arabia' (An-Naim 2006: 11), pointing to the fact that knowledge of Arabic does not necessarily imply superior understanding of the *Qur'anic* text.

Sachedina reinforces this by saying that

> ... translations of the Qur'an, however faithful to the original Arabic, cannot be regarded as more than an interpretative translation of the Word of God into a language in which it was revealed in the first place. Moreover, the translation is bound to be conditioned by the understanding of the Qur'anic message in its entirety by the translator .... (Sachedina 1988: v)

There exists, therefore, a robust debate in Muslim and non-Muslim scholarly circles regarding the primacy of Arabic for an authoritative understanding of the primary sources of the Islamic legal tradition. While this debate continues with no end in sight, it is evident that readings and understanding of the *Qur'an* and *hadith* from the Arabic text or through translations by a diverse community of Muslims around the world have implications for the transformative processes within the tradition.

Systemically Closed, Cognitively Open? Some Examples of the Transformative Processes in the Islamic Legal Tradition

It would not be an overstatement to say that, in light of our earlier discussion, there is scant possibility of a homogenous and monolithic articulation of what might constitute 'Islamic' law. Muslim legal history is replete with examples of this phenomenon, due mainly to the autonomy inherent in the Islamic legal tradition. Under the apparent rigidity of the system, some significant evolution has taken place – both drawing upon principles of Islamic law as well as responding to needs of time and place. But this observation poses the question: If the Islamic legal tradition, as presented above, is evolutionary and susceptible to transformation, why is there a reluctance – indeed, a total denial by some – of this fact?

A number of contributory factors may be responsible for this approach among Muslim jurists, scholars and communities. There is the ever-present interpretative diversity in application of the religious text, both historical and contemporary. Renewal (*tajdid*) and reform (*islah*) through *mujaddids* (revivalists) denotes an established belief of transformative process within the Islamic belief and tradition. These processes, in light of the sources of Islamic law, imply 'moving forward and applying broad principles of the religion to accommodate contemporary changes. A consistent attempt at *tajdid* and *islah* dispels the myth of Islam being a traditional religion at odds with modernisation and resistant to change' (Hamid 2001: 19).

Further, there appears to be a reluctance to admitting the role and importance of '*urf* or custom as evidence of 'the living law', and acknowledging how this feeds into law and legal practice as well as Muslim state practice. Custom is an evolutionary vehicle, propelling laws and legal frameworks informing law and state practice as well as how Muslims order their lives. One way of understanding this is the abundance of literature concerning legal pluralism in Muslim societies, including how it has overtaken and undermined as well as modified historical, traditional understandings of what is Islamic law and what is not.[10] That Muslim state practice meekly follows this trend while keeping up appearances of being 'Islamic', is also a reality that Muslim communities experience yet fail to recognise.

Although a number of examples may be advanced in support of the proposition that the Islamic legal tradition is systemically closed but cognitively open, four will suffice here: *as-siyar* or Islamic international law as an evolving body of legal norms; Muslim diasporic communities as discursive sites of transformation; changes in Muslim family law; and the institution of *ifta*. These will be dealt with in succeeding sections of this contribution.

Contemporary As-siyar *as an Evolving Normative Framework within the Islamic Legal Tradition: Some Key Developments in Muslim State Practice*

The interaction of Muslims with notions of 'modernity', the nation-state, its structures and institutions, in addition to the international community and its organisations, has been for the most part an uneasy one. Global developments, including those in the political, economic, technological, educational and social arenas, have propelled Muslims and Muslim state practice onto the international stage. The processes of globalisation and internationalisation have had a bearing on *as-siyar* and *ummah*, eliciting responses that are transformative in nature. As I have stated elsewhere, and I quote at length,

> The contours of contemporary *as-Siyar* as well as its sources have undergone an enormous modification both structural as well as ideological. It no longer draws inspiration from a pristine *Shari'a* based on the primary and secondary sources of Islamic law but is subject increasingly to *siyasa* (state power) *Shari'a*. In other words, Muslim states have acquired unto themselves the power to make laws (*qanun*) based on their understanding of the norms of *Shari'a*. Muslim state practice in the domestic and international arena has thus undergone major reconstruction (Arabi 2001: 18). The presumption of universality of *as-Siyar* encompassing the Muslim Ummah becomes questionable in the face of *siyasa Shari'a* and individual Muslim states promulgate overriding laws of entry and exit for persons within their jurisdiction. State practice of Muslim jurisdictions has moulded *as-Siyar* to become more open to contemporary realities of co-existence in an increasingly globalised world including engagement with human rights law. (Ali 2007b: 93)

---

[10] For a most inspiring account of the legal pluralism at play in Muslim communities and the vast array of competing religious and social norms that Muslims navigate in their daily life, see Bowen (2003).

These transformative processes have thus affected the entire spectrum of the Islamic legal tradition, including international law (*as-siyar*). A significant example is membership by Muslim states of the United Nations organisation, active participation in formulation of various human rights and other treaties, accession to these treaties (albeit with reservations in the name of Islam), as well as formation of the Organisation of the Islamic Conference (OIC) by Muslim states in 1969. Its Charter, among other statements, contains pronouncements implying agreement to conduct relations with other states on the basis of equality and reciprocity, and recognising core universal human rights norms (Moinuddin 1987: 14). The preamble of the OIC affirms this position by stating the following:

> Reaffirming their commitment to the United Nations Charter and fundamental Human Rights, the purposes and principles of which provide the basis for fruitful cooperation among all people.[11]

The principles and objectives of the OIC, formulated in contemporary human rights language as enunciated by its Charter, is an example of present-day *as-siyar* as there is clear acceptance of the United Nations as a world organisation comprising nation-states other than Muslim states. Likewise, the Arab Charter on Human Rights adopted by Muslim member-states of the Arab League in 1994 (with a revised version adopted in 2004) also invokes international human rights instruments as follows:

> Reaffirming the principles of the Charter of the United Nations and the Universal Declaration of Human Rights, as well as the provisions of the United Nations International Covenants on Civil and Political Rights and Economic, Social and Cultural Rights and the Cairo Declaration on Human Rights in Islam. (The Preamble, Arab Charter on Human Rights 1999)

More importantly, there is an explicit commitment to peaceful coexistence and engagement with the international community. More recently, ratification of the United Nations Convention on Rights of the Child (CRC) and the United Nations Convention on the Elimination of All Forms of Discrimination Against Women (CEDAW), and a host of other international treaties, despite the reservations in the name of Islam, attests to the evolutionary dimension of the Islamic legal tradition in the international arena. In entering reservations to various human rights treaties, there is evidence of autonomy and diversity in the interpretation of Muslim states in their determination of the different articles of treaties reserved as 'unIslamic' (Ali 2006: 245; Ali 2000: 358; Ali 2007a: 100).

The Moroccan Family Code (*Moudawana*) 2004 is a fascinating example of contemporary Muslim state practice wherein, alongside the *Shari'a*, a domestic

---

[11] At www.oic-oci.org/english/main/charter.htm, accessed 12 September 2007.

law acknowledges the Kingdom's internationally recognised human rights treaties in the following words:

> ... [the King] provided the Commission with his constant enlightened guidance and advice in order to prepare a new Family Code bill, and insisted upon the fidelity to the provisions of *Sharia* (religious law) and Islamic principles of tolerance, and encouraged the use of *ijtihad* (juridical reasoning) to deduce laws and precepts, while taking into consideration the spirit of our modern era and the imperatives of development, in accordance with the Kingdom's commitment to internationally recognized human rights. (The Preamble, Moroccan Family Code; Moudawana 2004)

Finally, there are increasing examples of Muslim state practice in the field of international trade and financial transactions vis-à-vis international financial institutions including the International Monetary Fund, the World Bank and others, that move beyond commonly held understandings of Muslims. Thus a number of Muslim states have acquiesced to interest-based monetary transactions, accepting loans from these bodies at exorbitant rates of interest in clear violation of established principles of the Islamic legal tradition. On the other hand, one of the fastest-growing body of scholarship and practice consists of Islamic Banking and Finance and its responsiveness to contemporary international issues in the field. It is interesting to note the growing international collaboration between Muslim and non-Muslim jurisdictions; banks located in the 'west' are developing 'Islamic' financial instruments and products to attract Muslim clientele, and Muslim countries and institutions are accommodating these developments within their economies.

Muslim Diasporic Communities as a Discursive Site for the Islamic Legal Tradition

As a recurring theme of the present contribution, it is evident that transformative processes of the Islamic legal tradition are also having an impact on more than one key concept within *as-siyar*. Muslims living in diasporic communities of non-Muslim jurisdictions including India, Europe, North America and Canada do not subscribe, either individually or collectively, to a dichotomous world comprising *dar-al-harb*[12] (territory of war) *and dar-al-Islam*[13] *(*territory of Islam/Muslim

---

[12] This consists of all states and communities outside the territory of Islam. Its inhabitants were called *harbis*, or people of the territory of war (Khadduri 1956: 359).

[13] *Dar-al-Islam* denotes territories under Islamic sovereignty. Its inhabitants were Muslims by birth or conversion, and people of the tolerated religions (Jews, Christians and Zoroastrians) who preferred to remain non-Muslims and paid the special tax (*jizyah*) (Khadduri 1956: 359). See also Mahmassani 1966: 250–52; Hamidullah 1977: part II.

country) as prescribed by historical *as-siyar* or Islamic international law.[14] It would be truer to suggest that the above-mentioned non-Muslim jurisdictions today fall into an intermediate classification known as *dar-al-sulh/dar-al-ahd/dar-al-aman/ dar-al-darura*.[15]

The concept of *dar-al-sulh* is historical, based upon security offered to (non-Muslim) people of *dar-al-harb* who were either passing through or chose to live in *dar-al-Islam*. It is premised on unconditional promise of security or *aman*, the *dhimmi* status that made Christians, Jews and members of other religions included as *ahl-al-kitab*, protected semi-citizens, and the *muwada'ah* or *pacta sunt servanda*, the recognition of the binding nature of treaties that cannot be revoked without prior notice.

Contemporary international law and geopolitical reality today means that, in place of non-Muslim protected persons in Muslim jurisdictions, the reverse situation prevails. Millions of Muslims have made a conscious decision to adopt non-Muslim jurisdictions as their homes, voluntarily and permanently. This is an eventuality that historical *as-siyar* had neither contemplated nor prescribed rules of engagement for. Norms of *as-siyar* have, therefore, perforce been transformed and modified to present contemporary contours of *dar-al-Islam*, *dar-al-harb* and its intermediate constituency of *dar-al-sulh*, *dar-al-ahd* and/or *dar-al-darura*.

At the outset is the acceptance that peaceful coexistence constitutes the 'normal' relationship between Muslim and non-Muslim states, and treaties of amity need not be confined to a fixed duration (as was the case historically). A further distinction is the fact that there is no single 'Islamic' or 'Muslim' state, but a number of political entities in the international community that have a predominantly Muslim population. Likewise, there is no single 'other' *dar-al-harb* territory but numerous independent states (and groups of states such as the European Union) where the dominant population consists of non-Muslims.

Bearing in mind the above discussion, we now arrive at the point of explaining the extent to which the definition of *dar-al-Islam*, *dar-al-harb* and *dar-al-sulh* has evolved and been modified in contemporary times in order to answer the question as to whether India, North America, Canada and European countries constitute *dar-al-sulh* or even *dar-al-Islam*. All three categories have undergone changes over the centuries. States that would have come within the purview of *dar-al-harb* previously no longer answer to that description. A broad definition of *dar-al-Islam* is 'any territory whose inhabitants observe Islamic law'. Supplementary questions in this regard would be: Are there any prerequisites for numbers of people observing Islamic law in a territory for it to qualify as *dar-al-Islam* (the majority of the population as opposed to any number of people)? Are Muslims able to freely fulfill their religious obligations? One test comprised whether Friday

---

[14] See for instance Busuttil 1991; Mushkat 1987.

[15] Land of peace, land of treaty, land of protection, land of necessity respectively.

and Eid[16] congregational prayers could be held in that jurisdiction (Khadduri 1956). On this trial alone, British India was considered by Muslim scholars as *dar-al-Islam* (Rahim 1995: 396–7). Other tests include the ability of Muslim inhabitants to comply with the five pillars of Islam (reciting the unity of Allah and the last Prophethood of Muhammad, saying *salat* or the five daily prayers, fasting, undertaking *haj* [17] and carrying out *zakat*[18]) and to enjoy the availability of *halal*[19] meat, to name but two. In summary, therefore, the criteria for *dar-al-Islam* include whether Muslims can fearlessly implement and observe the five pillars of Islam and believe that their life, property and honour are protected by the state. On the basis of this analogy, might we argue that Western states (of Europe, the United States of America and Canada) qualify for consideration as *dar-al-Islam*?

In order to address this question, it is important to make the point that classification of the world as *dar-al-Islam* or *dar-al-harb* is a political rather than religious issue as proposed by the late Zaki Badawi. He is of the opinion that *dar-al-Islam* and *dar-al-harb* are related to the power to implement *Shari'a* in a given polity (Badawi 2000: 39). The central ingredient of *dar-al-Islam* is the supremacy of Islamic law in that jurisdiction or, at the very least, the ability of the political authority to advance legal formulations on that basis. Additionally, the population must believe that they can comfortably and without risking confrontation with state and civil society practice their Islamic tenets. If this be the case then some Muslims may adopt the position that most countries, whether Muslim or non-Muslim, would qualify as *dar-al-sulh*: Muslims are able to fulfill their five pillars with a degree of confidence and protection, but political power may be either unable or unwilling to implement principles of Islamic law (*Shari'a*). This interpretation, surely, is a clear movement beyond historical notions of *as-siyar*.

---

[16] These are the two major feasts of Muslims. The first, *Eid-al-Fitr*, falls after the month of *Ramadan* (fasting month), and the second, *Eid-al-adha*, is celebrated after the annual pilgrimage to Makkah known as *Haj*.

[17] The annual pilgrimage to Makkah that is obligatory for Muslims once in their lifetime.

[18] The annual voluntary offerings obligatory upon Muslims, subject to certain conditions. Normally a Muslim beyond a certain level of income gives 2.5 per cent of his/her annual savings to deserving people (rules are laid down for who is 'deserving' of *zakat*).

[19] Food is either permitted (*halal*) or prohibited (*haram*). Meat of permitted animals, however, must be slaughtered in a particular manner for it to qualify as *halal* meat. The difference between *zabiha* (meat of animal slaughtered in the prescribed manner) and *halal* is to be noted. Lamb, cow and chicken meat is *halal*, that is, permitted, but if not slaughtered in the prescribed manner is not *zabiha*.

Evolution in Muslim Family Law: Cracks in the Citadel?

Emphatic pronouncements reverberate throughout the Muslim world and among individual Muslims that family law is the remaining bastion of a universal Muslim identity and governed solely by an unadulterated 'Islamic' family law. Reality reflects the striking fact that this area of law has evolved with tremendous alacrity, especially over the past century. Its evolution is both procedural and substantive. At the level of procedure, an individual *qadi* is no longer the sole judge of a case. An entire hierarchy of courts is present in Muslim jurisdictions and described as family courts, appeal from which is (in most cases) possible to the High Court and Supreme Court of the land. Secondly and more importantly, there appears to have become entrenched the trend of an adversarial legal system, sidelining the Islamic principle of 'equality of arms' that appears to have receded into the background. Most women in Muslim countries are less likely to cope successfully within the adversarial regime of the legal system; hence the obligations of the *qadi* to ensure an investigation into the facts of the case and to provide speedy justice. With the advent of the 'modern' nation-state in Muslim jurisdictions, this safety net has now sadly been withdrawn.[20]

On the substantive side, family law in the Islamic legal tradition has moved progressively towards codification, starting with the Ottoman Empire and continuing until present times. An impressive array of what are termed personal status laws mushroomed consistently during the 20th century in virtually all Muslim countries. The transformative element embedded within this codification is distinctive in that these are also reformative measures to overcome some of the strictures within one or other school of juristic thought in Islam. Refreshing is the revival of the use of juristic techniques of *ijtihad, talfiq, takhayyur, maslaha*, and so on. Examples include laws relating to the right of adult Muslim women to consent to marriage without intervention of the *wali*; laws permitting dissolution of marriage;[21] laws prohibiting *talaq ul bidda* or triple *talaq* – inhibition – in some cases; laws disallowing polygamy; laws protecting the rights of inheritance of grandchildren, and so on.[22] The latest examples of women-friendly reform in Muslim family law include the Moroccan Family Law[23] and Egyptian law on *Khul'*, the latter adopted in 2000.[24]

---

[20] Most states of the North (including most European States and Canada) have attempted to redress this inequality by instituting effective legal aid programs. This facility, so deeply enshrined in the Islamic legal tradition, appears absent from the majority of Muslim jurisdictions.

[21] The Dissolution of Muslim Marriages Act 1939 (India, Pakistan, Bangladesh); Muslim Family Laws Ordinance 1961 (Pakistan, Bangladesh).

[22] Muslim Family Laws Ordinance 1961; *Moudawana* 2004.

[23] The Moroccan Family Law (*Moudawana*) 2004

[24] The Egyptian Law on Khul', Law No. 1/2000.

At the level of local communities, this transformation takes the form of law as discursive site. Elements of 'classical' Islamic legal tradition are juxtaposed against the personal interests of parties. Thus, for instance, in the presence of polygamy as a right of the male Muslim, it is impossible for families to deny this outright. A strategy conceived over centuries is to stipulate an exorbitant amount as *mahr* (dower) to inhibit the husband from taking another wife. This is a resistance to polygamy as constructed and applied by society. Likewise, excluding women from inheritance, especially land, is common in South Asia, although clearly prescribed by Islam. Granted that this denial of rights is not legitimated in the name of Islam, nevertheless its practitioners are Muslim and society appears to provide tacit approval. Interestingly, a number of courts take this denial very seriously and a review of case law of the superior courts of Pakistan shows that women's rights in this area are restored unequivocally (Arif and Ali 1998: 163, 180).

A final example in the transformative processes of the Islamic legal tradition is the trend of some governments to 'Islamise' their laws. In Pakistan this came in the wake of General Zia-ul Haq's regime; the General declared a drive of 'Islamisation' in the country. But ensuing and continued resistance shows the distance between his perception of Islamic-ness and that of the population at large. One such law that was 'Islamised' is Article 17 of the Qanun-I Shahadat or Law of Evidence (1984), which states that in financial transactions reduced to writing the evidence of two men or one man and two women will be required. Courts in Pakistan have not invoked this law because the 'living' law has evolved towards an acceptance of women as equal witnesses. But the state once held hostage to this black letter inclusion is unable and unwilling to accept or concede this reality for fear of rousing public unrest (on the part of citizens who never made the demand for this law in the first place!). Strangely enough, there are no demands in court for leading evidence according to this provision of the Law of Evidence, and it was placed on the statute books as part of a political agenda of so-called Islamisation during the era of General Zia-ul Haq and that too in a watered-down version. Similarly, there were no demands for reducing women's evidentiary capacity prior to this law, which begs the question of reasons for its inclusion.

From Individual to Collective Fatwa? *Institution of* Ifta *as Transformative Vehicle in the Islamic Legal Tradition*

One of the most powerful vehicles of interpretative and transformative processes within the Islamic legal tradition lies in the role played by the institution of *ifta*. The *fatwa* or non-binding opinion of a *mufti* given in response to a question (posed by a *qadi*, a private person or an institution) 'formed the vital link between academic theories of pure scholarship and the influences of practical life, and through them the dictates of the doctrine were gradually adapted to the changing needs of Muslim society' (Coulson 1994: 142–3).

Over fourteen hundred years of Islam's legal history, public institutionalised application of Islamic law has existed side by side with private and autonomous initiatives of legal interpretation. The *fatwa* is perceived by many as the 'meeting point between legal theory and social practice' (Caeiro 2006: 661), serving a number of functions ranging from a legal tool assisting the adjudication process (employed by a *qadi*) to a social instrument (in the form of questions provided by private persons in the community), a means of political discourse (seeking a *fatwa* in relation to an act of state or government either within the state or in another state or states), and as a device for reform (where a *mufti*, in response to a question, presents his viewpoint for reform in existing practice).

Although not mutually exclusive, this interpretative exercise falls under binding judgments issued from within an institution of the state by judges (*qadi*) and non-binding advisory opinions (*fatwa*; *fatawa*) by jurisconsults (*mufti*) in response to an individual question, as well as formal requests of opinions by *qadis*. Hallaq defines a *fatwa* as 'a question (*sua-al*, *istifta*), addressed to a jurisconsult (*mufti*), together with an answer (*jawab*) provided by that jurisconsult' (Hallaq 1994: 31). He states that there exists strong evidence to indicate that *fatwas* went beyond simply responses to individual questions and played a considerable role in the growth and evolution of Islamic substantive law (ibid.). This is likely to have been the case, as *fatwas* issued by leading jurists were often collected and published and used as authoritative precedents.[25] The history of *fatwas* is therefore uniquely placed within the Islamic legal tradition as it stands at the crossroads between theory and practice of Islam, the formal and non-formal structures of authority and their relational location within Muslim communities. It thus provides both 'text' (the *fatwa*) and context (the space within which the question is posed and to which it applies), as well as the link between the two.

I would argue that, while the *fatwa* contributed to legal discourse within the Islamic legal tradition, it was also an important social instrument and helped in shaping societal views on issues from the mundane to the sublime. This point is significant in the transformative processes of the Islamic legal tradition and contrary to assumptions that statute laws would eventually marginalise this genre, leading to its extinction. In particular, it is important to bear in mind that, in view of the high rates of illiteracy among Muslim populations and their dependency on the mass media (radio and television), reliance on 'verbal' *fatwas* delivered to an audience has increasingly become a popular offering of radio and television channels. It is this aspect of the transformation of the *fatwa* as a response by an individual *mufti* to an individual question that appears to have taken a grip on the institution of *ifta* in contemporary times.

The *fatwa* represents a bottom–up approach to informing and influencing the formal legal system, and is representative of the ordinary Muslim's concern regarding 'Islamic-ness' of actions and issues around her/him (legal and non-legal). The *qadi* pronounces binding judgments in response to questions arising from the litigant public and at times with the assistance of *muftis*. *Fatwas*, on the

---

[25] The list of such *fatwa* collections is too lengthy to be included here. For some of the most prominent *fatwa* collections, see Hallaq 1994: 31.

other hand, have a wider and more informal remit in responding to questions that were not necessarily litigational (in the legal sense). They could be clarifications of existing circumstances and/or legal rules, moral or social, and ethical, political and economic questions.

Fatwas have acquired a different legal complexion in diverse Muslim populations and jurisdictions; and in today's era of globalisation, they represent the common Muslims' short-cut access to 'Islamic' knowledge on a range of subjects. In particular, *fatwas* appear to be acquiring increasing popularity as scores of troubled Muslims, young and old, lose faith in their respective governments and turn towards an '*Ummatic*' response from scholars anywhere in the world so long as they belong to the Muslim *Ummah*.

Summing up this discussion on the structure, evolution and dynamics of the institution of *ifta*, it is fair to state that a number of parallel normative developments have emerged. On the one hand, there exists the definitiveness of divine text (the *Qur'an*) and divinely inspired text (*Hadith*) that remains the foundational basis of the structure of the legal edifice. Simultaneously, individual and collective autonomy of thought and action through *fatwas* have contributed to a responsiveness within Islamic law and jurisprudence. I submit that there appears to have evolved an invisible hierarchy within the Islamic legal tradition regarding its sources and techniques. The top–down sources appear to remain incognisant of initiatives from below (that is, through '*urf* or *fatwa*) despite the fact that both these institutions feed and enrich its evolution and make it contemporary. Conversely, *fatwas* challenging and undermining the prerogative of governments in Muslim jurisdictions appear to have created parallel institutions appealing to Muslims in cities, towns and rural areas over and above the head of governments. These opinions have also brought into prominence the ever-present fluidity of concepts including *as-siyar* and *jihad* within 'formal' legal writings on Islamic law, and have highlighted how these concepts are understood and internalised by resistance movements (for instance in Iraq and Afghanistan, in Palestine and in Pakistan) as tools for liberation. Indeed, the ongoing communication revolution and the role of the mass media, including internet sites seeking *fatwas*, are playing a significant part in developing a responsive Islamic legal tradition.

The use of internet technology has brought about a revolutionary change in the process of *fatwas*: entire websites are dedicated to their issuance by religious scholars and institutions There are dozens of websites and online forums where these *fatwas* are published and religious scholars belonging to different sects and schools of thought respond to questions and discuss a wide range of issues. Commenting on this rising trend, Shmuel Bar believes that

> The age of information has opened up a new venue for Muslims to acquire religious instruction without coming in direct contact with the consulting Sheikh. The Internet now allows a Muslim to send a query to any learned Sheikh by E-Mail and to receive a ruling either directly or in the public domain of websites dedicated to such *fatwas*. (Bar 2006: 4)

'Surfing' *fatwa* websites, it is evident that these reflect the multitude of sects, cults and groups that come within the fold of what we call Islam. Adherents to these groups vary in size and influence, and can range from tens of millions to a few thousands. Even within the same sect, there can be fundamental differences in interpretation of the Quran and the *Hadith*, and rival *muftis* from the same sect can issue contradictory *fatwas*. What constitutes legitimate *jihad* in relation to the Iraq war, and whether the terrorist attacks of 9/11 and 7/7 fall within its remit, is interpreted from diverse perspectives. Some religious scholars do not justify the use of force and terrorist acts being committed in the name of *jihad*, while others have expressed a dissenting view by justifying those acts in the name of Islam.

Some Concluding Observations

This contribution has attempted to explore the extent to which there exist transformative processes within the Islamic legal tradition. It highlights the fact that, over the centuries, the religious text in Islam (mainly comprising the *Qur'an* and *Ahadith*) has been employed to evolve a dynamic legal tradition, a grudgingly accepted reality not universally ascribed to among Muslim communities. Historical, political and social events have created legally plural and often competing normative frameworks within which Muslims must navigate. Culture, custom, tradition, religion, as well as statute law and international laws, operate in a legally fluid environment. Increasingly, these processes appear as 'fractured modernities', negotiating ever-shifting boundaries of engagement within themselves and other spheres of legality and illegality. On the one hand, modern-day constitutions of Muslim jurisdictions pronounce Islam as the state religion and as the main source of laws. In the very same documentation, there appear equality and non-discrimination provisions that are controversial within mainstream understandings of the Islamic legal tradition.

Muslim jurisdictions make selective use of Islamic injunctions and ignore those clear rules of the *Qur'an* and *Sunna* that pose a challenge to unbridled political, economic and social power of the ruling elite within these countries. A veneer of immutability is cast over the legal system, emanating from the Islamic religion despite the full knowledge that this is no longer the case.

Transformative processes have neither been all negative nor entirely positive, and each development must be seen in light of its impact on peoples' lives. Thus financial and commercial rules of transactions permitting the impermissible *riba*' (interest) are still the norm in a number of Muslim jurisdictions. Pakistan is a prime example of this position: here the Supreme Court has yet to provide conclusive guidance on the way forward. Explicit *Qur'anic* injunctions regarding obligations of Muslim states towards their citizens in civil and political fields, and economic, social and cultural rights, remain unfulfilled. One has only to look at the Human Development Index to realise that Muslim countries with high GDPs fall far below their comparateur countries in terms of human development and the resources they dedicate to provide access to basic human rights of health, education, clean drinking water, access to justice (to name a few).

This contribution has also attempted to initiate a conversation, a dialogue, and hopefully an initiative towards bringing together differing understandings regarding the Islamic legal tradition. What emerges convincingly to my mind is the fact that the Islamic legal tradition, Muslim communities and states have for the most part accepted the fact of engagement among peoples, laws, states and governments. There is ample evidence among state practice to establish this point. What is not appreciated adequately, however, is the complexities of values, norms and legal systems that Muslims negotiate today. It is important for a Western readership, mostly trained in legal centrism, to comprehend this dynamic at play within the Islamic legal tradition.

A further inference of this contribution is that, in the maze of history and under the influence of disparate legal developments (for example, the colonial project, to which many Muslim jurisdictions were subjected), some of the pillars and distinctive features of the Islamic justice system were weakened and almost disappeared from legal memory. Thus the principle of access to justice for all and equality of arms (in the sense of availability of equal legal representation to all parties) gave way to a common law system of adversarial procedure before the courts. Likewise, speedy provision of justice in family cases by an individual *qadi* to minimise suffering of often vulnerable women and children was buried under a more 'modern' edifice of a hierarchical court system.

To close, the globalisation of religion as an emerging phenomenon is likely to prove a vital element in the transformative processes within the Islamic legal tradition. The increasing number of websites offering services for *ifta* points to the effect of the mass media and mass communications on access to contemporary responses to modern (Islamic) legal questions. Local, national and international institutions and their actions are being questioned by people approaching *muftis* on these websites and soliciting responses in light of the *Qur'an* and *Sunna*. The *fatwas* are therefore contributing towards this evolving tradition.

In summary, it is submitted that this contribution is very much a work in progress, and I welcome comments and observations that may effect a useful dialogue and ongoing exploration of the subject.

References

Al-Faruqi, I.R. (1978). 'Islam and Other Faiths', in A. Gauhar (ed.), *The Challenge of Islam*, London: Islamic Council of Europe, pp. 82–111.
Ali, S.S. (2000). *Gender and Human Rights in Islam and International Law: Equal Before Allah, unequal Before Man?*, The Hague: Kluwer Law International.
Ali, S.S. (ed.) (2006). *Conceptualising Islamic law, CEDAW and Women's Human Rights in Plural Legal Settings: A Comparative Analysis of Application*

of CEDAW in Bangladesh, India and Pakistan, Delhi: UNIFEM Regional Office.

Ali, S.S. (2007a). 'A Comparative Perspective of the United Nations Convention on Rights of the Child and the Principles of Islamic Law. Law Reform and Children's Rights in Muslim Jurisdictions', in S. Goonasekere (ed.), *Protecting the World's Children: Impact of the UN Convention on the Rights of the Child in Diverse Legal Systems*, Cambridge: Cambridge University Press, pp. 142–208.

Ali, S.S. (2007b). 'The Twain Doth Meet! A Preliminary Exploration of the Theory and Practice of As-Siyar and International Law in the Contemporary World', in J. Rehman and S. Breau (eds), *Religion, Human Rights and International Law*, Leiden: Martinus Nijhoff Publishers, pp. 95–136.

Ali, S.S. (2007c). 'Religious Pluralism, Human Rights and Muslim Citizenship in Europe: Some Preliminary Reflections on an Evolving methodology for Consensus', in T. Leonon and J. Goldschmidt (eds), *Religious Pluralism and Human Rights in Europe: Where to Draw the Line?*, Antwerp: Intersentia, pp. 57–79.

Allot, A. (1980). *Limits of Law*, London: Butterworths.

An-Naim, A.A. (ed.) (2002). *Islamic Family Law in a Changing World: A Global Resource Book*, London: Zed Books.

An-Naim, A.A. (2006). 'Global Citizenship and Human Rights: From Muslims in Europe to European Muslims', Inaugural Address as Professor to the W.G. Wiarda Chair, Utrecht University.

An-Naim, A.A. (2007). 'Global Citizenship and Human Rights: From Muslims in Europe to European Muslims', in T. Loenen and J. Goldschmidt (eds), *Religious Pluralism and Human Rights in Europe: Where to Draw the Line?*, Antwerp: Intersentia, pp. 13–55.

Arabi, O. (2001). *Studies in Modern Islamic Law and Jurisprudence*, The Hague: Kluwer Law International.

Arif, K., and S.S. Ali (1998). 'The Law of Inheritance and Reported Case Law Relating to Women', in F. Shaheed et al. (eds), *Shaping Women's Lives: Laws, Practices and Strategies in Pakistan*, Lahore: Shirkatgah, pp. 163–80.

Badawi, Z. (2000). 'New Fight for Minorities', Muslims of Europe in the New Millenium Conference, 9–10 September 2000, Regent's College London, AMSS (UK) and Islamic Cultural Centre, Ireland, cited in I. Yilmaz (2005) *Muslim Laws, Politics and Society in Modern Nation States: Dynamic Legal Pluralisms in England, Turkey and Pakistan*, Aldershot: Ashgate, p. 39.

Baderin, M. (2003). *International Human Rights and Islamic Law*, Oxford: Oxford University Press.

Balz, K. (1995–96). '"*Sharia*" and "*Qanun*" in Egyptian Law: A Systems Theory Approach to Legal Pluralism', in E. Cotran and C. Mallat (eds), *2nd Yearbook of Islamic and Middle Eastern Law*, vol. 2, London: Kluwer Law International, pp. 37–53.

Bar, S. (2006). *Jihad Ideology in Light of Contemporary Fatwas*, Center on Islam, Democracy, and the Future of the Muslim World, Washington DC: Hudson Institute.

Bowen, J. (2003). *Islam, Law and Equality in Indonesia: An Anthropology of Public Reasoning*, Cambridge: Cambridge University Press.

Busuttil, J. (1991). 'Humanitarian Law in Islam', *The Military Law and Law of War Review*, 30, pp. 111–45.

Caeiro, A. (2006). 'The Shifting Moral Universes of the Islamic Tradition of Ifta: A Diachronic Study of Four Adab al-Fatwa Manuals', *The Muslim World*, 96:4, pp. 661–85.

Coulson, J. (1957). 'The State and the Individual in Islamic Law', *International and Comparative Law Quarterly*, 6:1 (January), pp. 49–60.

Coulson, N. J. (1994 [1964]). *A History of Islamic Law*. Edinburgh: Edinburgh University Press.

Doi, A.R.I. (1984). *Shari'ah: The Islamic Law*, London: Ta Ha Publishers.

Fyzee, A.A.A. (1974). *Outlines of Muhammadan Law*, 4th edn, Delhi: Oxford University Press.

Hallaq, W.B. (1994). 'From *Fatwas* to *Furu*: Growth and Change in Islamic Substantive Law', *Islamic Law and Society*, 1, pp. 29–65.

Hamid, A.F.A. (2001). 'Islamic Resurgence: An Overview of Causal Factors, A Review of Ummatic Linkages', *IKIM Journal*, 9:1, pp. 15–47.

Hamidullah, M. (1977). *Muslim Conduct of State: Being a Treatise on Siyar, that is Islamic Notion of Public International Law, Consisting of the Laws of Peace, War and Neutrality, Together with Precedents from Orthodox Practices and Precedent by a Historical and General Introduction*, Lahore: Sh. Muhammad Ashraf.

Hassan, R. (1980). 'The Role and Responsibilities of Women in the Legal and Religious Tradition of Islam', unpublished paper from biannual meeting of Trialogue of Jewish–Christian–Muslim scholars on 14 October, Joseph and Rose Kennedy Institute of Ethics, Washington DC.

Jordanian Law of Family Rights (no. 92) of 1951.

Kamali, M.H. (2003). *Principles of Islamic Jurisprudence*, 3rd edn, Cambridge: Islamic Texts Society.

Khadduri, M. (1956). 'Islam and the Modern Law of Nations', *American Journal of International Law*, 50:2, pp. 358–72.

Law No. 1/2000 adopted by the People's Assembly of Egypt on the Reorganisation of Certain Terms and Procedures of Litigation in Personal Status Matters (the Khul' Law of Egypt).

Mahmassani, S. (1966). 'The Principles of International Law in the Light of Islamic Doctrine', *Recueil des Cours de l'Académie de Droit International*, 117:I, pp. 201–328.

Mernissi, F. (1991). *Women and Islam*, Oxford: Basil Blackwell.

Moinuddin, H. (1987). *The Charter of the Islamic Conference and Legal Framework of Economic Co-operation Among Its Member States*, Oxford: Clarendon Press.

Moors, A. (1995). *Women, Property and Islam: Palestinian Experiences 1920–1990*, Cambridge: Cambridge University Press.

Moroccan Code of Personal Status, 1958.

Moroccan Family Code (Moudawana) 2004, at http://hrea.org/moudawana.html, accessed 14 March 2009.

Mushkat, R. (1987). 'Is War Ever Justifiable? A Comparative Survey', *Loyola of Los Angeles International and Comparative Law Journal*, 9:2, pp. 227–317.

Muslim Family Laws Ordinance VII of 1961 (Pakistan, Bangladesh), at http://www.vakilno1.com/saarclaw/pakistan/muslim_family_laws_ordinance.htm, accessed 19 March 2009.

Organisation of Islamic Conference, at www.oic-oci.org/english/main/charter.htm, accessed 12 September 2007.

Ottoman Law of Family Rights, 1917.

Parwez, G.A. (1960). *Lughat-ul-Quran*, Lahore: Idara Tulu' e Islam.

Pearl, D., and W. Menski (1998). *Muslim Family Law*, 3rd edn, London: Sweet & Maxwell.

Rahim, A. (1995). *Muhammadan Jurisprudence*, Lahore: Mansoor Book House.

Ramadan, T. (1999), *To Be a European Muslim*, Leicester: The Islamic Foundation.

Rehman, F. (1979). *Islam*, 2nd edn, Chicago, IL: University of Chicago Press.

Sachedina, A. (1988). 'Preface', in M.H. Shakir (trans.), *The Holy Quran*. New York: Tahrike Tarsile Qur'an Inc.

Sonbol, A. (ed.) (1996). *Women, the Family and Divorce Laws in Islamic History*, Syracuse, NY: Syracuse University Press.

Syrian Law of Personal Status (no. 59) of 1953.

The Dissolution of Muslim Marriages Act VIII of 1939 (India, Pakistan, Bangladesh), at http://www.vakilno1.com/bareacts/dissolutionmarriageact/dissolutionofmuslimmarriageact.htm, accessed 19 March 2009.

Tucker, J. (1997). *In the House of the Law: Gender and Islamic Law in Ottoman Syria and Palestine*, Berkeley, CA: University of California Press.

Welchman, L. (2000). *Beyond the Code: Muslim Family Law and Shari Judiciary in the Palestinian West Bank*, The Hague: Kluwer Law International.

Chapter 10
Clashes and Encounters: Challenges in Nordic Legal Cultures Related to Law and Religion

Kjell Å Modéer

From a Modern Static Historical Argumentation to a Late Modern Dynamic One

Shaheen Sardar Ali's contribution 'Systematically Closed, Cognitively Open' is a most stimulating read for a Nordic audience, as it gives inspiration for a comparison between different normative systems and their cognitive structures. From a Pakistani as well as a global position she is opening up a possibility for any reader within the Western and secular legal tradition to understand Islamic law in a new way: as a transformative processes during a *longue durée*, with deep structures of law actually going back to a Mosaic and Abrahamaic legal tradition. By quoting G.A. Parwez, Shaheen Sardar Ali is describing the breadth and reach of *Shari'a* by using the metaphor of the well, the watering place, necessary for human life, providing 'the source of water ... [as] a flowing stream or spring'. It's the same metaphor the prophet Amos used in the Old Testament (5:24) when he described justice 'roll[ing] on like a river, righteousness like a never failing stream', a metaphor used frequently within the Western legal rhetoric tradition. *Shari'a* is like justice not a stagnant concept; it's a dynamic model adjusted and implemented differently in diverse contexts. Shaheen Sardar Ali analyzes the Islamic legal tradition by using a special term, 'evolving tradition', which in its content is transformative over time and space. Legal tradition is a concept that lately has been used extensively by the Canadian comparatist H. Patrick Glenn, who in his acclaimed book *Legal Traditions of the World* has brought new light to this notion in terms of recognizing orally transmitted law as a way to break with the dominating and established Western concepts in trying to include all legal systems of the world. By doing so, Glenn observes that the most dominating legal traditions are those related to the world religions – so the Jewish, the Christian, the Islamic etc. This dynamic concept of 'traditions' demonstrates the flexibility, the adjustments and the transformations within the legal traditions – expressively the Islamic – depending on time and space, and depending on integration in different contexts (Glenn 2007).

A keyword in Shaheen Sardar Ali's contribution is 'dynamics', for example the organic and evolutionary transformative processes that historically have defined the Islamic legal tradition, of course based on a belief in the Qur'an as the Word of God. This means that her analysis is based on two sides of a historical argumentation: the static and the dynamic. The static historical argumentation is in this case based on the religious text, and the dynamic argument is based on the religious context, the culture, the tradition: 'A tradition or *Hadith* is composed of the *matn* (text) of the tradition and the *isnad* (chain of transmitters)' (p. xx). From a Nordic perspective, this insight resonates particularly with regard to the more general transformation of the Nordic legal systems and their continuously changing cognitive structures. Also in the Nordic countries the historical argument during the last twenty years has changed, from the critical argumentation of the modern welfare state in the 20th century to the dynamic case of the late modern society of the early 21st century. Today the dynamic historical argumentation is visible in the discourses within Nordic legal science (Modéer 2009). Additionally, within the interdisciplinary field of law & religion a discourse related to a more dynamic argumentation has been observed (post-secularism, de-secularization).

Legal Culture as a Context for the Religious Legal Culture

A Chinese colleague of mine characterizes European legal systems as transparent in contrast to those of the Chinese. In that respect *The Great Wall* is useful as a metaphor for the Chinese legal culture. For centuries Chinese law and society have been looked upon as closed from outside influences in comparison with the situation in the European countries where foreign ideas and elements have been received regularly into the different national systems.

A dominating comparative law discourse in the post-war period defined the Western legal systems as organized in *legal families*. The Nordic countries were identified as the Nordic legal family. This family was regarded as exceptional. It was neither a *civil law* country with a codification, nor a *common law* country with a case law system. It was regarded as occupying the space in between these definitions. The Nordic legal family was characterized by its common history and harmonized legal systems (Modéer 2008). All the Nordic countries were homogeneous also in the respect that their religious life was dominated by Evangelical Lutheran State Churches.

This homogeneous view of legal and religious life in the Nordic countries has recently been transformed and challenged by on the one hand different affiliations to supranational institutions within the EU and the European Council, and on the other hand the late-modern pluralistic society with its increasing multiculturalism and multi-religiosity. The welfare state model of the post-war period also created differences between the Nordic countries regarding legal regulation, due to diverse social, political and economical positions. Sweden didn't like the other Nordic countries' active participation in World War II. Sweden itself started out from a quite different economical situation than the other Nordic countries, and the Swedish welfare state for decades became a strong model for its neighbour countries, also within the law.

The harmonization process of the Nordic legislation ran increasingly into a blind alley when Sweden wanted to speed up the modernization of its legislation. The year 1972 is regarded as a milestone in that respect. At a centennial Nordic Convention for the Jurists, the representative of Swedish government bluntly declared that Sweden wanted to break up from the century-old Nordic cooperation and continue modernization at its own pace. The same year Denmark in a referendum decided to be a member of the European Communities. Divergence substituted convergence within the members of the Nordic legal family.

The breakdown of the Berlin Wall and the abolition of the Soviet Union resulted in a quite new geopolitical context for the legal cultures in the Nordic countries. The referenda in 1994 on the Maastricht Treaty (1992) demonstrated that the divergence between the Nordic countries related to affiliation to the European Union. Finland voted clearly for a membership, Sweden's membership was more reluctant, and Norway voted not to be a member. Denmark voted against the Maastricht Treaty, but accepted after negotiations regarding the preservation of the national identity.

Since 1 January 1995 the Nordic countries have been separated definitively due to different attitudes to their national legal identity and culture. So from a legal perspective the legal cultures in the Nordic countries have undergone a shift from being homogeneous to becoming heterogeneous, from emphasizing similarities to highlighting differences, and to demonstrating a consciousness regarding the identity of each country's position on the legal map. This also has parallels to what's going on within the religious cultures in the Nordic countries.

East is East and West is West – and Never Do They Meet?

The historically based relation between State and Church has been questioned and discourse within the Nordic countries has been ongoing since the end of World War II. In recent years the diversity of attitudes within the Nordic countries to this topic has been demonstrated.

Since the Reformation in the early 16th century, the geopolitical situation in the Nordic countries for centuries was fixed in an eastern part (with Sweden and Finland) and a western segment (with Denmark, Norway and Iceland). Even if the Napoleonic Wars created a new political map regarding the Nordic countries in the early 19th century, the position of the Evangelical Lutheran Church as a state institution didn't change. Only in Finland, from 1809 to 1917 under Russian rule, was there a change, as the Russian Orthodox Church also became a constitutionally protected state church. The big difference between the Nordic state churches was related to their internal political power. In Finland and Sweden the synod was introduced in the 19th century. In the west Nordic countries, to date the political power of the Church emanates from the government directly.

The claim for autonomy within the Swedish state church started as early as the 1950s. Parliamentarian commissions continuously produced investigations without results. In the late 1990s, however, a political solution opened up for a separation between State and Church. This separation took place in the year 2000 (Modéer, in print).

The autonomy of the Swedish Church has resulted in interesting discourses in the other Nordic countries. In Norway an investigation on the same matter was published in February 2006 (*Staten og Den norske kirke*, 2006), resulting in a compromise adopted by the Norwegian parliament on 11 April 2008, but upholding the relation of State and Church (Det kongelige kultur- og kirkedepartement 2007–2008). In Denmark the strong relationship between Church and State has been an important part of the current domestic politics. This demonstrates two things: (1) Religion is back in the public square in the secular Nordic countries, and (2) the concept of Scandinavian exceptionalism has changed from being identified by harmonization and convergence to being increasingly dominated by national identity and divergence.

Within late modernity, religious discourses on *identity* and *autonomy* have occurred, with both concepts becoming important keywords. The Nordic state churches of the 20th century were to a great extent involved in the societal process regarding democracy. The democratic breakthrough around 1920 and its political implications became an important context also for the Nordic folk churches. The democratization of the folk churches took place in a zeitgeist where the state churches not only had almost-monopoly in the national religious culture but also involved a qualified majority of the nation's citizens. The state churches were identified not only with the state but also with its political culture. In retrospect, an interesting research project would be to analyze to what extent the adjustments of the Nordic folk churches to the democratic policies of strong secular welfare state were the result of a new theologian hermeneutic or more an expression of political correctness.

To what extent can the democratic folk churches of today as religious communities handle the concepts of identity and autonomy in our time of fragmentization and multi-religious societies? Does religious freedom also include religious equality, or is the Evangelic Lutheran Church in the Nordic countries still a part of the national identity? And is democracy an obstacle also for both the autonomy of the Swedish Church, since 2000 separated from the state, and for Norway, since 2008 involved in a political process towards autonomy? These internal perspectives are of course important additionally for the Nordic *folk churches* as majority churches in relation to other religious communities like the Catholic Church and Islam.

Secularism vs. Islam – and Christianity in Between

The domestic political and legal conflicts related to religion that have been visible in the Scandinavian countries – namely, the Muhammed Cartoon Crisis in Denmark; the Åke Green case on freedom of religion regarding discrimination of homosexuals in Sweden (High Court Decision, 29 November 2005); and the Folgerø case in Norway on the compulsory subject of 'KRL' (Christianity, Religion and Philosophy) in the European Court of Human Rights 2007 (European Court of Human Rights, Decision 29 June 2007: Case of Folgerø and Others v. Norway, Application 15472/02) – have all brought religion out into the public square.

In my opinion, all these cases are related not only to the visibility of minorities in Scandinavian multicultural society, but also to secularism. The negative freedom of religion – that is, the right not to have a religion – has been the prevailing attitude to religion during the era of the modernity. In Sweden, this discourse has predominated since the early 1950s.[1] Religion was consequently reduced to a private matter. In a recent work the British theologian Hugh McLeod describes the 1960s as a 'hinge decade' with a transformation in Europe – in contrast to the US – from a 'Christian Country to Civilized Society' (McLeod 2007). The secularization of the far greater social welfare orientation of the Scandinavian nations, or even most of Europe, contrasted increasingly with the religiosity prevailing in the US with its market orientation. One of the most interesting changes in the attitudes related to law & religion is the return of religion to the public square in late modern society. The return of the visibility of religions has also meant an increase in activity from its critics, atheists. In Sweden the Swedish Humanist Association (Humanisterna) has been very active in public media, and in Norway the parallel organization, the Norwegian Humanist Association (Human-Etisk Forbund) also played an active role in the Fogderø case, as the parents of the Applicants were members of that organization. The Norwegian Humanists also played an active role in the revision of the legislation regarding KRL due to the decision in the Human Rights Court.

The most visible religion in the contemporary Nordic public arena, however, is not Christianity but Islam. This is partly due to Islam's 'foreignness'. For the local citizen, Islam with its mosques and headscarves has a 'foreign', 'oriental' and even 'exotic' character. Those symbols are closely affiliated to Muslim immigrants in an increasingly multicultural society. Another reason for Islam's visibility is that *Shari'ah* in Muslim countries is regarded as a public norm system. The *Shari'ah* as a parallel norm system, however, is more controversial for the members of the Humanist Association than for the members of the Catholic congregation, for instance. Autonomous religious jurisdictions have been a part of European society since at least medieval times. The *Suum*-principle (*suum cuique tribuere*)[2] in Roman law formed part of European legal culture up to the time of the Enlightenment. Abolishing privileges and introducing legal equality into modern rational society also meant eradicating the *Suum*-principle.

---

[1] The Swedish Professor of Practical Philosophy at Uppsala University Ingemar Hedenius (1908–82) in 1949 published his work *Tro och vetande* [*Belief and Knowledge*] that triggered a major discourse regarding organized Christianity (Nordin 2004).

[2] 'Give to each what belongs to him/her.'

Today there are reiterated appeals for public acceptance of the *Suum*-principle in late modern society. There are no public *Shari'ah* courts in the Scandinavian countries, but just as members of Catholic congregations regularly go to confession, and ministers of the Catholic Church act as mediators and advisers in family law matters,[3] the members of Islam in the same way are consulting their *imam* regarding family law regulation in their *Shari'ah* law. In criminal law, Nordic courts in several cases have decided that they are not accepting *Shari'ah* law. However, in those countries that have ratified international private law conventions, *Shari'ah* law is implemented and used.

Some years ago a female Swedish MP applied to the Ombudsman against ethnical discrimination, arguing that the female members of the Islamic congregation in Stockholm were discriminated against as during the prayers they were obliged to use the balcony in the mosque. Of course the Ombudsman dismissed the case, but the application demonstrated the lack of knowledge regarding the *Suum*-principle relating to religious matters. The MP evidently was ignorant not only about Islamic religious habits but also about former Swedish Church habits, where during Mass the women sat in the left banks of the church – wearing headscarves – while the men were seated on the right banks.

In his critical analysis regarding the concept of legal culture, the British legal theorist Roger Cotterrell has abandoned a legal–sociological perspective of legal culture (an outsider's perspective) and instead used the cognitive systems of lawyers (the legal profession) themselves as an instrument to define legal cultures (Cotterell 1997). It's a concept based on ideologies of different arts, and including religions. Such legal cultures have been looked upon as more or less homogeneous, but regarding the Islamic law tradition within a boundless global transformation of legal thought and the appearance of legal pluralism, cognitive structures are merging and we are observing increasingly mixed legal systems and cultures. One tendency is the appearance of *diasporas* in European nation-states: in France the appearance of a French Islam, in England an 'Islamic Shari'ah Council', and a German Islam has also been identified.

So what we can observe today is that foreign legal and religious norms want to be integrated into Western legal systems. Professor Mathias Rohe at the University Erlangen-Nuremberg has argued for the integration of what he calls 'Euro-Islam' into the European legal systems, and he has noticed how German judges have accepted this adaption of the Islamic law tradition where it is adjusted to be able to fulfil the requirements of German basic law (Rohe 2000). In a couple of decisions in the German Constitutional Court, judges have agreed to integration of Islamic law within the German context. Regarding the principles within Egyptian *Shari'ah* law, the court argued that the Islamic sources were 'subject to discretionary interpretation and may alter with changes of time and space, in order to ensure their flexibility and vitality'. In a decision of 1994, the judges declared '… that the

---

[3] The Nordic Catholic congregations are using the Stockholm diocese as canon law jurisdiction in family law matters.

opinion of one canonist – concerning matters of difference in interpretation – are not sacred and may be amended or replaced, and that Islamic Shari'ah is therefore not rigid but subject to evolution in its basic fundamentals.' This statement of the Constitutional Court demonstrates that the judges within their practice have in fact adopted the main subject of Shaheen Sardar Ali's paper: the transformative processes of Islamic law in an international context.

References

Cotterrell, Roger (1997). 'The Concept of Legal Culture', in David Nelken (ed.), *Comparing Legal Cultures*, Aldershot: Dartmouth, pp. 13–32.

Det kongelige kultur- og kirkedepartement (2007–2008). [Ministry of Church and Culture], St. meld. nr 17, *Staten og Den norske kirke* [*The State and the Norwegian Church*; in Norwegian only].

Glenn, H. Patrick (2007). *Legal Traditions of the World: Sustainable Diversity in Law*, 3rd edn, Oxford: Oxford University Press.

McLeod, Hugh (2007). *The Religious Crises of the 1960s*, Oxford: Oxford University Press.

Modéer, Kjell Å (2008). 'Adjustment or Reluctance? Scandinavian Exceptionalism in Legal Cultures', in Hanne Petersen, Anne Lise Kjær, Helle Krunke and Minael Rask Madsen, *Paradoxes of European Legal Integration*, Aldershot: Ashgate, pp. 287–98.

Modéer, Kjell Å (2009). 'Det historiska argumentet i senmodern rättslig diskurs' [The Historical Argument in Late-Modern Legal Discourse], *Svensk Juristtidning*, 94, pp. 340–52.

Modéer, Kjell Å (in print). 'The Long Way Towards Traditional Autonomy: The Swedish Church and the Law 1968–2008', in Lisbet Christoffersen et al. (eds), *Law and Religion in the 21st Century: Nordic Perspectives*.

Nordin, Svante (2004). *Ingemar Hedenius*, Stockholm: Natur och Kultur.

Rohe, Mathias (2000). 'Rechtliche Perspektiven eines deutschen und europäischen Islam', *Rabels Zeitschrift*, 2, pp. 256–98.

Chapter 11
Law and Religion in Europe

Silvio Ferrari

The New Religious Plurality of Europe

Religious plurality is a well-known fact in Europe. For centuries Europe had been split up into Catholic, Protestant and Orthodox communities, with dividing lines that frequently crossed the same town or the same region. But this plurality was contained within a shared horizon, defined by reference to the same sacred books (Old- and New Testament) and the same interpretative corpus (Patristic). Of course, Jewish and Muslim communities have been living in Europe for a long time. The Jews, however, were faced quite early on with the alternative between assimilation or persecution (and they chose the first, without avoiding the second), and the Muslims were confined to a peripheral region of Europe after the Catholic 'reconquista' of Spain in the fifteenth century. As a consequence, religious plurality in Europe has predominantly been intra-Christian, and the religious conflicts that divided Europe after the Great Schism and above all the Protestant Reformation did not create insuperable cultural divisions. It is true that the relations between man and woman, citizen and State, State and religion were and partly still are conceived in a different way in the Catholic, Orthodox and Protestant countries, but this difference did not become so huge as to generate incompatibility and to prevent mutual understanding. The unification process of Europe, with all its shortcomings, is proof that a shared notion of citizenship does exist.

This common horizon has become progressively weaker. Two factors – the first internal and the second external to Europe – have played an important role in this weakening process and have paved the way to the birth of a culturally and ethically plural society.

The first factor is immigration, which brought into Europe an increasing number of people who do not know and do not share some central features of the European cultural heritage. The manner in which political or family relations are conceived, or, at a more day-to-day level, the way people dress or what they eat, marks a difference between a part of these immigrant groups and the majority of Europeans. It is not only a difference of religion, but something larger that concerns lifestyles, beliefs, values, behaviour: in a nutshell, a cultural difference.

Second, there is individualism, which questions assumptions that used to be taken for granted (Hervieu-Léger 2002). Secularization had already weakened the control historical Churches exercised on the central passages of human life, birth, marriage, death, and so on: now the way these experiences are conceived and lived is in the process of changing. The range of possibilities has become far larger and the individual is in a position to make choices that were unconceivable only a few years ago. Europe is moving towards the coexistence of different ways of procreating, marrying and dying that correspond with the diverse ethical views of individuals and that enjoy the same legal legitimacy. Both the debate on bioethics all over Europe and the recent reform of family law in a number of European countries show that the historic Churches have largely lost their capacity to lead the public debate on central ethical issues and to influence the corresponding political decisions (although there are exceptions, and I am thinking of Italy, which should not be overlooked).

What I have said confirms that today we are faced with something more than simple religious plurality: we have to deal with a veritable cultural and ethical plurality. But to understand this new challenge properly, we need to take into consideration its most interesting feature. This cultural and ethical plurality is by no means a result of the dissolution of the religious dimension in contemporary society: on the contrary, it is frequently characterized by a strong religious connotation or, at least, takes place in a context still dominated by the 'return of God'. On the one hand, the decline of the historical Churches' power to speak on behalf of European society in its entirety has been balanced by the development, within these same Churches, of new groups and movements, such as the Pentecostals and the 'Born Again Christians' in the Protestant field and 'Communion and Liberation' and Opus Dei within Catholicism. All are motivated by the aim to manifest their strong religious identity in all aspects of human life; consequently, they want to affirm the religious foundation of ethical, cultural and political choices. On the other hand, the distinction between religion, ethics, culture and politics that had been accepted – willingly or unwillingly – by most Christian churches is not part and parcel of the heritage of many religious communities that have arrived in Europe in the last forty years, starting with Islam and some of the new religious movements. Thus cultural and ethical choices are frequently justified through a direct reference to religion. The affair of the Islamic headscarf is a good example: what had been regarded, until a few years ago, as an ethnic custom is now perceived primarily as a religious expression. But there are equally clear examples in the Catholic domain: in Italy the distinction between religion and politics is much weaker now than when the Christian Democrat party ruled the country. At that time providing Italian political life with a Christian orientation was the task of those laymen who were engaged in politics; after the end of the Christian Democrat Party, the same task has been taken up by the bishops, who did not hesitate to give very precise and stringent political indications regarding the referendum on artificial fertilization and registered partnerships.

The final outcome of this mix of religion, culture, ethics and politics has been that negotiation and compromise are much more difficult today than in the past: when ethical and cultural choices are directly connected to the will of God, they tend to become non-negotiable.

Religious Plurality and Legal Change

What are the legal consequences of this transformation of the European religious landscape? What is its impact on the systems of relations between States and religions? Today the traditional legal mechanisms that regulated the different areas where human activity takes place do not seem to work properly: confronted with a pluralism that is at the same time cultural, ethical and religious, such mechanisms have difficulty in granting the freedom of social communities without falling into the anarchy of particularisms. This struggle can be explained by reflecting on how these mechanisms were born. They started taking shape as a way of putting an end to the wars of religion of the sixteenth and seventeenth centuries. The central question was then how to make possible the coexistence in the same country of subjects with a different religious faith: it was religious, not cultural and ethical, pluralism that created problems – and these could be solved through the neutralization of the impact of religion on public life. Although the (never completed) secularization of the public institutions began as late as the start of the nineteenth century, the theoretical solution had been found much earlier with Grotius's 'etsi Deus non daretur'. This approach shifted the focal point of religion from the public sphere to private life, while at the same time moving the centre of gravity of law from divine law to natural law based on reason. In other words, in order to make peaceful coexistence possible between Catholics, Protestants, Anglicans and so on, politics, the law, the economy and the other areas of public life had to be secularized, placing them under the exclusive rule of reason and freeing them from the control of religion. But this solution, which granted the religious peace of Europe for a long time, cannot be easily applied today: first, the connections between religion, ethics and culture make repetition of the process of secularization much more difficult; and second, the assumption that religion is a private matter that should not influence public choices is exactly what is currently being questioned. It is necessary to find legal mechanisms that take into account the new public role of religions. But how is it possible to so do without falling into 'communautarisme', which erodes the hard core of shared principles and values and risks endangering social cohesion?

The answer to this question has varied from State to State, according to different history and tradition. But these responses have some common features. First, the legal discipline of Church–State relations is in constant flux all over Europe. There are many examples of these changes: in Portugal, a law on religious liberty was enacted in 2001 and a new concordat with the Catholic Church was concluded in 2004; in Spain, the financing of religious communities and the teaching of religion in public schools were reformed in the last three years. In France, three official reports were published at short intervals and prompted a number of legal reforms, some of which are still in progress: the Debray report on teaching religion in schools (2002), the Stasi report on *laïcité* in the Republic (2003), and the Machelon report on the relations of religious communities with the State (2006). In Italy, new agreements with minority religions were signed in 2007, while in Romania a new law on religious liberty was approved during the same year.[1] Outside the European Union, things are no different: in many public schools of Russia, the old homeland of State atheism, classes of Orthodox Culture have started in recent years – on the reform of the State–Church systems in post-Communist European countries, see Ferrari et al. 2003 – and in Norway the decision has been taken to abandon the old system of the State Church (Plesner 2002: 263–70). These changes are too many and too close in time to be explained as simple coincidences: one has the impression that the socio-religious transformations of Europe have at last been noticed by the national legal systems, which have entered a process of adaptation of their content to the new situation.

The second common feature lies in the convergence of the Church–State systems of the European Union countries. This convergence is not the consequence of any direct intervention by the EU, which has no competence in this field, but is due to the growing EU presence in other areas, which has influenced indirectly the national legislations concerning religious communities.[2] An analogous role has been played by the European Court of Human Rights both within and outside the EU borders: some anomalies of national legal systems, such as the need to obtain the authorization of the Greek Orthodox Church to build a place of worship in Greece, have been removed through the decisions of the Strasbourg Court (Papastathis 2007: 6). Finally, the constitutions of the post-Communist countries, which since 1989 have had to build their systems of State–Church relations *ex novo*, were influenced initially by the United States and the international organizations (OSCE, Council of Europe, and so on) that played a significant role in their preparation; after a few years, however, this influence decreased, and the most recent laws – particularly those on religious freedom and associations – are closer to traditional European models (Ferrari et al. 2003: 411–27).

Still, without further stressing what these legal reforms have in common, the real question concerns the direction they are going to take. Do they follow a definite course, and is it possible to identify it?

States and Religions in Europe

Although this classification is outdated and does not answer the needs of contemporary societies, we can start with the distinction between countries in which Church and State are separated, countries where concordats and agreements with religious communities have been concluded, and countries that adopted the system of Church of State. The first fact to emerge from a legal analysis of these

---

[1] See also the contributions published by the *European Journal for Church and State Research*.

[2] The same has happened in other legal fields. For example, the EU has no competence in family law: nevertheless the national legal systems of the EU member-states became closer.

models is the decline of the last category. On the one hand, all the post-Communist countries – even those with a strong Lutheran tradition – avoided endorsing the Church of State system in their new constitutions, and some of them went so far to exclude this option also for the future. On the other hand, Sweden gave up its Church of State; Norway is in the process of doing so; Iceland passed a law that strengthens the independence of its National Church; and Finland modified the system of State Church in its central component, transferring the power to appoint bishops from the Head of State to the faithful of the Lutheran Church.[3] Extending the analysis from North- to South-East Europe, this conclusion is confirmed. The legal systems based on a constitutionally dominant religion, which represents the Orthodox *penchant* of the Protestant Church of State,[4] show a parallel decline: the example of Greece, whose constitution defines the Greek Orthodox religion as the dominant religion of the country, has not been imitated by any of the post-Communist countries where the Orthodox religion is the majority religion (Peteva 2003: 47–72; Kalkandjieva 2007).[5] The English system of Established Church fares a little better, because the Church of England quickly understood the need to accept religious pluralism and chose to exercise its prerogatives and political power in favour of all religions existing in the country: the Anglican bishops who are by law members of the House of Lords frequently act as representatives of the different religious communities and not only of the Church of England (Davie 2006: 30). But it is still open to question whether, in the long run, this strategy will succeed in balancing the demands for 'disestablishment' that are regularly voiced by important sectors of English public opinion. Why are the systems with a Church of State, a dominant or an Established Church in decline? The most convincing answer is that they do not fit a religiously fragmented society, particularly if religious membership is no longer merely a private choice but also a public expression of identity. The State choice to have an official religion presupposes a religiously homogeneous country: when people are divided among different faiths, the State adoption of one of them becomes a weakness because it prevents a number of the citizens from fully identifying with the public institutions. In conclusion, the process of transformation of the European religious landscape

---

[3] On the reform of State–Church relations in the countries of North Europe, see the proceedings of the conference held in Höör (Sweden) in August 2006 in the context of the research programme on the notion of 'national Church' (*L'année canonique*, 48 [2006], pp. 65–136). See also Lisbet Christoffersen et al. (eds), *Law and Religion in the 21st Century: Nordic Perspectives* (forthcoming).

[4] On the idea of Church–State relations prevailing in Orthodox countries see the articles published in *L'année canonique*, 43 (2001).

[5] In Article 13 of the Bulgarian Constitution, the Orthodox religion is defined as the 'traditional' religion of the country, while the Romanian law 489/2006 on the 'Freedom of Religion and the General Status of Denominations' recognizes 'the important role of the Romanian Orthodox Church' (Article 7). On this law see Eva Synek, 'Das Rumänische Religionsgesetz', *Österreichisches Archiv für recht & religion*, 3 (2006), pp. 427–32.

shows that the new religious, ethical and cultural pluralism has outdated the systems of Church–State relations that are characterized by the legal identification of the State with one religion.

A second observation pertaining to a legal analysis of the three models mentioned above concerns those countries that have a system of separation between the State and religious communities. Separation is a very common word in the constitutions of the European post-Communist countries, perhaps because of the influence of the United States on their preparation. But if these constitutions are considered more closely, it becomes clear that this separation excludes neither recognition nor support of religious communities by the State. It has little to do with the separation affirmed in the French law of 1905 that prevents the State from recognizing or subsidizing any religious community: on the contrary, it is a friendly and cooperative separation, which does not rule out the conclusion of concordats and agreements between the State and religious communities and coexists with constitutional statements that oblige the former to cooperate with the latter (for a few examples, see Ferrari 2003: 417–21). An analogous process of transformation took place in the country that is the symbol of separation: France. Today in France there is an institute, the *Institut européen en sciences des religions*, which is financed by the State and has the mission to train State School teachers about the place and impact of religion in society; there is also a foundation, the *Fondation pour les œuvres de l'Islam de France*, a private law foundation supported by the State and enjoying the status of foundation of public utility, whose task is to promote the building of Muslim worship places; additionally there is a ministry, the Ministry of Interior, which played a fundamental role in the creation of the Muslim representative institution, the *Conseil Français du culte musulman*. These examples show that even in France separation has become much softer and no longer excludes State interventions in areas that, until a few years ago, were considered outside the boundaries of interest and competence of public institutions (Messner et al. 2003). Once more, we need to ask why separation has acquired a different meaning and why even those States that had made it the banner of their religious policy have changed their attitude. This time the answer lies in the new significance acquired by religion and collective religious identities on the political stage. After the decline of the great secular ideologies, religions seem to be the only forces still capable of speaking the language of collective identities, of offering their faithful an interpretation of reality and a sense of membership: all this gives them the power to mobilize significant groups of followers (Pace 2004: IX–X). This power is too important to be ignored by governments that on the one hand fear that religion is exploited for creating political and social unrest, and on the other hand are tempted to make use of religion to achieve their own goals of internal and foreign policy. All this cannot be attained without meddling with religion and establishing relationships with religious communities, and therefore without giving up strict separation.

Starting from these remarks, it is possible to conclude that a process of convergence from the extremities towards the centre is taking shape in Europe.

The extremities are constituted by the systems of Church of State on the one hand and of rigid separation on the other: but what is the centre, that is, what is the direction this movement has taken? A closer examination of the Swedish case can be of help. In this country, giving up the Church of State model did not imply the adoption of separation of State and Church, but opened the way to a complex system where the legal status of the Lutheran Church is defined by a special law and that of the other religious communities is dependent on their registration. This arrangement maintains a special position for the old Church of State and, at the same time, makes it possible to affirm the *laïcité* and impartiality of the State towards all religious communities, also at the symbolic and formal level (Friedner 2005: 537–52). Similar models have been adopted by most post-Communist States and in Western Europe by those countries that have recently reformed their system of Church–State relations (for Austria see Potz 2005: 391–418; for Portugal Canas 2005: 439–468, for example): religious communities can register in different forms and, depending on the type of registration they are able to obtain, they receive State support accordingly. This solution offers a public recognition to religious communities and gives the State some control over them and also the possibility of grading its support according to their importance (Friedner 2007). Finally, the proliferation of concordats with the Catholic Church and of agreements with other religious communities should be underlined: they satisfy the request of these communities to have a legal status that reflects the particular identity of each of them.[6] In conclusion, the centre of gravity of the European system of Church–State relations seems to be shifting towards a group of national systems that are different yet share some common features – the acceptance of the public statute of religious communities, the recognition of their specific features, a certain degree of State control over them, and the selective and graded cooperation of public institutions with religious communities.

This analysis of the European pattern of Church–State relations seems to confirm Jonathan Fox's conclusion: modernization does not imply Church–State separation but a moderate involvement of States with religions.[7] This statement should be more precisely defined, however, as State involvement with religion is the consequence of the particular modernization that is taking place today in Europe, characterized by pluralism and the public role of religions. These are the two main engines of today's transformations, as confirmed by the examination of the most important fields of State–religion relations. For example, if the teaching of religion in State schools is taken into consideration (Kuyk et al. 2007; Jackson et al. 2007), there is a quite evident conclusion: everywhere in Europe – including Russia, the other post-Communist countries, and France – States regard the teaching

---

[6] The last one was signed on 12 January 2009 between the Holy See and the German Land of Schleswig-Holstein. For more in general, see the contributions published in *Quaderni di diritto e politica ecclesiastica*, 1 (1999).

[7] See 'World Separation of Religion and State into the 21st Century', *Comparative Political Studies*, 39:5 (2006), pp. 537–69.

of religion as part of their educative task. The models are different and range from the denominational teaching of a specific religion to non-denominational information about diverse religions: the difference is not negligible, but, in both cases, the old dogma that assigned to the family and the Church – and not to the school – the task of providing religious education seems to be outdated. Even a secular State cannot afford to ignore the importance of religion as an instrument for understanding today's world.

But this involvement too has to face the individualism and pluralism that characterize contemporary society and affect also the legal systems that have been including for a long time a certain degree of State involvement in religious matters. Teaching of religion in public schools is a good example of this influence. In those countries where, until a few years ago, only one religion could be taught (Portugal, Spain and Italy, for example), it is now possible to teach a number of different religions according to the requests of the students and their parents. Moreover, these requests can change from year to year. Pluralism and individualism have left their mark and have opened the school doors to some religious minorities that in the past had been excluded. At the same time individual choices, which in the past were limited to the demand to be exempted from the teaching of religion, have now gained a central importance. This trend is confirmed by an examination of the systems that some European countries have adopted to finance religious communities: they have enlarged the number of religious communities that can enjoy State support while structuring this support in ways that give a central place to individual choices (the tax-payer has the right to indicate the religious community that should be supported and, as in the previous example, can change this choice every year).

A good injection of pluralism and individualism into the legal systems that are emerging as the new centre of gravity of Church–State relations in Europe is desirable: it could contribute to frame the State's 'moderate involvement' in ways that are compatible with democracy. If this path is not followed, it is likely that the European model of Church–State relations will fall into decline, to be replaced by other models closer to the separation of the United States or the neo-confessionism of some Eastern European States.

Islam and the European Model of Relations between States and Religions: Some Comments about Sardar Ali's Contribution

Which is the role that Islam is going to play in this quickly changing context? Islam is currently undergoing a transformative process from an immigrants' religion into a religion that by full right is part of the European reality. This process requires to be accompanied by appropriate legal initiatives aimed at fully integrating Muslim communities in the European model of relations between States and religions, or, in other words, at transforming this model so that it is able to accommodate the needs of the Muslim communities. It is unlikely that a European Islam may take shape, substance and stability before this process is completed. It must be therefore pursued and carried out without delays and uncertainties, bearing in mind that, on the one hand, it will involve bringing relevant changes to the laws of most European States, and that, on the other hand, it will question traditional Muslim practices and doctrines that do not seem compatible with those laws.

Sardar Ali's contribution published in this book offers many good arguments in favour of Muslim communities' capacity to cope successfully with the changes required by the European context where they live. She convincingly stresses the extent of the 'transformative processes within the Islamic legal tradition' and the existence of 'legally plural and often competing normative frameworks within which Muslims must navigate'. The author also makes a strong plea for 'abandoning the orientalist (or indeed, occidentalist) approach to scholarship on ... Islamic legal tradition by creating deeper linkages and ongoing dialogue between the Islamic legal tradition and its Western counterpart'.

Sardar Ali is right in denouncing the ideological character of this approach and the damages it can provoke. Europe is not lacking in opinion leaders who maintain that the Islamic legal system is static, closed and inherently incompatible with 'European values'. As a consequence, Muslims are often the target of some pointed questions that are not addressed to the faithful of other religious communities: are Muslims capable and ready to accept democracy, the secular State, equal rights of men and women? In other words: are Muslim immigrants a particular genus of the larger species of immigrants and do they raise problems different in nature from the problems posed by any other immigrant community? Consequently, do they require a specific legal regulation, different from that which is applied to other immigrants?

To overcome the ideological nature of this approach, the role of lawyers is of decisive importance: lawyers are well equipped to provide a case-by-case assessment of this alleged Muslim specificity and to evaluate whether it is confirmed or denied by the problems that Muslim communities raise regarding family law, dietary rules, places of worship, ritual slaughtering, etc. This facts-based examination is the only way to disengage the debate from the unproductive stalemate to which it is often confined.

But at this point Sardar Ali's contribution raises a couple of questions. First, the assumption that the Islamic legal tradition is systematically closed and cognitively open at the same time is appealing, but it underscores the connection between the systemic and cognitive dimensions: the transformative processes that take place at cognitive level – where 'the imperatives of evolving norms, the 'living law' and changing needs of people and time' are taken into account – cannot overcome the boundaries fixed by the legal system. The systemic and cognitive dimensions are not two independent variables, as the system provides a horizon within which the cognitive efforts have to be confined. 'The unchanging status of the *Qur'anic* texts' – as well as that of the Bible or the Gospels – cannot be too lightly dismissed as something irrelevant, as it has an impact on the interpretative work and, therefore, on the evolution of the legal system.

Second, the cognitive work is not independent from the social and cultural context within which it takes place. Sardar Ali offers many and good examples of transformations of Islamic law; however, they are mainly taken from countries where Islam is the majority religion and has shaped the country's cultural horizon. In Europe Islam is a minority and, in many countries, relatively new religion that has to come to terms with a cultural horizon that has been shaped by other forces. For example, stipulating 'an exorbitant amount as *mahr* (dower) to inhibit the husband from taking another wife' can be a successful strategy to prevent polygamy in an Islamic country, but it is not helpful to deal with this issue in Europe. The European context requires a different approach, which still has to be identified.

In conclusion, many indications confirm Sardar Ali's argument about the transformative capacity of the Islamic legal system. It makes for a promising starting point, but not yet a guarantee of success. It is likely that Islamic law will be able to positively interact with the European context, but this capacity still has to be fully tested against the secular values deeply embedded in European history and culture.

References

Canas, Vitalino (2005). 'State and Church in Portugal', in Gerhard Robbers (ed.), *State and Church in the European Union*, Baden-Baden: Nomos, pp. 439–68.

Christoffersen, Lisbet, et al. (eds). *Law and Religion in the 21st Century: Nordic Perspectives* (forthcoming).

Davie, Grace (2006). 'Is Europe an Exceptional Case?', in *State and Religion in Europe*, Istanbul: Center for Islamic Studies, pp. 23–33.

Ferrari, Silvio (2003). 'Church and State in Post-Communist Europe', in Silvio Ferrari, Cole W. Durham, Jr., and Elizabeth A. Sewell (eds), *Law and Religion in Post-Communist Europe*, Leuven: Peeter, pp. 411–27.

Ferrari, Silvio, Cole W. Durham, Jr., and Elizabeth A. Sewell (eds) (2003). *Law and Religion in Post-Communist Europe*, Leuven: Peeter.

Fox, Jonathan (2006). 'World Separation of Religion and State into the 21st Century', *Comparative Political Studies*, 39:5, pp. 537–69.

Friedner, Lars (2005). 'State and Church in Sweden', in Gerhard Robbers (ed.), *State and Church in the European Union*, Baden-Baden: Nomos, pp. 537–52.

Friedner, Lars (ed.) (2007). *Churches and Other Religious Organisations as Legal Persons*, Leuven: Peeters.

Hervieu-Léger, Danièle (2002). 'Les tendances du religieux en Europe', in *Commissariat Général du plan, Croyances religieuses, morales et éthiques dans le processus de construction européenne*, Paris: La Documentation Française, pp. 9–22.

Jackson, Robert, Siebren Miedema, Wolfram Weisse and W. Jean Paul Willaime (eds) (2007). *Religion and Education in Europe: Developments, Contexts and Debates*, Münster: Waxmann.
Kalkandjieva, Daniela (2007). 'Traditional Religion vs. Secular Law in Post-Communist Bulgarian Society', paper given at the Copenhagen conference on 'Religion in the 21st Century', 19–23 September 2007.
Kuyk, Elza, Roger Jensen, David Lankshear, Elizabeth Löh Manna and Peter Schreiner (ed.) (2007). *Religious Education in Europe*, Oslo: IKO–ICCS.
Messner, Francis, Pierre-Henri Prélot and Jean-Marie Woehrling (eds) (2003). *Traité de droit français des religions*, Paris: Litec.
Pace, Enzo (2004). *Perché le religioni scendono in guerra?*, Roma-Bari: Laterza.
Papastathis, Charalambos (2007). 'Changes in Greek Law on Worship Places', *European Consortium for Church and State Newsletter*, July, p. 4.
Peteva, Jenia (2003). 'Church and State in Bulgaria', in Silvio Ferrari, Cole W. Durham, Jr., and Elizabeth A. Sewell (eds), *Law and Religion in Post-Communist Europe*, Leuven: Peeters, pp. 37–56.
Plesner, Ingvill Thorson (2002). 'State and Religion in Norway in Times of Change', in *European Journal for Church and State Research*, 9, pp. 263–70.
Potz, Richard (2005). 'State and Church in Austria', in Gerhard Robbers (ed.), *State and Church in the European Union*, Baden-Baden: Nomos, pp. 391–418.
Synek, Eva (2006). 'Das Rumänische Religionsgesetz', *Österreichisches Archiv für Recht & Religion*, 3 (2006), pp. 327–43.

Secularism and State Politics

Chapter 12
Republicisation of Religion in France

Sébastien Tank-Storper[1]

For the past twenty or thirty years, we have been witnessing a return of religious discourse in public policy or, to be more precise, a return of religious discourse legitimacy in the public sphere of European democracies. Spokespeople for religions are invited to express themselves regarding biotechnologies, for instance; they are called to fight against new forms of poverty or to assist authorities during political, social or ethnic troubles. At the same time that the Roman Catholic Church mobilises its political networks to obtain, at the European level, official recognition of the 'Christian cultural roots' of Europe, the issue of the recognition of Islam and Muslims in European countries becomes one of the most important political topics.

This 'return' of religion to the public scene (let us use this term for the moment for lack of a better one) appears problematical in the political context of democracy. Theoretically, religion in a democracy must restrict its activities to the private sphere. Ideal-typically, democracy was built as a result of a movement towards emancipation from the domination of a hegemonic religious institution that excluded religion from public policy. The separation of religions and states and the assignation of religion to the private sphere were thus fundamental elements in the building of modern democracy. As José Casanova writes:

> To say that 'religion is a private affair' is nonetheless constitutive of Western modernity in a dual sense. First, it points to the fact that religious freedom, in the sense of freedom of conscience, is chronologically 'the first freedom' as well as the precondition of all modern freedom. Insofar as freedom of conscience is intrinsically related to the right of 'privacy' – to the modern institutionalization of a private sphere free from governmental intrusion as well as free from ecclesial control – and inasmuch as 'the right of privacy' serves as the very foundation of modern liberalism and of modern individualism, then indeed the privatization of religion is essential to modernity. (Casanova 1994: 40)

There is yet – still according to Casanova – another sense in which the privatisation of religion is intrinsically related to the emergence of the modern social order. To say that in the modern world 'religion becomes private' refers also to the very

---

[1] I would like to thank Eli Commins, Anne Raulin and Ann Cand for their linguistic contribution.

process of institutional differentiation that is constitutive of modernity – namely, to the modern historical process whereby the secular spheres emancipated themselves from ecclesiastical control as well as from religious norms (ibid.).

The process of the privatisation of religion appears thus as a constitutive element of the process of modernisation and secularisation. In this context, does this process of 'deprivatization' of religion, as José Casanova (1994) calls it in his book *Public Religions in the Modern World* (a term I address later), translate into a global movement of the revitalisation of religions in Europe? Does it invalidate the whole corpus of theories of secularisation, as Peter Berger (1999) argues in his book *The Desecularization of the World*?

The key idea of the current contribution is that this paradox is not necessarily in contradiction with the theories of secularisation. In Europe, we are not witnessing a movement of 'counter-secularization' (Berger 1999), which would give back to religions their political power and their capacity to regulate individual beliefs and behaviours. All indicators suggest, on the contrary, an increase in the process of secularisation, translating into religious disaffiliation and the deregulation of beliefs.

The empirical observation of a return of religions to the public sphere has to be analysed in relation to forms of religiosity, and to their manifestation in politics or society. If religions return to the public sphere, it is not necessarily in the sense of a return to a previous order. It is rather a redefinition of religion in the public democratic space, which is possible in the unique condition within which religions become privatised. My purpose thus is to describe how religions return to the public sphere while becoming more private and individual; that is, how the logic of the republicisation of religions can be compatible with the process of the individualisation of religious belief.

The return of religions to the public sphere could be explained by the redefinition of boundaries between public and private within the new context of what could be called 'concrete individualism'. In this perspective, the 'republicisation' of religion does not take place according to a principle of domination (in the Weberian sense of the term), but rather according to the logic of identity recognition in the democratic public space.

The majority of my presentation of this issue is based on France, which has represented a challenge to adopt a new type of *laïcité*, taking Islam into account. The radical split between religion and State should be reconsidered in the present transformation of public and private religion in Europe. The religious situation in France may function as an ideal-type of a contemporary challenge of relations between religion and politics.

The Individualisation and Privatisation of Religious Beliefs in Europe: From Heteronomous Religion to Identity

It may not be necessary to present in this contribution the empirical facts that demonstrate the validity of secularisation theories applied to Europe. Even Peter Berger, in his book *The Desecularization of the World*, underlines the idea of a European exception:

> In Western Europe, if nowhere else, the old secularization theory would seem to hold. With increasing modernization there has been an increase in key indicators of secularization, both on the level of expressed beliefs (especially those that could be called orthodox in Protestant or Catholic terms) and, dramatically, on the level of church-related behavior – attendance at services of worship, adherence to church-dictated codes of personal behavior (especially with regard to sexuality, reproduction, and marriage), recruitment to the clergy. These phenomena, long observed in the northern countries of the continent, have since World War II rapidly engulfed the south. [...] There is now a massively secular Euro-culture, and what has happened in the south can be simply described (though not thereby explained) by that culture's invasion of these countries. It is not fanciful to predict that there will be similar developments in Eastern Europe, precisely to the degree that these countries too will be integrated into the new Europe. (Berger 1999: 9–10)

We can also refer to the book edited by Danièle Hervieu-Léger and Grace Davie, *Identités religieuses en Europe* (1996) [*Religious Identities in Europe*], which addresses this idea that Europe may be the only geographic area where secularisation is going to occur.

But saying that Europe 'left the realm of religion' (to use Marcel Gauchet's term for describing the social process of emancipation from religion) does not mean that religion has disappeared (Gauchet 1998: 11–30). To understand the contemporary situation, we have to keep in mind that secularisation designates the whole process of decomposition and recomposition of religions in modern society, rather than the end of religion (Hervieu-Léger 1996: 19).

This process of religious recomposition corresponds above all to a process of believing in privatisation and individualisation. Privatisation and individualisation of religion have an important impact on the internal functioning of the religious sphere itself. They undermine religious authority and the sense of obligation (such as going to Mass, for example). The consequences of individualisation can also be observed in the degradation of the status and number of clerics as well as in the rarefaction of rituals. It can also be seen through the decline of moral values of sacrifice or discipline, and through individual ways of life, in which self-realisation dominates. Women and men become mobile and stray away from inherited identities (Hervieu-Léger 1999).

The most important consequence of the process of individualisation and privatisation of religion is the radical switch from a religion conceived as a principle of heteronomy to a religion conceived as an identity and a support for individuals in an uncertain modern society.

Analysts observe a global 'slippage' of the scope of beliefs that tends to move away from a vision of the afterlife to a focus on the here and now. This global process of the 'mundanisation' of beliefs is apparent, for example, in the increase in the belief in reincarnation (rather than resurrection), which, in the year 2000, concerned around 20 per cent of European Catholics (Lambert 2002). This is indicative of the difficulties the Catholic institution has regulating the beliefs of its followers. It also illustrates the process of mundanisation, according to which salvation has left the heavens for the here and now.

The mundanisation of beliefs is also apparent in the theme of 'self-regeneration' expressed by a large number of religious groups and that is ideal-typically represented by the 'born again' and the convert: the one who, with the help of a powerful faith, is reborn after a life of wandering, of sin and suffering. The theme of regeneration entails a process of 'desymbolisation' of religious content, which is consistent with the modern culture of performance and efficiency. Religion is not a 'meaning code' or a heteronomous system anymore, but a support to help live one's life in what Zygmunt Bauman (2007) calls a 'liquid society'.

Claiming a Public Religious Identity: The Emblematic Case of Young Muslims in France

Going beyond mundanisation, religion tends to become a frame for social identities, and especially for minority identities.

The case of young Muslims in France is emblematic of this process. For these young women and men whose parents immigrated to France (and whose parents, to a great majority, did not transmit their religion to their children), Islam is mobilised as a paradoxical way to evolve and to project themselves in the mainstream society. It is a minority identity that gives content to their social and economic marginality. Islam is referred to as a positive symbolic resource for the individual, the parents and the global society. Muslim identity is the language that enables them to challenge the negative representations of themselves that are projected by society. Thus Islam is a means to convey a serious and rigorous image of themselves. The young man who appropriates Islam may not be perceived as an anomic young man anymore, but as a conscientious Muslim worshipper (Khosrokhavar 1998).

Islam may also be a way for young women to free themselves from parental control. For example, the public affirmation of religious belonging and practices (above all by wearing the *hidjab*) allows young women to combine family tradition and autonomy (Kakpo 2007: 105). This is proof of faithfulness to the familial tradition that allows those young women to project themselves in modern society and to emancipate from strict family tradition. By demonstrating their religious conformity and their moral rigour, they can escape from some traditional rules (like a precocious marriage) and follow their studies in universities, which are sometime distant from home (Liogier 2006: 119).

For certain schoolgirls, the public demonstration of Islamity through the *hidjab* may also be a way to protest against a conception of the individual that negates their singularity, in a school system where 'ostentatious' (*ostentatoires* in French) religious signs are forbidden.

The French model of *laïcité* is typical of a conception of citizenship that conceives the citizen as an abstract reasonable individual limited in his personal expression. Access to citizenship, knowledge and reason requires the dissociation of the individual from his religion, from his family, and from his geographic origin. According to this conception, the link between individuals and institutions is one-dimensional. Each individual is defined according to his role and status. A schoolgirl and a schoolboy have to be schoolgirls and schoolboys at school, a patient has to be a patient in the hospital, and a prisoner has to be a prisoner in prison. Ideally, the individual plays one role at a time, without expressing personal requests (Singly 2005: 64).

As a consequence, there is theoretically no intermediary political level of belonging between State and individual. In French democracy, the social link is no longer religious, ethnic or dynastic, but political. Living together is not sharing the same religion, being born from the same ancestor, but rather being a citizen of the same political organisation. Citizenship is built by transcending particularism. Individuals do not act as concrete individuals, with their particular characteristics, but as citizens, as abstract individuals (Schnapper 2005: 11).

Thus, public space is considered free from religion. The public space is not 'laic' because all religions can express themselves within it, but because it has been emptied of all sorts of religious signs. This theoretical model is evident in the public school system, where all 'ostentatious' manifestations of religious identity are to be banished.

This conception of religious neutrality as religious invisibility was built in a historical context of a clerical and secular forces conflict, which has been resolved by the law of separation of Churches and State in 1905. But it is important to correct the image of a static ideological conception of French *laïcité*; in fact, both the concept and the materialisation of laicity do not constitute a closed static model. They adopt pragmatic accommodations and conflict conciliations.

According to Jean Baubérot (2004), two historical periods of French secularism can be defined. First, from the French Revolution to the law of separation of Churches and State in 1905, the *régime concordataire* institutes the control of Catholic clergy (but also of the Protestant and Jewish institutions) by the state (clerics become state functionaries) in exchange for the recognition of the public utility of religion. This *concordataire* model could be analysed as a first step of laicisation, which implies:

1. the institutional differentiation of religion (religion does not organise the whole social life);
2. the recognition of the social utility of religions;
3. the recognition of religious pluralism.

This model, where State and religion overlap, was very conflicting. Clerics profited from their institutional prerogatives to try to extend their influence on society (and above all on school systems, considered as the best way to keep people under the influence of religion). Secular partisans were fighting to exclude clerics from public positions, and above all from schools, in order to restrict Catholicism's influence on society.

This conflict, named *conflit des deux France* (the Two France Conflict), for over 150 years opposed clerical partisans and secular partisans. It was temporarily resolved by the 1905 Law of Separation between Churches and State and the *pacte laïc* (secular pact). This law, still valid, instituted a second step of laicisation characterised by:

1. the dissociation between the State and the religious establishment;
2. the absence of recognition of the social utility of religions;
3. the freedom of consciousness as a fundamental right.

The French model of *laïcité* results from the tension between politics and religion: the emancipation of the public sphere from the domination of religions, on the one hand, and the protection of religions from the State's intervention, on the other hand.

The law of 1905 consecrated the idea of a hermetic compartmentalisation of the two spheres. But in fact, the notion of privacy has been literally translated from the Christian distinction between private and public. Although a Catholic or a Protestant can fully practise his/her religion without leaving the private sphere (because laicity has made compatible Christian religious practices with public space), this is not the case for Jews or Muslims. To go back to the case of the *hidjab*, for example, it has to be worn in a public place rather than at home, which creates a conflict with the principle of laicity.

Thus, publicising of Muslim identity by wearing an ostentatious sign such as the *hidjab* enables one to express self-autonomy through conflict. This is a very modern way to build and publicise an authentic religious identity: a dominated population mobilises a depreciated sign of their culture to claim the material and symbolic exclusion that they feel by using in their own way the dominant values of individualism (Liogier 2006: 122). And it can be analysed as a conflictual way to be recognised in French society as full citizens.

The 'Muslim headscarf affair' can be analysed as a new crisis of the French model of laicity. In this case, the purpose was not, or most precisely was not *only*, to emancipate politics from religion, or to guarantee the freedom of consciousness, but to integrate a large religious-minority group into *laïcité*.

This political debate has been extremely tense because it questioned a redefinition of the previous consensus of laicity. It revealed the limits of the universality of the French model of *laïcité*, and how it can be a source of inequality. The French conception of religious neutrality as invisibility is culturally connoted. As Tariq Modood writes:

> This way of structuring space and of deciding what is public and what is private can be a source of power and inequality. In so far as subordinate, oppressed or marginal groups claim equality, what they are claiming is that they should not be marginal, subordinate or excluded; that they, too, their values, norms, and voice, should be part of structuring of the public space. (Modood, 2007: 54)

Thus, consequently, the 'Muslim headscarf affair', which terminated with the total exclusion of all ostentatious religious signs from the school system, requires an acknowledgement of Islam in French society compatible with the laws of 1905. The constitution of the Conseil Français du Culte Musulman meets this challenge. But in the French case, the politic of recognition is also a most traditional politic of control and domestication of a religion and a population perceived as 'savage' and exogenous. To quote the Minister of the Interior and Religious Affairs in charge of this policy:

> The situation of Islam in France is not good. [...] A large part of the national community fears Muslims and Islam. They ask sometimes with ideological background about its compatibility with the French Republic. On the other hand, Muslims feel stigmatised as Muslims in other people's eyes. In fact, the reality is that Islam is here. There are 4 to 5 million Muslims in France. To deny this reality entails the emergence of an 'Islam of cellars and garages'. We have a lot to fear of this underground Islam, because clandestinity impels to radicalism, while public existence impels to integration then to a form of normalisation. (Nicolas Sarkozy, interview in the newspaper *Liberation*, 23 February 2003)

This process of institutionalised Islam is very close to the *concordataire* model, trying to apply to Islam the Catholic pattern of organisation (it was applied in the same way to Judaism by Napoleon). Such a vision of politics of recognition as politics of domestication raises the third challenge of French laicity (and in my view, the most important and the most problematic, because it is the most implicit). The 'Muslim headscarf affair' and the constitution of a 'French Islam' question the possibility of the recognition, by French politics, of the autonomy of religious individuals. The rhetoric used to ban headscarves at school reveals such a vision, as it was done for the sake of young Muslims girls. Wearing headscarves was interpreted as a sign of oppression and domination of those girls by their parents, and therefore the school of the *République* had to emancipate them, exclude them, and send them back to their oppressive environment. Behind this argumentation hides a historical blindness to religious reality, which is only conceived as a fact of domination and which is, typically, incompatible with self-autonomy (Bobineau and Tank-Storper 2007: 47).

The Republicisation of Religion

Recognition rather than Domination

The friction between the old French model of *laïcité* and the need for recognition of French Muslims is emblematic of the tension between two different conceptions of citizenship: an old conception based on the idea of an abstract individual, and a new conception based on the affirmation of a concrete individual who claims his/her originality, authenticity and independence (Singly 2005: 59). Moving from an abstract emancipated individual to a concrete authentic individual, the compromise of the previous period is undone according to the paradigm of individual rights. Schoolgirls and schoolboys do not want to be just schoolgirls and schoolboys anymore, but want to express their own singularity. In other words, the individual claims to express other dimensions of his/her identity than those officially requested by the situation or the institution (ibid.: 71–2).

Moreover, individuals now claim to project themselves in public space with their authentic identity. There is an imperative of fusion between statutory and intimate identity. Interiority has to coincide with exteriority; belonging becomes constitutive of personal identities, precisely because it becomes more subjective.

The demand for greater publicity by French Muslims must be analysed as a public claim for the legitimacy of Muslim presence in France. It does not correspond to a will to dominate or bully French society – as some politicians would claim. The purpose is not to impose an Islamic society, but to obtain the recognition of their full citizenship, that is to say, the recognition of the right to express their concrete identity in public space.

That is why I suggest the term 'republicisation of religious identity' rather than 'deprivatisation of religions', which conveys the idea of a return to a previous situation.

The concept of 'deprivatization' defined by José Casanova means that:

> Religious institutions and organizations refuse to restrict themselves to the pastoral care of individual's souls and continue to raise questions about the interconnections of private and public morality and to challenge the claims of the subsystems, particularly states and markets, to be exempt from extraneous normative considerations. One of the results of this ongoing contestation is a dual, interrelated process of repolicization of the private religious and moral spheres and renormativization of the public economic and political spheres. This is what I call, for lack of a better term, the 'deprivatization' of religion. (Casanova 1994: 6)

While I agree with the observation that some religious institutions, such as the Catholic Church, or some tendencies of European Islam, for example, still have difficulty abdicating their pretence to influence political affairs and to try to norm individual behaviours,[2] I am more cautious about their capacity to succeed, at least in western European countries.

In this respect, Italy is interesting. It is, along with Poland, the European country where the Catholic Church is supposed to have maintained the largest influence on the political and individual levels. But in fact, most of its attempts to direct its ethical orientation on Italian society by intervening in the public debate have failed.

For instance, on 28 January 2002, Jean-Paul II publicly encouraged judges and attorneys to act in order to prevent laws on divorce being applied. Not only did this not have any impact on the number of divorces, but this intervention was also received poorly by the population. A survey showed that 87.5 per cent of Italians condemned the intervention of the Pope, and that only 11.6 per cent of Italian Catholics agreed with him (Ormières 2005: 260).

In other words, the attempt of 'deprivatization' of the Catholic institution does not necessarily mean that it has the effective capacity to reintroduce religious norms in European societies. All the surveys emphasise that European populations, in large majority, do not give religious institutions the legitimacy to intercede in the public sphere in a normative way. Religion has to remain a 'private affair' and, in fact, the concrete life of European individuals is increasingly disconnected from religious prescriptions concerning nuptials and birth rates, divorce, as well as sexual behaviours (these are all historical domains of religious prescription).

Furthermore, these ultimate attempts of the Catholic Church to politically impose its prescription on an increasingly secularised society could be translated as its growing fragility rather than its vitality. As Alexis de Tocqueville suggests regarding North America, we can express the hypothesis of a reversed relation between religious political commitments and their social influence in Western democracies:

> As long as a religion is sustained by those feelings, propensities, and passions which are found to occur under the same forms at all periods of history, it may defy the efforts of time; or at least it can be destroyed only by another religion. But when religion clings to the interests of the world, it becomes almost as fragile a thing as the powers of earth. It is the only one of them all which can hope for immortality; but if it be connected with their ephemeral power, it shares their fortunes and may fall with those transient passions which alone supported

---

[2] For example, the previous pope Jean-Paul II broke with the policy of his predecessor by claiming the legitimacy of the Catholic public intervention, and his first collaborator Joseph Ratzinger, current pope Benedict XVI, wrote in 1987 that 'the restriction to the private sphere, this integration in the pantheon of the relative global system values, is opposed to the pretence of truth, which is a public claim' (Ormières 2005: 267).

them. The alliance which religion contracts with political powers must need be onerous to itself, since it does not require their assistance to live, and by giving them its assistance it may be exposed to decay. ...

In America, religion is perhaps less powerful than it has been at certain periods and among certain nations; but its influence is more lasting. It restricts itself to its own resources, but of these none can deprive it; its circle is limited, but it pervades it and holds it under undisputed control. (Tocqueville 2005: tome 1, 403)

The process of modernisation, and more specifically the process of privatisation and individualisation of religion, can enable us to understand the new articulation between public and private religion. According to Marcel Gauchet (1998), we are witnessing the 'publicisation of private identities' rather than the deprivatisation of religions, which means that religion will stop being a 'private affair' and will regain its previous public status. More than ever, religion keeps private, and it is because it keeps private that it can find a new place in public space.

The Double Secularisation of Religion and Politics

This does not mean that religion is excluded from the public sphere. As I said previously, there has been a return of the legitimacy of religious discourse in the public sphere of European democracies over the past twenty or thirty years. But this 'comeback' has had to strictly conform to democratic political culture. What is rejected is normative intervention, which does not mean that religions cannot be consulted alongside other actors of civil society.

This tendency is also apparent when French authorities asked religious representatives – most specifically, Muslims authorities – to intervene during the *émeutes de banlieues* (suburban riots) to keep order. The fact that State authorities ask civil society to intervene as mediators in social disorders is not new. But the fact that religious institutions are perceived as legitimate actors of civil society reveals that political authorities do not consider religious actors as private anymore. But the comeback of religion into public space is legitimate so far as it does not arrive of its own accord, but on the State's behalf: it constitutes an allied force, very much under the control of the government.

Religion's resources are also mobilised in a pragmatic way to define political orientations and put forward an ecumenical ideal of civil concord that surpasses social and ideological differences. This is the case, for instance, with the recent ecological consultation in France. The State Secretary for Ecology Nathalie Kosciusko-Morizet had dinner with religious representatives to evoke their role in the 'green evangelization' of their followers. Kosciusko-Morizet reported that the newspaper *Libération* wanted to multiply such informal dinners all along the 'Grenelle' – a sort of consultation of civil society around ecological problems – with mathematicians, but also with writers and architects (Libération, 15

September 2007). She said also: '*without the reflection of religions, we'll never be able to organise the ecological rupture*'.

Those consultations are always pluralistic. In this case, religion advice cannot be limited to one particular religion, and must reflect the plurality of religious options. By publicising religious and political concord, and further by broadcasting inter-religious cooperation through ecumenical meetings, political and religious institutions work together to celebrate democratic values of pluralism. We are indeed very far from a religion that prescribes its norms to society. Religion is incorporated in the democratic game rather than being a normative principle.

My hypothesis is that this process of republicisation of religion in democratic countries has to be linked with a more global context of what we could call a process of 'internal secularisation of politics'.

Again in reference to the French case, Jean Baubérot demonstrates how the historical process of laicisation, in the beginning, was more a process of 'totalization' of politics in a 'civil religion', according to Bellah (1975), than a real process of institutional differentiation and autonomisation. The political sphere was hegemonic and pretended to interfere in the religious sphere (concretely the Catholic Church) through the model of 'gallicanism' (Baubérot and Mathieu 2002: 63–6). In this way, instead of being a 'private affair', religion was, during the first period of the French Republic, a 'public affair'.

The contemporary process of the republicisation of religion in the French democratic public sphere (and more generally in the European democratic public sphere) could be understood through the progressive process of 'secularisation' of this 'civil religion', which passes a turning point with the dismantling of the welfare state at the European level since the 1980s. According to neo-classical economic theories, the State should not want to attain universal competence. It should rather focus its activities on ministries with major central administrative functions (justice, police, defence), and leave others' social activities to the civil society (such as the economy, education, health, moral and ethical issues).

This is close to the process of internal secularisation of religion conceptualised by François-André Isambert. Analysing the Vatican II Council, he defines the process of internal secularisation as the recognition from the religious sphere itself that some aspects of social life are out of its competence (Isambert 1992).

The fact that politicians ask for religious advice on subjects such as euthanasia, human cloning or, as we saw, ecology (alongside other civil actors such as scholars or philosophers) can be explained by the conjunction of those processes of internal secularisation that affect both the political and the religious spheres. This is because politics no longer claims to have a monopoly on such ethical subjects that it requires collegial deliberation to define public morality. And because religions are mostly privatised and politically harmless, the political power can reintroduce them in the public place through such ethical deliberations. When religion stops being a political danger, that is, by not seeking to dominate society, it can be reintroduced in the public sphere as a legitimate actor of civil society.

But we can wonder if the religious presence in such ecumenical ethical commissions does not contribute to reinforcing its decline by increasing its relativity. Enclosed within a role of 'ethical consultant' beside other religious discourse and non-religious discourses, religion becomes a 'voice' beside other voices and loses its absolute character. Finally, the republicisation of religions could maybe contribute to an increase in its relativisation in modern democracies. But conversely, it may also reinforce all religious groups that do not deal with politics, this is to say, all dissident religious groups that are not invited to the political game (new religious movements, sects, religious radicalism, and so on).

References

Baubérot, J., and S. Mathieu (2002). *Religion, modernité et culture au Royaume-Uni et en France*, Paris: Seuil.
Bauman, Z. (2007). *Le présent liquide*, Paris: Seuil.
Bellah, R. (1975). *The Broken Covenant: American Civil Religion in a Time of Trial*, New York: Seabury Press.
Berger, P. (1999). *The Desecularization of the World*, Cambridge: Eerdmans Publishing.
Bobineau, O., and S. Tank-Storper (2007). *Sociologie des religions*, Paris: Armand Colin.
Casanova, J. (1994). *Public Religions in the Modern World*, Chicago, IL: University of Chicago Press.
Gauchet, M. (1998). *La religion dans la démocratie. Parcours de la laïcité*, Paris: Gallimard.
Hervieu-Léger, D. (1999). *Le pèlerin et le converti. La religion en movement*, Paris: Flammarion.
Hervieu-Léger, D., and G. Davie (1996). *Identités religieuses en Europe*, Paris: La Découverte.
Isambert, F.A. (1992). *De la religion à l'éthique*, Paris: Cerf.
Kakpo, N. (2007). *L'Islam, un recours pour les jeunes*, Paris: Les Presses de Sciences Po.
Khosrokhavar, F. (1998). *L'islam des jeunes*, Paris: Flammarion.
Liogier, R. (2006). *Une laïcité légitime. Le France et ses religions d'Etat*, Paris: Entrelacs.
Lambert, Y. (2002). 'Religion, l'Europe à un tournant', *Futurible*, 277 (juillet–août), pp. 129–59.
Modood, T. (2007). *Multiculturalism: A Civil Idea*, Cambridge: Polity.
Ormières, J.-L. (2005). *L'Europe désenchantée*, Paris: Fayard.
Singly, F. (2005). *L'individualisme est un humanisme*, Paris: Editions de l'Aube.

Schnapper, D. (2005). 'Renouveau ethnique et renouveau religieux dans les démocraties providentielles', *Archives de Sciences Sociales des Religions*, 131–2, pp. 9–26.

Tocqueville, A. (2005). *De la démocratie en Amérique*, tome 1, Paris: Flammarion.

Chapter 13
The Meaning of Privatization and De-privatization

Martin Riesebrodt

Sébastien Tank-Storper has presented a very elegant and stimulating argument. He suggests that there is no necessary contradiction between theories of secularization and the 're-privatization' (Casanova 1994) or, as he prefers to call it, the 're-publicization' of religion. He correctly observes that the re-entering of religion into the public sphere does not represent a return to a previous order, but that religion takes on a new role in a democratic society. At least in Europe we are not witnessing a counter-secularization in which the traditional churches re-establish their power in the public sphere, but rather the use of religion as an expression of individualism, which he calls 'concrete individualism'. Whereas religion used to be conceived as a principle of heteronomy, a law imposed on the individual from the outside, it is now envisioned as an expression of autonomy, as a freely chosen identity and marker of difference. In other words, religion no longer represents a system of domination but rather an expression of 'authenticity'.

Tank-Storper acknowledges that not all religions have ceased to try to establish their public moral authority over their members, but – at least in Europe – they will no longer succeed and are actually de-legitimizing themselves by such attempts. Nevertheless, religion will not be absent from the public sphere, but will re-enter it in a democratic form controlled by the state. Religion becomes a moral voice among others and will be thereby even more relativized.

Tank-Storper presents many observations that are immensely instructive and offers important insights into the role religion plays in contemporary France, especially with regard to young second-generation Muslim immigrants. Also his focus on secularization mostly in terms of institutional differentiation avoids the confusion many authors create by not clearly distinguishing between institutional differentiation, disenchantment or changing mentalities, and deinstitutionalization or decreasing power of religious institutions over their members. However, there remain some questions to be asked and some assumptions to be challenged. Let me focus on two related topics, the question of individualism and of religion in a democratic society.

From 'Abstract' to 'Concrete' Individualism?

Tank-Storper links the changing role of religion and especially its 're-publicization' to the emergence of a new kind of individualism that he calls 'concrete' individualism. Whereas decades ago people were abstract role players without individual traits, they have now become highly individualized role players who no longer are expected to suppress their particularistic features.

Although there might be some truth to this distinction, I wonder if this transition is not more complicated and must be explained in terms of a process of pluralization instead of a transition from one type of individualism to another. There has always existed a tension between 'abstract' and 'concrete' individualism. If one recalls, for example, Max Weber's speech on 'Science as a Vocation' (1917), one understands that 'abstract' individualism has been highly contested already, nearly one hundred years ago (Weber 1992). Many of Weber's colleagues and young students wanted to be professors and political prophets at the same time, fusing their official task with their personal convictions. The ideal of 'abstract' individualism is the ideal of a bureaucratic state. Although Weber defended 'abstract' individualism as an unavoidable evil of our bureaucratic age rather than an ideal, for him – in contrast to Durkheim (1984, 1973) – 'concrete' individualism is not a danger to society, but rather bureaucracy is a danger to individualism.

But I would go even further. 'Abstract' individualism might have been an ideology rather than a reality in an ethnically and religiously relatively homogenous, authoritarian, rationalizing bureaucratic society. In 19th- and early 20th-century Germany, for example, 'abstract' individualism meant suppression of individual features primarily for those who did not belong to the establishment or the majority, like Jews and other minorities. Without too much exaggeration one could argue that women in public life had to act like men, Jews like Christians, workers like members of the middle-class, in order to be accepted. Middle-class Christian men, however, could always act like middle-class Christian men, thereby appearing as 'abstract' individuals dedicated solely to their tasks, but in fact expressing their 'concrete' individuality rather freely. 'Abstract' individualism therefore might be best described as an ideology claiming that the establishment or the majority has no particularistic features – only minorities or outsiders do. If I recall it correctly, Marx made a similar point when he criticized Hegel's understanding of bureaucracy (Marx 1962 [1844]).

In other words, what Tank-Storper describes is less a general transition from 'abstract' to 'concrete' individualism, than it is the debunking of a myth as well as the liberalization of a norm. Now more categories of people and social groups can freely express their 'concrete' individualism instead of suppressing it by attempting to conform to the norm of the dominant individualism. This seems to be confirmed by the American experience, which made that transition much earlier. Since its disestablishment religion has always played the role of an identity marker in the United States as a country of immigrants. But even under those much more pluralistic conditions, until 2009 no woman, African–American or Jew has ever been president. Tank-Storper's observation of a transition from 'abstract' to 'concrete' individualism therefore might be primarily via the decentralization and especially pluralization of French society.

Religion in Modern Democracies

Tank-Storper is certainly correct when he claims that religion serves as a marker of identity in modern societies. However, he fails to explain why people in growing numbers choose religion as such a marker, especially since he insists that secularization has indeed taken place. Moreover, to see in religion nothing but a marker of identity would obviously underestimate the role religion actually plays in the lives of people. Religion is much more complex than other markers of identity, like tattoos, piercings, flags or fashion statements, because it has a social dimension and a commitment to a certain conduct of life, especially when it is newly chosen and not inherited from the parent generation, as is the case – according to Tank-Storper – for the young generation of Muslims in France.

I also disagree that religion in its seemingly individualized forms does not exert authority over its followers. Certainly if one associates authority primarily with a hierocratic church structure, Tank-Storper is correct. However, voluntary associations also exert authority and social control over their members, maybe in more subtle and less visible but also much more effective ways than churches do (Weber 2002). Tank-Storper's argument seems to rely too much on a metropolitan French or European experience. In order to understand religion in modern democracies, it might be helpful to pay more attention to provincial politics and to compare the French case with others, especially the American example.

Similarly to my comment on the distinction between 'abstract' and 'concrete' individualism, I would also suggest that the concept of 'de-privatization' or 're-publicization' of religion is problematic. Religion has never ceased to play a role in democratic politics. For example, Christian parties that – at least nominally – base their politics on Christian values have been in existence in Europe for many decades. More important, the individual who brings religion into the public sphere via his or her 'concrete identity' is by no means a new phenomenon. Tank-Storper approvingly quotes José Casanova, that freedom of conscience is the first freedom in the modern West on which all others freedoms rest. But, this privatization of religion is meant to protect the individual from the state, not the state from religion. Therefore, when members of parliament vote on important issues, they are expected to vote according to their conscience. If this conscience happens to be religiously formed, religion unavoidably enters the democratic political process, making a private belief a public fact.

Moreover, the 'de-privatization' of religion does not mean that an essentially public phenomenon that had been reduced to a private one, now re-enters its proper domain. The Roman Empire already distinguished between the public cult and private cults. All salvation religions have a private and individual dimension, since they have to be appropriated subjectively in order to be practiced, and usually salvation is understood as individual salvation. And in the Christian traditions there have always been denominations that never sought political power but rather despised the world of politics or at least, like Lutheranism, clearly distinguished the realm of the world from the realm of the divine.

I hope that my comments adequately convey how stimulating and thought-provoking Tank-Storper's talk has been.

References

Casanova, J. (1994). *Public Religions in the Modern World*, Chicago, IL: University of Chicago Press.
Durkheim, É. (1973). *On Morality and Society: Selected Writings*, ed. R.N. Bellah, Chicago, IL: University of Chicago Press.
Durkheim, É. (1984). *The Division of Labor in Society*, New York: Free Press.
Marx, K. (1962 [1844]). 'Kritik des Hegelschen Staatsrechts', in H.-J. Lieber and P. Furth (eds), *Karl Marx. Frühe Schriften*, Darmstadt: Wissenschaftliche Buchgesellschaft, Bd. 1, pp. 258ff..
Weber, Max (1992). *Wissenschaft als Beruf, 1917/1919. Politik als Beruf, 1919*, ed. W.J. Mommsen, W. Schluchter and B. Morgenbrod, MWG, Bd. I/17, Tübingen.
Weber, M. (2002). *The Protestant Ethic and the 'Spirit' of Capitalism and Other Writings*, ed. P.R. Baehr and G.C. Wells, New York: Penguin.

Denmark and the Cartoons

Chapter 14
The Settled Secularity of Happy Denmark

David Martin

I am interested in whether the secularity of happy Denmark should be understood as a harbinger of the global future or as a nice niche available to the Danes (and to fellow Scandinavians) due to special circumstances. I am also curious about the uniformity of a broadly Social Democratic political culture throughout the five Nordic countries as it has emerged in the wake of an equally uniform secularised Lutheranism. The Nordic countries appear to illustrate in an unusually obvious form my belief that religious and political cultures mirror each other quite closely. So I ask just how the doctrines of the two kingdoms, of the priesthood of all believers, and of salvation by personal experience of trusting faith, assist the emergence of a modest monarchy, a settled attachment to believing in your own way, and the principle of universal entitlement to the benefits of the flexi-security system.

I propose to address these issues in comparative perspective, as follows. First I want to set Denmark in the context of the low-lying Post-Protestant plain stretching from Birmingham to Tallinn by way of Amsterdam, Hamburg, and its capital – Berlin. That implies two sets of comparisons between very different patterns of secularisation: the Anglo-Scandinavian set, in which I include New Zealand because it is the British Isles upside down, and the Post-Communist set, in particular the former DDR and Estonia, but including the Czech Republic. Next I look at societies that are as religiously homogeneous as Denmark but have been or remain vigorously practicing: Ireland, Poland and Greece. The former two countries have a special interest because they are outposts of Catholicism at the western and eastern ends of the northern plain. Then I summarise the data as presented in the excellent study *I hjertet af Danmark* (Gundelach, Iversen and Warburg, 2008), offering some British comparisons. Finally I look at this curious tendency of Lutheranism to mutate into semi-secular Social Democracy. Not only do I think that religious and political cultures mirror each other; the ensemble they represent has to be set in a geographical and geopolitical niche, both within the national boundaries and beyond them in the whole continental context. Within the national boundaries one has to consider the regional cultures likely to develop along the coordinates north and south, east and west, allowing for the contingent effects of mountains or their absence (since in Denmark the highest point is 500 feet), or of islands and peninsulas. It is important that Denmark is a small peninsula with islands at the crossroads of the Baltic Sea and the North Sea, whereas Britain is made up of two large islands, with something like a natural break between the north and south of the larger island, and looking towards the Atlantic. To some extent geography is destiny, so Denmark is more likely to be religiously and politically homogeneous than Britain. The internal differences likely in Britain will arise not only in the natural ecological niches of Scotland and England, Wales and East Anglia, but in the north and south of England, Scotland and Wales respectively, each with a different religious complexion. In Denmark, by contrast, the main difference occurs between east and west. It also makes a difference where the capital is situated. London, for example, is strategically situated in the southeast near the estuary of the principal river, directly facing the mouth of the Rhine and Europe, while Copenhagen stands furthest east in the country, controlling the narrow strait into the Baltic. It is a maritime axis and the bridge from Scandinavia to Central Europe. What I am suggesting here is a contrast between Britain and Denmark within the wider religio-political universe of Anglo-Scandinavia, rooted in geography, whereby Britain is unusually diverse and Denmark unusually homogeneous. The implications are wide-ranging. Denmark has a good chance of an even-paced development where problems arise in a manageable sequence, and where mutual tolerance and compromise are preferred over revolutionary change or civil war. In the case of Britain the revolution and the civil war came very early, and the result was that Britain enjoyed centuries of relatively peaceful change, marked by compromise between contending parties, to a degree only exceeded by Denmark. Another consequence of the exceptional homogeneity of Denmark is that the ethnic cleansing characteristic of the romantic era of national mobilisation proved unnecessary, in part because losing the war with Germany in 1864 partly solved the problem of the ethnic minority, and reinforced the national consciousness of a somewhat diminished Denmark. At the same time Denmark was confronted by immediate neighbours who were not all that different and shared the same Lutheran religion. The Danes could distinguish themselves from the Swedes, who had taken Scania from them, and even more from the Germans, who had taken Schleswig-Holstein, without nurturing the sense of radical difference and injury felt by the Catholic Irish in relation to Protestant English and Northern Ireland. They were saved from that kind of political poison.

So far I have suggested that the ecological niche occupied by Denmark makes for a degree of homogeneity and settled evolutionary change greater even than that found in Britain. The data show that this homogeneity is associated with strong identification between Church and people, Church and nation, so that the majority of Danes are baptised and confirmed, and count themselves members. In typical Scandinavian fashion, strong identification is further associated with weak practice when it comes to regular worship as distinct from entering a church building. However, in Europe as a whole homogeneity is not necessarily accompanied by weak practice, and if we take the cases of Ireland, Poland and Greece quite the reverse is true. That is because these three countries lie at a disputed ethno-religious frontier and have been dominated by alien empires. Once freed from foreign domination the alien religious and/or ethno-religious minorities have to this or that extent been extruded. With the lessening of tension over Northern Ireland

and increasing prosperity, practice in the Irish Republic has dropped, whereas in Greece continuing perceptions of threat to national or cultural identity on the part of Turkey, as well as the EU, have stimulated a greater degree of religious mobilisation. Such perceptions of threat from a traditional 'other' have barely existed in either Denmark or Britain. The only exception relates to the arrival in both countries of a substantial number of Muslim migrants, making up some 3 per cent of the total population. In both Britain and Denmark an enhanced awareness on the part of the home population of being in some sense Christian has been reinforced by the sort of global tensions represented by terrorist attacks in Britain and by the international furore and flag burnings over cartoons of Mohammed printed in Denmark.

A rather different contrast to that provided by other cases of religious homogeneity like Ireland, Poland and Greece, can be found in other Lutheran societies that were up to 1989 subject to Russian-supported Communist domination. In East Germany, Latvia and Estonia a Lutheran culture proved much more vulnerable to state-sponsored secularisation than the Catholic culture of Lithuania. Arguably East Germany and the Lutheran Baltics have adopted a kind of self-conscious secularism considerably more dramatic than the passive semi-secularity of Scandinavia. The same is to a lesser extent true of the Czech Republic, which, while Catholic, acknowledges a Protestant founding myth and for a long period resented Austrian domination of the Czech Catholic Church. In a similar way Estonia and Latvia have nourished resentment over German cultural hegemony, including domination of the Lutheran Church. The case of the sometime Lutheran DDR is complicated. East Germans were offered absolution from Nazi crimes provided they identified themselves as proletarian victims of Nazi rule liberated to achieve their true Communist and atheist potential after the Russians conquered Eastern Europe.

We now turn more directly to the portrait provided by Gundelach, Iversen and Warburg in *I hjertet af Danmark* (2008), which ranges rather more widely than religion to include superstition and spirituality as well as the national ethos, and institutions like family and school. Clearly the family and its rituals stands at the emotional centre of Danish everyday life, in spite of the changes that have accelerated since the 1960s. These are the end of the patriarchal family, a greatly increased female participation in the workforce, and a higher divorce rate. The pattern day by day resembles contemporary Britain: the children are taken to nursery after breakfast (though nursery facilities are much cheaper than in Britain), there is an empty house during the day, and quality time in the evening between parents and children including a shared meal. However, the sixties do not seem to have been a time of major cultural upheaval, and in particular the changing roles of women do not appear to have affected their participation in the Church in the way postulated by Callum Brown in the context of Britain (Brown 2001).

Politically the dominance of Social Democrats has been more assured than in Britain and the result has been a political consensus based on tolerance and compromise, for example between potentially rival social groups like farmers and industrial workers. Danes acquired a universal education system and democratic rights earlier than most, and today they are entirely wedded to universalism as a principle of social provision and to an egalitarian social structure where the skilled workers do as well as middling professionals. The data show the Danes happy with this situation, with their lot and with themselves, more so than in Britain, where social and political inequality and distance are markedly greater. Maybe the fact that Britain has ten times the population of Denmark has something to do with this. Both countries show a decline in trade union power, and some ambivalence towards such power as remains. In Denmark high taxes make possible a very high level of what is known as flexi-security. Apart from the family there is a unified school system, socialising Danes into a common culture, and one still influenced by the religio-social ideals of Grundtvig in the nineteenth century. There is nothing in Denmark like the English independent school system, with its Anglican ethos, for the better-off. Nor are there Founding Fathers and iconic national heroes such as used to be celebrated in Britain.

The authors of *At the Heart of Denmark* explain that there is a certain reticence about Danes, and certain customs in the preparation and sequence of dishes that delay the assimilation of aliens and strangers until appropriate sensitivities have been acquired. Since Danish is not spoken by a large number of people, Danes are more insistent that migrants speak the language as part of acquiring the culture than has been the case in Britain, at least up till recently.

All the data just summarised provide a necessary background to the pattern of Danish religion, and may even have some explanatory value if one shares Inglehart's view that religious practice and intensity is positively related to greater inequality and lower levels of prosperity (Inglehart and Norris 2004). Inevitably in a highly developed and financially secure society modern media play a larger role in the formation of religious attitudes than the Church, and of recent years there has been more debate about the role of religion, as there has also been in Britain, in part stimulated by very different conceptions of the place of religion among the minority Muslim population. The media have also stimulated an interest in astrology and alternative healing, but there seems not to have been quite the growth of alternative spiritualities reported by Woodhead and Heelas in the English town of Kendal (Heelas and Woodhead 2003). Alternative lifestyles are accepted, even if they offend against the Danish ethos of hard work, providing those who adopt them accept the costs. Given that Danish Lutheranism is more a habit of the heart than a dogma or a belief, there has been a long tradition of accommodation within the boundaries of a very broad Church. Whereas in England, Wales, and Scotland, Evangelical and Revivalist movements have occurred outside the Church as well as inside it, in Denmark revival and dissent have largely remained within the Establishment, even more so than in the rest of Scandinavia where there are major regional variations. It was, of course, precisely this fractious and fissionable spirit in Britain that, when transported to North America, helped inaugurate a culture of universal pluralism and a degree of individualism greater than anything found in Denmark. The kind of individualism that Bellah and his associates in *Habits of the Heart* called 'Sheilaism' does not have much appeal in Denmark (Bellah et al. 1985).

The greater degree of internal difference and overt pluralism in Britain serves to introduce further comparisons between Denmark and Britain. The object here is to bring out the specific character of Danish homogeneity and even maybe to suggest that Denmark is more of a nice niche than our universal global future. I suggested earlier that countries tend to have a regional east and west, as is the case in Denmark, and also a north and south. In the time of the English Civil War the country was divided into roughly east and west, with the King raising his standard in Oxford, and Parliament drawing its support from Puritan and radical London, and East Anglia, including Cambridge. In the course of the nineteenth century with early industrialisation and urbanisation all three countries of the main island divided into a north and a south, with the north roughly corresponding to upland areas and the south to flatter country. In Scotland the Presbyterian central lowlands encroached on the Catholic highlands, while in England religious Noncomformity (and the progressive Liberal party) established itself in the north and west, particularly Wales and the south-west peninsula. Then with increasing migration Irish Catholics in particular traversed the country from Liverpool in the north-west to Birmingham and London, leaving an Anglican belt running from Dorset in the south-west through Oxford to Lincoln in the east Midlands. Jewish and later Muslim migration reversed the Catholic trajectory by fanning out from London to the Midlands and the north-west. All these regional differences and varied migratory trails had political correlates too complicated to go into here, except to say that the English and adherents of the Anglican Church were more likely to be Conservative, while other ethnicities and faiths were more likely to vote Liberal or Labour. In part this reflects the greater heterogeneity of Britain, but it also illustrates the consequences of the British Empire, since substantial populations migrated from ex-imperial territories – Christian Blacks from the Caribbean and Africa, and Muslims, Sikhs and Hindus from India. Due to their imperial experience the English came to distinguish home from abroad, and to nostalgically imagine spring in England just as Danes imagine summer. Danes and English alike are much exercised by the vagaries of the weather. Moreover the long centuries of relatively peaceful change in England have resulted in an attachment to 'the country' as a place, and to the law of the land as an accumulated practice rather than a set of principles.

The point here is that the English live in a relatively understated manner at the heart of two islands where the other groups define themselves more distinctly in ethnic and – at least historically – in religious terms. Anglicanism and Englishness are as much conditions related to an ancient sense of place, in particular pastoral place, as they are a corpus of beliefs and a national identity. In times of crisis and peril an iconic pastoral landscape is summoned up, even though England is one of the most urbanised countries in the world. The same sense of an iconic landscape and the same understated self-consciousness is to be found in Denmark, but there seems also to be a greater awareness of a distinct and bounded nation. If one thinks only of the Anglican Church, its core of worshippers is almost identical with the core worshipping community of the Danish Church: 2 per cent per week, perhaps twice that number in the course of a month. However, the presence of many other traditions means that overall regular practice in England has been higher than in Demark. Over recent decades in Denmark the level of regular practice has remained stable, whereas in England it has been declining.

I turn now to the interesting question of the mutations of Lutheranism that have had such uniform consequences throughout the Nordic countries. Perhaps the most obvious mutation relates to the contribution of the vernacular Bible and liturgy to the formation of a distinct national consciousness. Church and nation became so closely bound together that I recollect a Norwegian telling me that his friend was a Methodist, not a Norwegian. That helps explain how a prominent Dane could ask why anyone should attend church on Sunday when there was opportunity to be part of the nation every day.

Luther's stress on individual faith and trust is easily transformed into the idea that everyone is a Christian in his or her own way, while the priesthood of all believers downgrades hierarchy as such, not only the dogmatic deliverances of ecclesiastical hierarchy. The idea of Christian brotherhood mutates into notions of mutual cooperation in the local community. That seems particularly clear in Grundtvigian invocations of a local community or parish focused on a folk high school, and one needs to remember that Danish Lutheranism is Grundtvigian, whatever the fame and influence of Kierkegaard elsewhere. The high valuation of experience mutates into empiricism and pragmatism just as it did in England, and the large-scale constructions of Hegelian philosophy gain little purchase. It is true that there was a great interest in German thought in England in the later nineteenth century, but in thinkers like T.H. Green the idealism was muted and generated a passion for social reform. In T.H. Marshall there emerged an interest in the idea of the rights and duties of citizenship as influential in Denmark as it was in England. The ties between the two countries are therefore intellectual as well as agricultural: in an early period the 'liberal Anglican' John Locke influenced the writings of Ludvig Holberg (Kent 2000: 217). In both countries movements of social reform placed a high value on hard work, which could be regarded as deriving from the Protestant work ethic, though any explicit reference has now disappeared.

Since Denmark and England share so much in common, whatever their differences, and an unfortunate clash in 1805, it is worth pointing out similarities between their musical traditions. Both countries share a certain reserve towards the vastly influential and indeed overwhelming Austro-German canon. Nielsen and Elgar were both strongly influenced by German romanticism in music, yet they both created a recognisable national style. Perhaps this is echoed in more widely held reservations about the EU as a project promoted together by Germany and France. There is a shared tradition of choral singing and hymn singing. The authors of *At the Heart of Denmark* claim that the Danes are the champion hymn singers among Nordic peoples. I have heard the same claimed for the Finns, but the crucial issue is the participatory practice of singing, promoted in the origins of

Protestantism, and by Luther's special interest in music. It would be interesting to know how far the tradition of hymn singing has survived the depredations of the mass media and their promotion of popular music. In England the tradition has gone into decline, along with the tradition of folk song, not least because educational policy has neglected alike the national music, the national history and the religious inheritance. I find no hint of that *trahison des clercs* or pedagogic alienation in the Danish data. What does surprise me is the relatively small democratic influence accredited to voluntary association such as Robert Putnam claims in a remarkably influential thesis, and one that highlights the role of choral societies (Putnam 2000). Perhaps Denmark is so compact and rooted that voluntary association is not as important as it is in the United States.

References

Bellah, R., R. Madsen, W.M. Sullivan and A. Swidler (1985). *Habits of the Heart: Individualism and Commitment in American Life*, Berkeley, CA: University of California Press.

Brown, C.G. (2001). *The Death of Christian Britain: Understanding Secularization 1800–2000*, London: Routledge.

Gundelach, P., H.R. Iversen and M. Warburg (2008). *I hjertet af Danmark. Institutioner og mentaliteter*, Copenhagen: Hans Reitzel.

Heelas P., and L. Woodhead (2003). *The Spiritual Revolution*, Oxford: Blackwell.

Inglehart, R., and P. Norris (2004). *Sacred and Secular: Religion and Politics Worldwide*, Oxford and New York: Oxford University Press.

Kent, N. (2000). *The Soul of the North*, London: Reaktion Books.

Putnam, R. (2000). *Bowling Alone: The Collapse and Revival of American Community*, New York: Simon and Schuster.

Chapter 15

Background of the Cartoon Crisis in Danish Mentality

Hans Raun Iversen

A Question of Mentalities

Books and articles on the Danish Cartoon Crisis have already been and are still being published by the hundreds. In a number of them the course of events of the crisis has also been described and analyzed (see Mogensen 2007; Riis 2007; and Gregersen 2009, for example). This contribution therefore limits itself to the background of the crisis in the special national, political and secular setting in Denmark.

I agree with Tariq Modood (2006), among others, that part of the story is about racism in the cultural, not in the precise legal, primarily biological based sense of the word: the stereotypization, marginalization and stigmatization experienced by Muslims in Denmark during recent decades do resemble the experience of, for instance, the immigrant Jews during the last 400 years in Denmark (Østergaard 2007). Intolerance to and fear of religion is not uncommon in secular people in Denmark. On the contrary, it is mixed with 'an avoidance of all deviations from local standards' (Riis 2007: 443). I do not think that *Jyllands-Posten* did the right thing in its attempt to teach Danish Muslims the lesson necessary for citizens in 'a modern, secular society', by attempting to make them ready for 'scorn, mockery and ridicule' with the help of the cartoons (Rose 2005). All of us surely need education, and that goes not least for the old ethnic inhabitants in Denmark, who are in need of 'education and refinement of their sensitivities in the light of changing circumstances and the specific vulnerabilities of new entrants' (Modood 2006: 61). The cartoon crisis was about the handling of an actual multicultural situation (Modood 2007), or rather the Danish lack of ability in this respect (Lægaard 2007; Andersen 2008).

Borrowing the term of Richard J. Bernstein, what happened in Denmark during the crisis can be analyzed as a 'clash of mentalities'. Bernstein defines mentality as

> ... a general orientation – a cast of mind or way of thinking – that conditions the way in which we approach, understand and act in the world. It shapes and is shaped by our intellectual, practical and emotional lives. Mentalities can take a variety of concrete historical forms. We never encounter a mentality in the abstract, but only in a particular historical manifestation. To fully understand a

specific historical manifestation of mentality, we need to locate its context, its distinctive character, and its sources. (Bernstein 2005: 18)

There is not much sense in talking about a clash of civilizations in Denmark, but there are significant differences between the personal experience-based secular mentality of most ethnic Danes[1] and the authority-based religious mentality found among Muslim groups of immigrant Danes, for example. To live in peace, a mutual understanding and recognition between the two mentalities is needed.

Ethnic Danes and Immigrant Danes

The most typical element in the Danes' approach to 'the others' is great openness to the world and globalization, and even to multiculturality, combined with a high degree of determination to protect themselves and their own cultural self-perception. The survey by *Epinion* for the weekly magazine *Ugebladet A4*, carried out in June 2006, strikes this doubleness very precisely with the reactions to the following five statements:

- 'It is positive to be a multi-cultural society.'
  Agree: 57 per cent.
  Disagree: 16 per cent.
- 'Globalisation constitutes no threat to Denmark.'
  Agree: 57 per cent.
  Disagree: 11 per cent.
- 'Denmark *had* to tighten its immigration policy.'
  Agree: 69 per cent.
  Disagree: 15 per cent.
- 'Islam is a threat to western society.'
  Agree: 57 per cent.
  Disagree: 25 per cent.
- 'Danish society rests on certain Danish values which it must protect.'
  Agree: 79 per cent.
  Disagree: 6 per cent.
  (Quoted from Per Michael Christiansen in *Politiken* 19 May 2007).

On the one hand, we can agree that this is a contradiction of the kind that the social comedian Niels Hausgaard illustrates with the Jutlander who is a strong supporter of atomic energy so long as the reactor is over on Zealand or at any rate on the other side of Funen. For, as he says, over by us it'll just be in the way! On the other hand, it is wise to acknowledge that the self-contradiction in the Danes' attitude to 'the others' is of a complex nature and much deeper than the well-known forms of

---

[1] The analysis of Danish mentality in this contribution builds on Gundelach et al. 2008.

local chauvinism. In the newest and most thorough survey of the conflict around the so-called new Danes, the political scientist Frølund Thomsen formulates the Danish dilemma in the following diplomatic yet also unambiguous way:

> It is clear in the Danish immigrant debate there is a democratic Achilles' heel regarding the immigrants' right to be culturally different from the majority Danish population. (Thomsen 2006: 67)

The *Background Report* from the Ministry of Integration's study of the values of ethnic groups (Gundelach and Nørregaard-Nielsen 2007) places the Danish weak spot in relief to the Achilles' heel that exists among the immigrants themselves. In a series of questions on their views of gender, marriage, sex, religiosity and obedience, the immigrants are seen to be more moralistic and old-fashioned than the present Danish average. For better for worse, their position resembles that of Danes born 75 or 100 years ago. This is not to imply that the immigrants will change their views just as quickly as our grandparents' grandchildren did, but it is nevertheless strange that the Danes, who are used to letting their grandparents think what they like, have relatively serious problems with the attitudes of the immigrants. The centre of the problem is mental: the Danes have only just got used to their new Danish mentality when along come the immigrants with a mentality that the Danes themselves have recently abandoned. That is the core of the mental difference between the Danes and the new immigrants. After a thorough study of the role of Danish mentality in media, Rosenfeldt (2006) argues for investment in an immigrant press comprising a mentality that does not offend the immigrants as easily as the Danish media that currently debate conditions of life in Denmark. This step, he believes, will encourage integration.

Because the Danes are so engaged in their own (new) mentality, they are – literally and politically – neglecting the results of the survey, which sets a question mark against the Danes' excellence. For example, the *Background Report* shows that in a number of crucial areas the immigrants are actually living up to what are often called the Danish core values better than the ethnic Danes themselves. Immigrants are more against travelling on public transport without a ticket, cheating the social services, and doing moonlight work than the ethnic Danes; they have more faith in equal treatment by the courts, the hospitals and the police; they are more prepared for their children to have friends from a different ethnic background; they are almost equally as prepared as the Danes to separate religion and politics; and they oppose more strongly than the Danes the introduction of a 'strong man' to take over power in the country.

The most problematic area of conflict over 'Danish values' is the 'freedom to hold meetings for extreme groups', which is supported strongly by only 39 per cent of ethnic Danes but by 65 per cent of immigrant Danes, who perhaps have always wanted such freedom rights. Only 40 per cent of ethnic Danes agree completely that you should 'be able freely to perform religious rituals', whereas the immigrant Danes, who are perhaps more experienced in this area, firmly support free religious practice with 80 per cent backing this aspect (Gundelach and Nørregaard-Nielsen 2007: 126ff.). Thus the majority of Danes are in marked opposition to the 19th-century national prophet, Grundtvig's (1783–1872) famous demand for 'freedom for Loke as well as for Thor', where 'the enemy', Loke, should have the same rights as 'the friend', Thor. The ideal of freedom in Denmark is cut to suit the needs of the majority Danes.

Summarizing, it is clear that the immigrants' attitudes reflect the cultures from which they have come on questions that can be regarded as moral. On the other hand, to a considerable extent the ethnic Danes' attitudes appear to be unconsidered products of a cultural and political normality with limited broad-mindedness towards people who think differently about politics and religion.

We're All in the Same Boat

Denmark is a small country with fewer than 5.5 million inhabitants. The defeat to Germany in 1864 led to the loss of roughly one-third of the kingdom, after which practically everyone in the remaining population was a Danish-speaking Dane. The fact that Greenland and the Faroe Islands still belong to the kingdom works as a kind of historical exception, which only goes to prove that Denmark is the Danes' Danish kingdom. The defeat to Germany also meant that Denmark had to face up to being a vulnerable nation whose continued existence was far from assured. The result was that the Danes staked their energies on a shared, people's Denmark, applying in practice the words attributed to the founder of the Danish Land Development Service, third-generation immigrant Enrico Dalgas (1828–94): 'Every loss has a compensation /An outward loss must lead to inward cultivation'. Dalgas was referring to both the loss of South Jutland and the cultivation of the Jutland moors, but the motto was also used about Denmark's situation in general. The Danes had to put their efforts into building up a nation internally strong with Danish culture and a national feeling of solidarity. With the support of the Grundtvigian movement and its focus on a Danish *folk*, language and history, a popular self-awareness was established despite the country's insignificant size and limited numbers.

There have been numerous rewritings of the old revue song, 'We're All In The Same Boat'. This was also the tune that Vase and Fuglsang turned to when they wrote new lyrics for the song, *Did we learn anyfink?*, about the Mohammed cartoon crisis, performed by Ulf Pilgaard at the Circus Revue in 2006. The picture they paint is extremely effective. What a single group of decision-makers says or does in Denmark often has consequences for everybody in such a small country. Further, most of us behave as if we are sitting on each other's laps in the same little boat. The image can therefore be used to appeal for unity and to urge moderation in attacking others while we are on the collective voyage.

Anthropologists from abroad who have conducted fieldwork in Denmark have often been tempted to describe the Danes as a tribal society in the classic anthropological sense – that is, a pretty much closed community, where everyone keeps watch on one another in order to ensure the group's survival, best of all without the intervention of those outside, who in any case do not belong to the tribe (Mellon 1992; cf. also Borish 1991 and Reddy 1993). Denmark's socio-economic structure, with record-high taxes (63 per cent as the top rate) and arguably more free common benefits than any communist country has ever had, both assumes and promotes a high degree of solidarity in the form of willingness to pay for joint enterprises. Conversely, in the area of existential ethics and religion the Danes are individualists, almost anarchists, without a sense of the importance of joint authorities, even though they discover most of their attitudes to life within the joint structures of the Danish forms of religion (see below). It is therefore reasonable to ask whether there indeed is a tribal mentality among the Danes that makes it difficult for immigrants to feel at home in Denmark.

At any rate, anthropologists describe the Danes as people who form a circle around themselves and each other, while simultaneously shutting out 'the others'. Anne Knudsen fastens on this circle that the Danes – children and adults alike – surround themselves with when problems are to be solved. Face to face with one another in this formation, everyone looks a little more like everyone else – that at any rate is the experience – and a natural desire arises to show regard for those who are similar to yourself when you can see who is at the table and who is not: 'The dislike of ambiguous identities is very widespread in Denmark,' reports Knudsen (1996: 13). The flipside is that in both a physical and a standpoint sense the Danes turn their backs on those who seem fickle or are outside the circle. 'This is something that especially immigrants and their descendants can feel,' she adds (ibid.).

Steven M. Borish (1991) takes up the round-table dialogue at the folk high schools (*folkehøjskolerne*), where it is a bit of a disaster if someone is unwilling to join in. The Danes are – or at any rate, once were – mostly disposed towards an arrangement where everyone joins in, as in the universal principles of the cooperative movement and the welfare society. Jonathan Schwartz (1985) uses the unique quadrangle shape of the Danish farmyard as a metaphor for Danish mentality: once you are inside the farmyard gate, it is really welcoming – here there is *hygge* (cosiness). But if you have no legitimate errand, you should stay outside the gate, where there is precious little *hygge* around. If a dinner party is to enjoy *hygge*, it must not be too large. Otherwise you must split into groups so you can cosy up to one another around the table with its candles and all the other accoutrements, as Prakash Reddy notes (1993: 157f.).

Most Danes today settle for insisting they are *Danes*, leaving it to the Swedes to aspire to be the best, as Hanne Sanders from the Centre for Danish Studies in Malmö has put it (Sanders 2006: 27). But the Danes live a good life in Denmark, and that is clearly not the case for people in a whole series of other countries. There must therefore be something special about Denmark and the Danes. At any rate, Danes are damned good at being Danes!

Church, Nation and People

The Reformation in 1536 made Denmark a Protestant Lutheran country, and thus one where faith became a personal matter. That belief has won through entirely today as all Danes claim to be Christians or whatever else 'in my own way'. The democratic Constitution of 1849 states that the church's 'organisation' is to be agreed on later, but this has in fact never happened in the form of the overall solution envisaged in 1849. The work of various commissioners never resulted in political agreement. So the state and the church are still interwoven. Church tax, paid by all members and used not least for church maintenance, is levied alongside ordinary income tax. The state pays 40 per cent of the clergy's salary and thus helps to finance important areas of the church's work. In return, the church carries out administrative tasks for the state by having responsibility for civil registration of all persons as well as being the public burial authority.

Religion and faith play an *implicit* role for Danes. There is an emotional affiliation towards, and at times participation in, church rituals and alternative religious practice, but there is little understanding of the religious content. It can be argued that Christianity is not present in Danish families, schools, workplaces, welfare systems and voluntary activities. But it can be equally claimed that a number of Lutheran–Protestant figures stand behind – or have helped to encourage – the Danes' attitudes to children, family, work, freedom, equality, commitment, solidarity, and so on. Just as history, culture and Christianity are present within the major Danish institutions and their mindset, so do they also make their presence felt in guiding individual attitudes.

The Danes' faith is not especially visible in day-to-day life. Like secular Jews in the USA, secular Lutherans in Denmark practise *incognito ergo sum* (Sachs 1999: 60). Few give active expression to belief: an occasional prayer is said, and faith in a spiritual power is more common than faith in a God corresponding to the personal image of God in Christianity. Yet Danish Christianity does contribute to creating an us-and-them relation to other faiths, particularly Muslims (Gundelach, Iversen and Warburg, n.d.).

The balance between community and individualism in the mentality of the Danes finds strong expression when we look at their faith in God. Incidentally the situation is portrayed better than anywhere else in the following brief dialogue, formulated by Woody Allen, without special reference to Denmark (quoted from Warmind 2005: 290):

> A: Do you believe in God?
> B: I'm not sure…
> A: Well, Kierkegaard says that if you're not sure, then you don't!
> B: Okay! Then I guess I do!

Only few Danes fully support the line by the well-known Norwegian hymn-writer Petter Dass that God will still be God if all men die (Dass 1698). Yet even fewer (approximately 5 per cent) strongly believe that there is no God! Most tend to believe in some kind of God: God as a spiritual power in man, or maybe God as a good person – not unlike Pastor Thorkild Grosbøll, who states: 'God is dead and that is good. Therefore we can come close to the man from Nazareth without running the risk of assault. He is a brother only' (Grosbøll 2003: 90). The great majority of Danes don't like outspoken pious Christians, confessed atheists, fanatical spiritualists or provocative pastors, preferring to emphasize that since the death of Jesus good human beings are themselves 'gods', even though it helps if, like Pastor Grosbøll, they insist that they are Christians. According to a study of more than 1500 contributions to the so-called Grosbøll Debate in Danish newspapers during 2003/2004, Danes prefer to find their place in the centre, as they have become accustomed to having their common religion peacefully and passively in a more or less secular way (Højsgaard 2005: 198).

Secular and National Lutheranism

Danes are afraid of too much religion, especially as they perceive it among Muslims and New Religious Movements. Paradoxically, at one and the same time Danes also have the feeling that religion should play a more significant role – probably as a stabilizing factor behind their fragile culture of Christianity (Larsen et al. 2002: 86–8). According to European Values studies, the main institution in the Danish Park of Religions, the National Lutheran Church (*Folkekirken*) is respected and trusted in the same way as the military, the school system, Parliament and the welfare system – and significantly more than the press and the trade unions. Social solidarity, good education and free hospitals are advantages to which most Danes are strongly committed. In the same way they are serious about some sort of religion, even though the majority personally claim that they are 'Christian in my own way'. They are right insofar as nobody ever put them under pressure to become Christian in a specific way. But they are wrong inasmuch as almost all of them end up 'choosing' their 'own' religion within the traditions in the common Park of Religions.

Denmark is a 'Christian' country. So say most Danes today – faced with immigration, the EU and globalization! A female factory worker agrees that Denmark's religion is Christianity, even though 'you don't have to engage in it' (Gundelach, Iversen and Warburg, n.d.). But for the folk church, it is a clear-cut case for most people: children are baptized and confirmed in the Christian Church (75 and 72 per cent respectively in 2005), so they live in a Christian country. A male carpenter adds that Denmark's Christianity is 'at a level where it's accessible. I don't think that if anyone mocked our religion we would burn their flag and stuff like that. That's way over the top, the idea, it's so distant...! We have to go a bit further south-east before the chain comes off the wheels – but I don't think they should have mosques here' (ibid.). A young shipping man sings the typically Danish tune about Christianity and the church:

> We're a Christian country, but we're not the kind that runs down to the church to hear the priest tell us about the actual religion. Christianity is like the Ten Commandments. It's more than being just God's things. It's like ... the way our society's built up. Like you can have several wives in other religions, but you mustn't in Denmark. In that way I think I'm Christian, because I live the Christian way, and of course it's also got something to do with the fact that I've chosen to believe in God, because I said yes to my confirmation. But I don't do anything about it in the form of the Church and that way. (Ibid.)

Ethnic Danes have a clear tendency to position themselves in relation to Muslims – and thereby to claim that they are Christian, or at any rate that they live in a Christian country, even though the content of their Christian knowledge and practice is modest. The question therefore is, how can Denmark be and remain a Christian country, if there is no one who practises or knows anything about Christianity?

Europe is the only continent that is markedly secularized. And in that respect Sweden and Denmark lead the way (Davie 2002). The Danish National Lutheran Church can be characterized as the world's weakest monopoly church (Iversen 2006). This weakness stems from the lack of support for its religious services and basic creeds, while expectations as to what use it has are very low in comparison with what we find in other countries. The monopoly it holds is due to the fact that there have never been any major active alternatives to its longstanding tradition for administering the four transitional rites of birth, confirmation, marriage and burial. Added to this is the crucial historical circumstance that Denmark is the only country in the world that since the Reformation has always retained its linking relationship between people, state and church. For this reason – and because the state/church discussion has never acquired widespread support – it remains a general view not only of the state but also of the church that 'It's all of us' – even though in 2006 'only' 83 per cent of Danes were members of the folk church.

Just ten or twenty years ago, very few would have considered religion and the National Lutheran Church as one of the seven institutional pillars of Danish society. It is also a moot point, since there has been no tangible increase either in religious activity or in church support during the period. What *has* risen – and by several hundred per cent in the last decade – is the extent of and interest in the politically influenced public debate on religion (see Rosenfeldt 2006; Højsgaard 2005). Since the 1970s and 1980s, when the individual was expected to decide for him-/herself about religion because the traditions could no longer accommodate their practice, more and more people are now feeling it necessary to take a stance, often arguing that they themselves – and 'we in Denmark' – are different from the Muslims who fill the newspaper columns and the TV and computer screens. If we are not actively practising our positive attitudes to Christianity we can, the Danes seem to think, at least be active in our negative attitudes to Islam.

Experiential Centrism

Danes have considerable international experience – at least as tourists. No current research can point to strictly racist or strongly ethnocentric attitudes among the Danes. When we must note with Thomsen that in the debate on immigration the immigrants' right to be culturally different from the Danish majority society is the 'democratic Achilles' heel' (Thomsen 2006: 67), we find a fair share of the explanation in the Danish form of experiential centrism. There are many historical, social and psychological factors in play, but it is striking how much the Danes keep to what they themselves have experienced.

This experiential centrism may hang together with the influence of the specifically Danish tradition in philosophy and theology of experiential life orientation. Since the beginning of the 19th century there has been a high degree of scepticism in Denmark towards the German idealist philosophers with their systems such as the Hegelian. Guided by their common contemporary mentors Poul Martin Møller (1794–1838) and F.C. Sibbern (1785–1872), both N.F.S. Grundtvig and Søren Kierkegaard were raised in this experiential and life-philosophical tradition. To this very day, Danish philosophy as a rule is either empirically analytical or phenomenologically orientated and is thus more engaged in experiences than principle thought-figures. This tradition, via the schools, culture and adult education, has most probably acquired a significant degree of popular approval. In a well-known popular mediation of the tradition, Grundtvig writes:

> And never lived that man
> who understood the span
> of what first he had not loved.
> (Grundtvig 1834)

This direction down the proper path of experience can mean that you must commit yourself in order to become wiser and acquire knowledge of others. That's a valid point. But it can also be interpreted to mean that 'the others', whom you do not yet know and certainly have not loved, are doubtless dangerous or wrong. The culturally optimistic slogan 'A stranger is a friend you haven't met' can easily become culturally pessimistic in practice when 'the other', whom I do not know, does not belong to 'us'. We need research into how close the connection is between the popular- and the philosophical way of thinking in Denmark, and how the Danish experiential centrism relates to similar mental forms in other parts of the world.

The crisis in February 2006 following *Jyllands-Posten*'s publication of cartoons of the Prophet Mohammed was in many ways a test case for the Danish mentality. 'Did we learn anyfink?', asked the song that summer. The Queen gave the authorized answer in her New Year's Eve Speech 2006. After several nuanced views on the necessity of respecting the cultures of others, she said:

> The year that is past has taught us something, not least about ourselves. We now know better what we stand for, where we neither can nor will sell out.

The following evening on New Year's Day 2007, Anders Fogh Rasmussen, then Prime Minister, interpreted the text:

> We stood guard over the freedom of speech, which is the most precious freedom-right we have ... It is the core of democracy. And it is the driving-force for enlightenment, education and development. It is the freedom of speech that has created progress in Denmark, in Europe and other free societies of the world.

There was nothing else to be learned, according to the Prime Minister, even though Danish diplomats have not without reason been retrained in the wake of the crisis (Branner 2007; Petersen 2006). Possibly the majority of Danish people concurred with the Prime Minister's conclusion, but there was far from overall agreement. In fact there are differences of opinion right down to individual families, for example in the elderly farming couple's comments with regard to the flag-burnings: 'It's those Muslims, they're stupid,' says she; 'Yes, yes, but there are enough Dannebrogs,' he adds (Gundelach, Iversen and Warburg, n.d.).

In Denmark only 10 per cent say that there cannot be truths in different religions. The corresponding figure for the UK is 23 per cent, rising to 57 per cent for Turkey and 86 per cent for Pakistan.[2] The reason why it is incessantly hammered home in Denmark that 'democracy always has the right of way over religion', and the reason why A.F. Rasmussen could go so far as to claim that freedom of speech is sacred and apparently the only sacred thing, is that there are evidently not many who disagree with the former Prime Minister in a population that deals *relatively* with its own and others' religion. The disagreement in Denmark has less to do with differing views of religion than with the political savvy of A.F. Rasmussen's absolutist, idealistic stance, which was aired, for example, during his opening speech to Parliament on 3 October 2006 in his refusal to sell out in the global 'battle of values' between 'intelligent enlightening and fundamentalist darkening. Between democracy and dictatorship. Between freedom and tyranny' (quoted in Petersen 2006: 31).

Nikolaj Petersen, Emeritus Professor of Political Science, characterises the former Prime Minister's simple dualist message as one of 'almost messianic pathos'. Together with his then-ally, George W. Bush, A.F. Rasmussen fought for 'democracy, freedom of speech and human rights'. In staging their respective speeches, the difference is that the dividing line for Bush runs between 'good and evil', while for Fogh Rasmussen it is between enlightened secularity and darkened religion. Who is the enemy and who is the friend, they often agreed upon.

It cannot be said that the Danes are without religion, only that it has little direct effect when it comes to major political questions such as war and peace.

---

[2] *Gallup International Millennium Survey*, no. 8/2000, p. 2.

The Danes' religion is 'pliable' and weak, so it does not present any barrier in moral or ethical questions. Their religion has to do with the Danes' personal identity and self-perception. Relationships to 'the others' are decided by and large on a secular basis, as A.F. Rasmussen urged in his wish to remove religion from the public sphere.

The secular, nationalist Danish lack of sensitivity towards other people's points of view reached a climax with Danish reactions to the diplomatic attempt by UN Secretary-General Kofi Annan to excuse the Danish behaviour by citing the nation's short experience of living with Muslim immigrants, paraphrased thus: Mr Annan must have been quoted wrongly or he has misunderstood the whole thing, as of course it is not the Danes who have to get used to living with immigrants, but the immigrants who must get used to living with the Danes (*Kristeligt Dagblad*, 27 February 2006)! It is the repeated claim by the Danish People's Party that most politicians are afraid to confront the issue, that the Muslims must understand 'us' and not the other way around (Rothstein and Rothstein 2006: 170).

A Clash of Mentalities

It is hard to find any 'clash of civilizations' in the Danish background of the Cartoon Crisis. There are different religions, and to some extent diverse cultures, but it is senseless to talk about different civilizations in Denmark since immigrant Danes tend to be more 'Danish' than ethnic Danes. What we find is what Richard J. Bernstein calls different mentalities. The dominant mentality in Denmark tends to think 'that affirming one's certitude and the depth of one's sincere conviction is sufficient to justify the claim of objective certainty' (Bernstein 2005: 14). The Muslim minority mentality insofar as it is strongly dependent on religious authority may have the same tendency.

This clash of mentalities had a clear expression in July 2007 when the leader of the Danish People's Party, Pia Kjærsgaard, won the court case raised against her by some of the Muslim leaders whom she had characterized as traitors against the nation because of those leaders' journey to some Middle East countries during the Cartoon Crisis. At the doorstep, leaving the courtroom, the spokesman of the Islamic Society of Denmark, Mr Kasem Ahmad, announced that the Muslims had to call for a *fatwa* now. Immediately the Danish press was filled with speculations on who was to be killed, knowing about *fatwas* only from the Rushdie case. To the Danish minds it was and still is incomprehensible that an adult man can appeal to religious leaders far away in order to learn how he should react to what he considers as injustice committed firstly against his prophet and then against himself. What we witness here is a clash between a self-dependent secular way of thinking and an authority-dependent religious mentality.

To Richard J. Bernstein, the alternative to the clash of mentalities is a 'pragmatic fallibilism' (2005: 39), meaning that we should abstain from claims of absolute truth in human and political relations. This is obviously difficult for

Muslims seeking religious security in a *fatwa*. It is, however, at least as difficult for a prime minister such as the previous Danish leader, who never admitted to a failure: not only was his handling of the Cartoon Crisis infallible, but so was his involvement in the Iraq war and whatever he accomplished during his term as Prime Minister from November 2001 to April 2009. His sincere experience was that he was always right. Whenever criticized, his answer was, 'There is nothing to come after'; everything is just in order.

Since 1901, the political form of rule in Denmark has been parliamentary government, where no minority, however powerful, can govern without a majority in Parliament. Since 2001, when the right-wing took over power with the support of the Danish People's Party, parliamentary government has allowed room for a modest majority to be able to determine important matters on Denmark's relation to the world (for example, participation in the war in Iraq and a tightening of immigration policy). In a number of other democratic countries there is a broader distribution of power and thus more powerful voices in the public debate than in Denmark. This may take the form of a president with his/her own mandate, a second democratically elected chamber, or courts with a strong legal basis for monitoring observance of the constitution. The Danish form of parliamentary government does not allow room for any of these. Whenever the Prime Minister is supported by a majority in Parliament he is always right, since there are no means to prove otherwise.

The Danes construct 'society' on the basis of their own experiences. There are – apart from the politicians – no powerful norm-setters to influence attitudes. Nor in general are there any strongly idealistic positions and traditions that can trump the individual's experiences. It seems that, for the Danes, as for the Danish philosophical tradition, it is experiences and reflection thereon rather than more principled explanations that stand at the centre. Far from being ethnocentric in a classic racist way (Thomsen 2006: 189–200), the Danes are experience-centred. However, since Denmark is a relatively open society where you can meet people of another culture nearly everywhere and where many have extensive international experiences, the Danes have varying attitudes to immigrants with a mentality different from their own.

As I have argued elsewhere (Iversen 2006), the National Lutheran Church might help the Danes by pointing to the religious experiences and traditions found in Christianity. Tied as it is to the state, and thinking in a manner almost as secular and nationalistic as the majority of Danes, there was, however, no statement from the Danish Church like the following issued by the World Council of Churches in the days of the crisis, February 2006:

> As people of faith we understand the pain caused by the disregard of something considered precious to faith. We deplore the publication of the cartoon. We also join the voices of many Muslim leaders in deploring the violent reaction to the publications. (Quoted in Riis 2007: 448)

Danes in general are not strong 'people of faith'. Even so, it should not be impossible for them to understand people of faith. Mutual understanding is primarily a question of will and education – as often found among Muslims in Denmark. Let me conclude by quoting a young Muslim girl who was interviewed in an investigation of cultural and religious encounters at the two most multiethnic secondary schools in Denmark. Having described her sincere and deeply felt religious commitment to Islam, quite different to the ethnic Islam of her parents, she ended up saying smilingly: 'Of course I am also pretty well able to analyse my religion in a critical way. I have after all been educated in Denmark, haven't I?' (Bektovic 2004: 86, 122) It might be useful if religious and not least secular Danes received the same Danish education as this young Muslim girl.

Was the Cartoon Crisis about religion? No – in Denmark it was about a clash of mentalities, each of course having its own religious dimensions. Religion does have some significance, but it is far from dominant in the Danish background of the Cartoon Crisis. As is more often the case, it is more about something else than about religion.

References

Andersen, Lars Erslev (2008). *Freedom of Speech, Battles over Values, and the Political Symbolism of the Muhammad Drawing*, ser. no. 6, Copenhagen: DIIS-Report.
Bektovic, S. (2004). *Kulturmøder og religion. Identitetsdannelse blandt kristne og muslimske unge*, Copenhagen: Museum Tusculanum Press.
Bernstein, R.J. (2005). *The Abuse of Evil: The Corruption of Politics and Religion since 9/11*, Cambridge: Polity.
Borish, S.M. (1991). *The Land of the Living: The Danish Folk High Schools and Denmark's Non-Violent Path to Modernization*, Nevada City, CA: Blue Dolphin.
Branner, H. (2007). 'Muhammed-krisen og den nye dobbelthed i dansk udenrigspolitik', *Den ny Verden*, 2, pp. 61–73.
Dass, P. (1698). 'Herre Gud! Dit dyre navn og ære', in *Den danske salmebog 2002*, Copenhagen: Det Kgl. Vajsenhus' Forlag, no. 7.
Davie, G. (2002). *Europe: The Exceptional Case: Parameters of Faith in the Modern World*, London: Darton, Longman and Todd.
Gregersen, N.H. (2009). 'On Taboos: The Danish Cartoon Crisis 2005–2008', *Dialog: A Journal of Theology*, 48:1, pp. 79–96.
Grosbøll, T. (2003). *En sten i skoen. Et essay om civilisation og kristendom*, Copenhagen: Anis.
Grundtvig, N.F.S. (1834). 'Nu skal det åbenbares', *Højskolesangbogen* 2006, Copenhagen: Folkehøjskolernes Forening i Danmark, no. 88.

Gundelach, P., and E. Nørregaard-Nielsen (2007). *Etniske gruppers værdier – Baggrundsrapport*, Copenhagen: Ministeriet for Flygtninge, indvandrere og integration.

Gundelach. P., H.R. Iversen and M. Warburg (eds), forthcoming. *At the Heart of Denmark: Institutions and Mentalities*.

Højsgaard, M.T. (2005). 'Gudstro i den danske offentlighed efter Grossbøll', in Højsgaard and H.R. Iversen (eds), *Gudstro i Danmark*, Copenhagen: Anis, pp. 183–203.

Iversen, H.R. (2006). 'Secular Religion and Religious Secularism', *Nordic Journal of Religion and Society* 2:19, pp. 75–92.

Knudsen, A. (1996). *Her går det godt. Send flere penge*, Copenhagen: Gyldendal.

Larsen, C.A., T. Cay, M.B. Klitgaard, M. Tobiasen, J.B. Jensen and J.G. Andersen (2002). *Danskernes forhold til religionen – en afrapportering af ISSP 98*, Aalborg: Institut for Økonomi, Politik og Forvaltning, Aalborg Universitetscenter.

Lægaard, S. (2007). 'The Cartoon Controversy as a Case of Multicultural Recognition', *Contemporary Politics*, 13:2 (June), pp. 147–64.

Mellon, Sir J. (1992). *Og Gamle Danmark. En beskrivelse af Danmark i det herrens år 1992*, Copenhagen: Centrum.

Modood, T. (2006). 'Obstacles to Multicultural Integration', *International Migration*, 44:5, pp. 4–7.

Modood, T. (2007). *Multiculturalism: A Civil Idea*, Cambridge: Polity.

Mogensen, M. (2007). 'The Danish Cartoon Crisis', in Lissi Rasmussen (ed.), *Bridges Instead of Walls*, Minneapolis, MN: Lutheran University Press, pp. 27–46.

Petersen, N. (2006). 'Handlerummet for dansk udenrigspolitik efter Muhammed-krisen', *Den ny Verden*, 2, pp. 31–60.

Reddy, G.P. (1993). *Danes Are Like That! Perspectives of an Indian Anthropologist on the Danish Society*, Mørke: Grevas.

Riis, O. (2008). 'Religious Pluralism in a Local and Global Perspective: Images of the Prophet Mohammed seen in a Danish and a Global Context', in P. Beyer and L. Beaman (eds), *Religion, Globalization, and Culture*, Leiden: Brill, pp. 431–51.

Rose, F. (2005). 'Muhammeds ansigt', *Jyllands-Posten*: *Kulturweekend*, 30 September, p. 3.

Rosenfeldt, M.P. (2006). *Muslimers medierepræsentation. En undersøgelse af grundlaget for at etablere en specialavis for muslimer i Danmark*, Department of Media, Cognition and Communication, University of Copenhagen.

Rothstein, K., and M. Rothstein (2006). *Bomben i turbanen. Profeten, provokationen, protesten, pressen, perspektivet*, Copenhagen: Tidernes Skifter.

Sanders, H. (2006). *Nyfiken på Danmark – klokare på Sverige*, Malmø: Makadam/Centrum for Danmarksstudier.

Sachs, J. (1999). 'Judaism and Politics in the Modern World', in P.L. Berger (ed.), *The Desecularization of the World: Resurgent Religion and World Politics*, Washington DC: Eerdmans, pp. 51–64.

Schwartz, J. (1985). 'Letter to a Danish Historian', *Den Jyske Historiker*, 33, pp. 123–4.

Thomsen, J.P.F. (2006). *Konflikten om de nye danskere*, Copenhagen: Akademisk Forlag.

Warmind, M. (2005). 'Ateisme i Danmark', in M.T. Højsgaard and H.R. Iversen (eds), *Gudstro i Danmark*, Copenhagen: Anis, pp. 279–94.

Østergaard, B. (2007). *Indvandrerne i Danmarks historie – kultur og religionsmøde*, Odense: Syddansk Universitetsforlag.

Chapter 16

The Politics of Lutheran Secularism: Reiterating Secularism in the Wake of the Cartoon Crisis[1]

Anders Berg-Sørensen

Introduction

The publication of twelve cartoons depicting the Prophet Mohammad on 30 September 2005 in *Jyllands-Posten*, a Danish daily newspaper, has given rise to passionate public debate, demonstrations and death threats in Denmark and abroad. In January and February 2006, this unrest spread to most Muslim countries and was reported worldwide: Danish flags and embassies were burned in the Middle East; there were reports of people dying in riots sparked by the cartoons; and Danish goods were boycotted in many countries.[2] In official discourse, the Cartoon Crisis was even labelled the worst crisis in Danish foreign affairs since World War II.

The original publication of the cartoons was accompanied by the following editorial statement: 'Some Muslims reject modern, secular society. They demand a special position, insisting on special consideration for their own religious sentiments. This is incompatible with secular democracy and freedom of expression, where one must be ready to put up with scorn, mockery and ridicule' (Rose 2005, my translation). Immediately after the publication of the cartoons, some people supported the publication of the caricatures, the implied denial of self-censorship, and the defence of the freedom of expression; others rejected the

---

[1] An earlier version of this essay was presented at the Political and Social Philosophy Research Seminar, Department of Philosophy, University of Amsterdam, 15 November 2007. I would like to thank the participants for their comments.

[2] Because an illustrator of a children's book on the life of the Prophet Mohammad wished to be anonymous for fear of reprisals, the editor of the Danish Daily newspaper *Jyllands-Posten* decided to highlight this case of self-censorship and asked the forty members of the Newspaper Cartoonist Association whether they would like to depict the Prophet Mohammad for publication in the newspaper. Twenty-five cartoonists responded: some refused to depict the Prophet Mohammad; others did not have the time; and twelve drew a cartoon for the newspaper. The rest did not answer. The focal point in the entire crisis is one cartoon in particular, in which the Prophet Mohammad is depicted with a bomb in his turban.

move as a childish way of defending such a crucial democratic value, pointing out how publishing the cartoons creates lines of division and opposition in society by offending the Muslim minority. Still others emphasised the implicit Islamophobia, perceiving the publication as symptomatic of the dominant climate of public debate and political attitudes towards immigrants, refugees and others with foreign roots living in Denmark.

The Cartoon Crisis thus illustrates in a nutshell the challenges of religious pluralism for democratic political regimes and communities, and it raises principled questions of the following: equal basic rights and liberties; equal or special treatment of minorities; blasphemy; tolerance; mutual respect and recognition; and social cohesion and harmonious coexistence in the encounter between secular and religious values. In political studies, the Cartoon Crisis has previously constituted an illustrative case for the construction of principled arguments for and against freedom of speech, freedom of religion, blasphemy, tolerance, mutual respect and recognition (Cf., for example, Asad 2008; *International Migration*[3] 2006; Lægaard 2007a and 2007b; Post 2007; Swaine 2006). That which has yet to be theorised in relation to the Cartoon Crisis, however, is a plausible frame for understanding the various forms of power and political processes in the encounter between secular and religious values in the formation and transformation of political orders and identities with reference to such constitutive norms and principles.

On the basis of some of the public debate over the cartoons depicting the Prophet Mohammad in Denmark, the aim of this essay is to elaborate theoretically on what could be referred to as *a politics of secularism*. The claim is, *first*, that when the Cartoon Crisis peaked in February 2006, a politics of *Lutheran* secularism was articulated in order to put religion in its place with reference to the Lutheran tradition of the majority of the Danish population constituting a dominant social imaginary of the proper relationship between religion and politics. *Second*, as an exercise of power, a politics of secularism operates by political-theologising and, thus, it produces the very paradoxes of secularism questioning its political ideals: liberty, equality, neutrality and impartiality.

The Politics of Lutheran Secularism

The point of departure for reconstructing what is termed *the politics of Lutheran secularism* is the stance on religion, politics and the public sphere taken by former Danish Prime Minister Anders Fogh Rasmussen in an interview aired in mid-February by the Danish Broadcasting Corporation, a position he expounded upon in May 2006 in an essay in *Politiken*, a Danish daily newspaper (Rasmussen 2006b). These points of view were reiterated on several occasions since then and,

---

[3] Special issue on 'The Danish Cartoon Affair: Free Speech, Racism, Islamism, and Integration', with contributions by Tariq Modood, Erik Bleich, Joseph H. Carens, Randall Hansen and Randall O'Leary.

thus, they constituted Rasmussen's political doctrine as expressed in his 'actual political thinking' concerning concrete political problems related to religion and politics raised by the Cartoon Crisis (Freeden 2005). The Prime Minister's position could initially be termed liberal secularism, having a difference-blind conception of equal basic rights and liberties in accordance with his liberal background. From this point of view, he emphasised the crucial role of freedom of expression for a democratic society, for example as stated in his New Year's speech of 2006: 'The freedom of expression is absolute. It is not negotiable' (Rasmussen 2006a: 63). Rasmussen generally referred to three principles of equal basic rights and liberties: (1) *the principle of liberty*, *in casu* the individual religious freedom that one must not impose one's own faith on others; (2) *the principle of equality* that every citizen has equal rights and liberties irrespective of religion – according to Rasmussen, that one should identify with these equal citizenship rights in political matters rather than one's religious belonging; and (3) *the principle of neutrality* that the state is neutral in religious matters and does not interfere in them, and conversely, the church refrains from interfering in political matters (Rasmussen 2006b).

These principles are to be understood in relation to the overall aim of Rasmussen's political doctrine. For the purpose of the strong sense of community and social cohesion characterising Danish society according to his conception together with the current challenges of religious fundamentalism in Denmark, he requested that religion not play a role in the public sphere with reference to religion as a private matter. In the essay, he writes: 'In order to guarantee social cohesion in the future, my opinion is that religion has to be less visible in the public sphere ... We have to distinguish between religion and politics. In my opinion, religion, faith, and religious commandments are personal matters' (Rasmussen 2006b, my translation). In other words, social cohesion based on the principles of liberty, equality and neutrality implies that one is able to distinguish between religion and politics. In that sense, Rasmussen's political doctrine was shaped along the lines of doctrines of secularism from the 16th century and onwards claiming religion and politics as separate spheres in order to guarantee social and political order by instituting universal principles of liberty, equality, impartiality and neutrality (Taylor 1998).

According to Rasmussen, however, this religion/politics distinction is made possible by the Lutheran doctrine of two kingdoms and the integration of this confession in the Danish Lutheran Church. Rasmussen continues:

> In my view on religion and society, I am strongly influenced by the renowned quote from Jesus Christ: *Give to the emperor the things that are the emperor's, and to God the things that are God's*. With reference to Luther's doctrine of two kingdoms, it would seem obvious to use this as point of reference for distinguishing between the secular and the religious, between politics and religion. To give God what is God's and the emperor what is the emperor's implies that the state must be kept as the one and only secular authority. (Rasmussen 2006b, my translation)

From the perspective of the former Prime Minister, the liberal principles of difference-blind equal basic rights and liberties are thus made possible by the unique Danish tradition of Lutheranism as institutionalised and interpreted in the Danish Lutheran Church and integrated in the public culture in Denmark. In that sense, his political doctrine differs from the doctrines of secularism from the 16th century and onwards. This emphasises the human ability of secular reasoning as the mode of justifying and authorising the universal principles of liberty, equality, impartiality and neutrality that guarantee a political order independent of religion.

In the process of articulating the politics of Lutheran secularism, one could claim that the former Prime Minister acted as a political–theological authority. He interpreted the Lutheran doctrine of two kingdoms and its effectual history in Danish political culture, and he justified his conception of religion and politics as separate spheres; and, thus, the organisation of a political order in a democratic society by this interpretation. In other words, he established what is conceived as neutral ground for equal basic rights and liberties with a theological reference. In that sense, the former Prime Minister's statements produced a paradox of secularism by installing a distinction between religion and politics itself made possible by his interpretation of the theology of the Danish Lutheran Church. This revitalisation of the theological tradition provided him with authority in regulating matters of religion and politics in the Danish context. Although his interpretation of the Lutheran doctrine of two kingdoms was contested in Danish public discourse, there seems to be widespread agreement both on the particular influence of this doctrine for Danish democratic society and on its ongoing value for regulating religion and politics in the Danish context.

However, this does not solve the paradox of secularism implied by a politics of Lutheran secularism. Rather, it emphasises the very paradox of a politics of secularism as regards the political ideals of secularism: liberty, equality, impartiality and neutrality. Considering the principle of liberty, Rasmussen paid special attention to religious freedom, i.e. that one must not impose one's faith on others. The question is, however, whether the reference to the Lutheran doctrine of two kingdoms and the reiterated institutional and cultural impact of this doctrine on Danish democratic society is not to compare with imposing one specific perspective on the religion/politics relationship on the citizenry in general and *in casu* on the Muslim minorities and their self-understanding as religious citizens. In order to understand themselves as fully integrated citizens in Danish democratic society, they must be able to distinguish between religion and politics in keeping with the Lutheran tradition and, thus, reflect upon their own religious belonging from this point of view. This paradox is reflected in the articulated opposition to religious fundamentalism based on literary interpretations of the religion's Holy Scriptures. This opposition includes the widespread celebration of the Association of Democratic Muslims, established at the beginning of February 2006, in opposition to what is conceived as a fundamentalist interpretation of Islam as represented by a handful of conspicuous imams. This association is celebrated on the grounds that it has successfully adapted to the crucial Western democratic values and unites Islam with democracy in an enlightened and self-critical manner based upon the religion/politics distinction.

This point is also emphasised by Rasmussen's interpretation of the principle of equality that every citizen has equal rights and liberties irrespective of religion, wherefore one ought to identify with one's equal citizenship rights in political matters rather than one's religious belonging. This civic-rather-than-religious identification presupposes one's ability to distinguish between religion and politics as sketched by Rasmussen and his interpretation of the Lutheran doctrine of two kingdoms. The principle of neutrality is therefore also undermined. The state is not neutral in religious matters; rather, the reiteration of the impact of Lutheran theology on political institutions and the culture of Danish democratic society grants priority to one religious tradition on behalf of others. In that sense, the former Prime Minister imposed the values of difference-blind equal basic rights and liberties made possible by the Lutheran tradition of the Danish Church on the Muslim citizens and, thus, his politics of secularism simultaneously includes and excludes the Muslim minority.

This reconstruction of Rasmussen's political doctrine as a politics of Lutheran secularism emphasises the dimensions at play in the exercise of power referred to as a politics of secularism in this essay (Cf., for example, Asad 2003 and 2006; Berg-Sørensen 2007; Hurd 2008). As illustrated by the former Prime Minister's reaction to the Cartoon Crisis, a politics of secularism operates at various dimensions from proclaimed universal principles of liberty, equality and neutrality embedded in particular religious and political institutions and cultures to the creation of 'proper' self-understandings and points of identifications imposed on the citizenry in order for them to become fully integrated citizens within the particular political community. In that sense, secularism is hardly an unambiguous and universal political doctrine claiming religion and politics as separate spheres with reference to principles of liberty, equality and neutrality. Rather, secularism is articulated in ambiguous political strategies for governing the citizenry embedded in particular religious and political institutions and cultures and reiterating the meaning of these particular traditions of political community. Furthermore, secularism operates in its exercise of power by political-theologising. This exists not only in the Danish case of the Cartoon Crisis. The Danish case is no exception. One could also consider the most well-known case of a politics of secularism, the reiteration of the French principle of secularism (*laïcité*) in the so-called headscarf affair (cf., for example, Asad 2006; Balibar 2004; Berg-Sørensen 2006; Bowen 2006; Roy 2007; Scott 2007).

In the French case, the politics of secularism refers to the principle of secularism as a pillar in the constitution of the fifth French Republic associated principles of liberty, equality and neutrality. These proclaimed universal principles are embedded in the particular French tradition of state sovereignty and, thus, institutionalised in public organisations and integrated in public culture. The public school system in particular is referred to as a crucial institutional framework for cultivating autonomous future citizens in accordance with these principles. In other words, the subject-matter in the headscarf affair with reference to the universal principles of secularism was the power of governing the citizenry by cultivating the schoolchildren and their self-understanding and understanding of others as autonomous individuals. This mode of governing implied the ban on the Muslim girls' embodied point of identification and, thus, it imposed a specific social imaginary on Muslim girls of how they must be and understand themselves in order to be fully integrated citizens, i.e. autonomous persons able to make up their minds without influence from religion. The question is, then, in which sense is this an exercise of power operating at various dimensions by political–theologising, as it seemed to be in the Danish case?

In the French case, it has been emphasised that the state operates as a political–theological authority by defining what religion and, thus, a religious symbol is by prohibiting religious symbols in public schools (Asad 2006). Rather than allowing headscarf-wearing girls themselves to define the meaning of their embodied points of identification, the state defines the headscarves as religious per se and therefore prohibited. This act of political–theological authority is even interpreted along the understanding of political theology forwarded by Carl Schmitt and the present reception of his work (Cf., for example, Agamben 2005; Schmitt 2006). This entails an association of political theology with the absolutist conception of sovereignty; the sovereign is the lawgiver not comprised by the law and, as such, the sovereign operates as a political–theological authority whose power of lawgiving transcends the law. This act of the sovereign use of power is characterised as a state of exception that suspends and (re)institutes the law. With reference to this conception of sovereignty, the French ban on religious symbols in public schools is interpreted as an act of the sovereign use of power without ambiguous power positions and resources and without contestation and negotiation in decision-making (Asad 2006). However, this mode of operating as a political–theological authority was contested in the fifteen-year political processes preceding the legislation prohibiting religious symbols in public schools. Even the interpretation of the French principle of secularism was highly contested in the process. Interpreting the political-theologising of a politics of secularism along this tradition of political theology and its implied absolutist conception of sovereignty would therefore appear excessive. As emphasised in the Danish case, political-theologising is a rhetorical figure used as political strategy in a field of contested narratives concerning the proper relationship between religion and politics.

Conclusion

The present essay has taken departure from the 'actual political thinking' constituting a political doctrine labelled a politics of Lutheran secularism articulated in reaction to the Cartoon Crisis, especially when it became a matter of Danish foreign policy. It has focused on the reconstruction of this politics of Lutheran secularism, the various dimensions of the implied exercise of power, and the production of the very paradox of secularism by operations of political-theologising. That which appears crucial in these political processes of articulating political strategies of secularism, however, is that they are also characterised by deliberation, negotiation and contestation between diverse narrative strategies and points of identification, perspectives and reasoning. Within this frame, the relationship between religion and politics is ambiguous and unstable, and subject to continuous democratic negotiations between diverse perspectives and reasoning. This also means that the categories of secular and religious could become mixed up in the processes of governing and authorising the use of power, for example the political-theologising with reference to a specific church tradition (Denmark) or state tradition (France). This emphasises the inherent tensions in democratic societies between the exercises of power in terms of *in casu* a politics of secularism and the religious and metaphysical pluralism constituting the political community in a democracy. A politics of secularism does not necessarily have the last word...

References

Agamben, G. (2005). *State of Exception*, trans. K. Attell, Chicago, IL: University of Chicago Press.
Asad, T. (2003). *Formations of the Secular: Christianity, Islam, Modernity*, Stanford, CA: Stanford University Press.
Asad, T. (2006). 'Trying to Understand French Secularism', in H. de Vries and L.E. Sullivan (eds), *Political Theologies: Public Religions in A Post-Secular World*, New York: Fordham University Press, pp. 494–526.
Asad, T. (2008). 'Reflections on Blasphemy and Secular Criticism', in H. de Vries (ed.), *Religion: Beyond a Concept*, New York: Fordham University Press, pp. 580–609.
Balibar, É. (2004). 'Dissonances within *Laïcité*', *Constellations*, 11:3, pp. 353–67.
Berg-Sørensen, A. (2006). 'Cultural Governance, Democratic Iterations and the Question of Secularism: The French Head Scarf Affair', *Nordic Journal of Religion and Society*, 19:2, pp. 57–74.
Berg-Sørensen, A. (2007). 'Politicising Secularisms', *Journal of International Affairs*, 61:1, pp. 253–6.
Bowen, J.R. (2006). *Why the French Don't Like Headscarves: Islam, the State, and Public Space*, Princeton, NJ: Princeton University Press.
Freeden, M. (2005). 'What Should the "Political" in Political Theory Explore?', *The Journal of Political Philosophy*, 13:2, pp. 113–34.
Hurd, E.S. (2008). *The Politics of Secularism in International Relations*, Princeton, NJ: Princeton University Press.
International Migration (2006) *International Migration*, 44:5.

Lægaard, S. (2007a). 'The Cartoon Controversy: Offence, Identity, Oppression?', *Political Studies*, 55, pp. 481–98.
Lægaard, S. (2007b) 'The Cartoon Controversy as a Case of Multicultural Recognition', *Contemporary Politics*, 13:2, pp. 147–64.
Post, R. (2007). 'Religion and Freedom of Speech: Portraits of Muhammad', *Constellations*, 14:1, pp. 72–90.
Rasmussen, A.F. (2006a). 'Nytårstale', in A. Jerichow and M. Rode (eds), *Profet-affæren. Et PEN-dossier om 12 Muhammed-tegninger – og hvad der siden hændte ... Dokumenter & argumenter*, Copenhagen: Dansk PEN, pp. 63–4.
Rasmussen, A.F. (2006b). 'Hold religionen indendørs', *Politiken*, 20 May [n.p.; one page only]..
Rose, F. (2006 [2005]). 'Muhammeds ansigt', *Morgenavisen Jyllands-Posten*, 30 September, in A. Jerichow and M. Rode (eds), *Profet-affæren. Et PEN-dossier om 12 Muhammed-tegninger – og hvad der siden hændte ... Dokumenter & argumenter*, Copenhagen: Dansk PEN, p. 14.
Roy, O. (2007). *Secularism confronts Islam*, trans. G. Holoch, New York: Columbia University Press.
Schmitt, C. (2006). *Political Theology: Four Chapters on the Concept of Sovereignty*, trans. and intro. G. Schwab, Chicago, IL: University of Chicago Press.
Scott, J.W. (2007). *The Politics of the Veil*, Princeton, NJ: Princeton University Press.
Swaine, L. (2006). 'The Mohammed Caricatures: Liberalism vs. Islam?', at www.opendemocracy.net, accessed 2 March 2006.
Taylor, C. (1998). 'Modes of Secularism', in R. Bhargava (ed.), *Secularism and Its Critics*, Oxford: Oxford University Press, pp. 31–53.

Chapter 17

Globalisation and Religious Diasporas: A Reassessment in the Light of the Cartoon Crisis

Margit Warburg

Globalisation implies, among other things, a liberated and intensified flow of money, goods, people and ideas across borders (Scholte 2000: 41–61). The large-scale, worldwide migration of the late 20th century is one of the salient features of globalisation. In West Europe the waves of immigration after World War II articulated the presence of religious traditions different from Christianity and Judaism. In Great Britain, immigration of Hindus, Sikhs and Muslims from India and Pakistan accelerated as early as the 1950s; in France, the immigration of North African Muslims was particularly significant; in Germany and Denmark, the first Muslim immigrants in the 1960s were guest-workers from Yugoslavia and Turkey, both Turks and Kurds (Coleman 1999; Pedersen 1999).

Many of the immigrants to Europe were drawn selectively from particular regions of their home countries, as exemplified by the nearly two million South Asian immigrants in Britain (Ballard 2003) and by the Anatolian Kurds in Denmark. Their contact with relatives back home was and remains frequent and lively, thanks to the cheap opportunities of rapid international travel and electronic communication, which is another distinct feature of globalisation (Scholte 2000: 99–101). Globalisation has thereby eased the upholding and survival of collective identities among immigrants coming from the same places on earth (Rudolph 1997).

Among scholars in different fields of the humanities and the social sciences the term *diaspora* has become widely used as a common descriptor of the societal position of these immigrant groups. Originally used about the scattered groups of Jews and later Armenians and Greeks around the world, the term was adopted by scholars to characterise nearly all groups who lived in several places outside their home country or another (attributed) place of origin (Anthias 1998; Schnapper 1999; Baumann 2000). It has furthermore been discussed whether the term can be extended to characterise the situation of Muslim immigrants in Europe and the USA in relation not to their home countries but to the imagined commonwealth of the Muslim *umma* (Saint-Blanchat 1995; Sayyid 2000; Samers 2003; Schumann 2007). With globalisation, the idea of a transnational Muslim commonwealth has actually gained more substance among Muslims worldwide (Roy 2004; Schmidt

2005), and a lively debate on the notion of the *umma* in an era of globalisation takes place on the Internet (see for example, Sajjad 2007).

In this contribution I shall use the crisis of the Danish Muhammad cartoons in 2005–2006 to discuss the analytical advantages and disadvantages of characterising Muslims in predominantly non-Muslim countries as a religious diaspora, which in the case of Muslims is used by several authors to mean a diaspora of the *umma*. The cartoon crisis is a useful case since it temporarily united Danish Muslims to a hitherto unseen degree, where they felt challenged as Muslims, first and foremost, rather than as immigrants. I concentrate on Denmark – and Europe – because the crisis was fuelled by secularist majority attitudes characteristic of Europe in particular.

I shall begin by discussing the analytical strength of the concept of diaspora, summarising its main characteristics. I shall also consider the proposition of having *religious* diasporas as a special sub-term. I shall then briefly sum up some of the events in the cartoon crisis that are relevant for a discussion of Danish Muslims' relation to the *umma*. My presentation concludes by disputing whether 'religious diaspora' is the most pointed concept for analysing the position of Muslim immigrants and their descendants. An alternative analytical frame based on established concepts in the sociology of new religions is proposed for understanding some of the Muslim groups and movements of Europe today.

Diaspora as an Analytical Concept

There has been a lively debate about the analytical usefulness of expanding the concept of diaspora to become as inclusive as to encompass, for example, Muslims in the West as a general category, because such inclusiveness implies a risk of blunting its analytical edge (Tölölyan 1996; Anthias 1998; Schnapper 1999; Safran 1999; Baumann 2000; Butler 2001). Critique has also been raised against the later political use of the term among post-modernist, cultural critics (Cohen 1998; Schnapper 1999; Baumann 2000).

As pointed out by, among others, political scientist William Safran, the vast majority of European immigrants to the USA, Canada and Australia do not consider their residence in these countries as living in diaspora, although they are aware of their descent (Safran 1999). However, at one time these immigrant groups might have qualified as diasporas; for example, Nancy Foner has convincingly documented that the Italian immigrants to the United States a hundred years ago behaved in all respects as a diaspora. They had lively contact with their home, and a considerable fraction of them actually moved back to Italy after having earned enough money to buy, for example, a house (Foner 1997). This suggests that being a diaspora may be a transitory situation, and it does necessitate a sharper definition of the concept of the diaspora.

Concluding from a number of articles dealing with definitions of the term (Tölölyan 1996; Safran 1999; Schnapper 1999; Butler 2001), I shall propose that a group must fulfill the following criteria to be characterised as a diaspora:

- It must have undergone a significant geographical dispersion from an original homeland to several destinations around the world. National minorities in border areas are not diasporas; their minority situation stems not from a dispersion but from the drawing of a border between two countries.
- Its members must be settled in the host country for an indeterminate period, living de facto as permanent residents/citizens of the host country, also for generations to come. A temporary exile in fugitive camps is not a diasporic situation.
- Its members must share a self-consciousness of a group identity different from that of the majority population in the host country.
- It must have some active relationship with its actual or imagined homeland; for example, frequent travels to the homeland, regular contacts with relatives in the homeland, regular transfer of money earned abroad to the homeland, and preference for endogamy (marriages with persons of the same national/ethnic group).

With a few notable exceptions, a diaspora is transitory, lasting only a few generations before the group merges with society at large. The exceptions are scattered ethno-religious groups such as the Jews, the Armenians, and perhaps the Sikhs.

For the sociologist of religion it is, of course, also obvious to consider whether the term *religious* diaspora is meaningful as a sub-category of diaspora. Martin Baumann has argued that the term is relevant for Hindu immigrant groups in Great Britain, since the establishment and operation of temples are a main focal point for upholding the social relationships within these groups (Baumann 1995). However, it can be counter-argued that these Hindus nearly all come from India, meaning that there is no clear separation of their religious and ethnic identity.

Muslim immigrant groups in Europe are regularly denoted as a Muslim diaspora (Saint-Blancat 1995; Sayyid 2000; El Hamel 2002; Schwartz 2003; Samers 2003). There is no doubt that, for example, the first wave of largely Muslim immigrant workers from former Yugoslavia and Turkey clearly formed Yugoslavian and Turkish diasporas in West European countries in the 1960s and 1970s (Safran 1999; Schwartz 2003). Also some of the Pakistanis form a diaspora, as expressed for example in the practices of sending children back for 're-education', and in choosing prospective spouses with roots in the local community back home.

However, the fact that immigrant groups from different Muslim countries each may fulfill the criteria of being a diaspora, does not immediately allow us to make the extrapolation and gather them into a communality of a Muslim religious diaspora. 'Muslims' are a diverse category in Europe who on average mainly show some social characteristics, notably by their disproportionally high representation among the lowest-paid and unemployed (Modood 2003). Accounting for religious diversity, it must be noted that immigrants from predominantly Muslim countries do not always themselves accept the tendency to have ascribed upon them an overriding Islamic identity on top of their ethnic identity (Schmidt 2002). Pushed to extremes, it is a question of respecting their atheism. In the Scandinavian countries, less than a quarter and probably far fewer of the immigrants from Muslim countries are practicing Muslims (ibid.). Thus, it is only a minority of these immigrants and their descendants who under normal conditions could be characterised as a religious diaspora, whereby I mean in this case a Muslim diaspora having the Muslim *umma* as its imagined homeland. However, sometimes extraordinary conditions prevail, and this was the case during the Danish Muhammad cartoon crisis of 2005–2006.

The Danish Muhammad Cartoon Crisis

The crisis was ignited when a leading Danish newspaper, *Jyllands-Posten*, decided to invite cartoonists to draw caricatures of Muhammad.[1] The motive for this invitation was to raise a debate about Danish Muslims' tolerance of a possible critique and ridicule of their religion (Rose 2005; Rose 2006). I shall not discuss here whether this was a sensible way of testing the limits to the freedom of expression as claimed by *Jyllands-Posten*, or if it was part of a current of anti-Muslim attitudes in Denmark – this discussion has been carried through both in Denmark and internationally (Modood et al. 2006; Lægaard 2007). Twelve satirical drawings were published in *Jyllands-Posten* on 30 September 2005, immediately causing some stir among Danish Muslims. Representatives of Danish Muslim organisations met on 9 October 2005 and issued a press release, signed by seventeen Muslim organisations in Denmark, in which they condemned the provocative act by *Jyllands-Posten* (Jerichow and Rode 2006: 21–2).

The crisis soon took an international turn. On 12 October 2005 eleven ambassadors from Muslim countries, headed by the Egyptian ambassador, wrote a joint letter to the Danish Prime Minister, in which they denounced both the publication of the cartoons and some earlier incidences that they conceived also to be discriminatory towards the Muslim minority in Denmark. The ambassadors asked for a meeting; however, the Prime Minister declined their request, arguing that the freedom of the press was not to be negotiated.[2]

After this, the situation rapidly got out of control: several Muslim countries recalled their ambassadors; a consumers' boycott of Danish dairy products was orchestrated in a number of countries, primarily in Saudi Arabia; and there were

---

[1] Ole Riis has written a thorough exposition of the affair for an international audience; see Riis 2007.

[2] See http://www.danmarkshistorien.dk/pdf/leksikon-og-kilder/vis/materiale/brev-fra-11-ambassadoerer-til-statsminister-anders-fogh-rasmussen-samt-anders-fogh-rasmussens-svar/, accessed 18 February 2010.

violent demonstrations against Denmark in many Muslim countries, with burnings of the Danish flag. In a few cases also Danish embassies were attacked and burned. This escalation of the crisis and the patterns of its course are characteristic of globalisation (Warburg 2006a, 2007). For example, the demonstrations and disturbances abroad did not spread from country to country over a certain period – they erupted simultaneously in several places that were geographically unrelated, demonstrating in the course of the crisis two salient traits of globalisation: simultaneity and deterritorialisation (Kanter 1995; Scholte 2000).

The Akkari–Laban Dossier

While the crisis developed, a group of Danish Muslim religious leaders assembled a dossier with documentary material, mainly dealing with the cartoon crisis.[3] A leading figure among these men was the now-deceased Abu Laban, a charismatic and controversial imam at a congregation called Islamic Society in Copenhagen. This is one of the major Muslim congregations in Copenhagen, and it attracts Muslims of different ethnic backgrounds, many second-generation immigrants, and also quite a few ethnic Danish converts (Kühle 2006: 115–28). Abu Laban authored the dossier together with Ahmad Akkari, who was the spokesman of the Islamic Society in 2005.

In early December a group of Danish imams[4] – all belonging to the same activist circles as Abu Laban – travelled to Egypt to present this material and discuss it with leading religious leaders and with government officials.[5] The Egyptian ambassador to Denmark, Her Excellency Mona Omar, played an active role in arranging the visits. The dossier was handed over by the Egyptian foreign minister to delegates of the Organisation of Islamic Countries (OIC). It was discussed at a summit on 6 December 2006, and the publication of the cartoons was denounced in the communiqué from the meeting (Jerichow and Rode 2006:

---

[3] The dossier was translated into Danish and published by the newspaper *Politiken* on 22 August 2006. The translation is rendered in Jerichow and Rode 2006: 43–8.

[4] The Danish party was generally denoted 'the imams', although not all of them regularly served as such.

[5] In addition to Ahmad Akkari the party included Raed Hlayel, an orthodox imam from a mosque outside Århus, where Akkari occasionally also functioned as imam (Kühle 2006: 118–20). Another outstanding member was Abu Bashar, who was connected to a mosque in Odense, where one of the imams is a pupil of Abu Laban (Dørge 2006). Abu Laban himself did not go to Egypt. He had close associations internationally with the Muslim Brotherhood and was *persona non grata* in Egypt and in the United Arab Emirates because of allegations of Islamist activities (*DR Nyheder*, 1 February 2006). In an interview to IslamOnline of 18 November 2005, Abu Laban expounded on his role in arranging the travels and he specifically mentions that the party wished to meet with Sheikh Yussef Al-Qaradawi, a leading figure in the Muslim Brotherhood (Qenawi 2005).

51–2). The travel to Egypt was followed up later in December by other travels to the Middle East, where the Danish imams met with a number of high-ranking religious leaders.

The Dossier and the Notion of *Umma*

Among other documents the dossier contained a copy of a letter dated 5 October 2005 and addressed to the ambassadors of eleven Muslim countries in Denmark.[6] The letter urged the diplomatic missions of Muslim states in Denmark to transmit the news about the cartoons, and concluded that 'an official protest is needed sooner before later'. The eleven countries represent the major part of the Muslim world, from Morocco in the west over Bosnia and Turkey to Egypt, Saudi Arabia, Iran, Pakistan and Indonesia. The nationalities of the spokesmen for the Danish Muslim organisations were not an issue here – it was clearly not an address to the respective 'home' countries of the different Muslim organisations giving support to the letter, but a joint address to governments in power in the *umma*.

United in Islam?

There is no doubt that Danish Muslims in general felt the cartoons to be intimidating. According to a survey conducted in early 2006, 81 per cent of Danish Muslims felt offended by the publication of the cartoons, and 53 per cent declared that they felt they were Muslims first and Danes next (Bræmer 2006a). Interviews and diary notes by Danish Muslims also show that the crisis led people to reconsider their identity. For example, a young woman reflected over the remarkable development that in three months her identity changed: rather than remaining no more than just 28 years old, a woman, a student in sociology, and so on, she was now 'MUSLIM, 28 years, woman, student in sociology…' (Hassan 2006: 27). If the feeling of being a religious diaspora of the *umma* would ever be relevant for Danish Muslims, this would have been the period.

Danish Muslim immigrants and descendants generally fulfill my first two criteria of being in a diasporic situation:

- They have undergone a significant geographical dispersion from their original homelands to several destinations around the world.
- They have settled in the host country (in this case, Denmark) for an indeterminate period, also for generations to come.

---

[6] The letter was sent to the Embassy of Saudi Arabia in Hellerup, Copenhagen.

During the crisis, the Danish Muslims – or at least a significant part of them – seemed temporarily to qualify as members of a religious diaspora, because they shared:

- a self-consciousness of a group identity different from that of the majority population in the host country – in this case as Muslims in an otherwise non-Muslim population.

The letter from the Danish Muslim organisations to the eleven ambassadors and the Danish imams' subsequent private diplomatic activities in the Middle East were certainly expressions of an:

- active relationship with an imagined homeland, in this case the *umma*.

The travel destinations were varied – Egypt, Lebanon, Qatar – and the journeys were meant to arouse the Muslim world:

> The [Danish Muslim] organisations have on the background of [the Danish Prime Minister's refusal to meet with the ambassadors] issued a second announcement, in which they demand the Muslim world to interfere in the case which has acquired an international character. Since the issue of the prophet – "peace be upon him" – not only concerns the Muslims of Denmark but all Muslims of the world, we cannot accept that our prophet is demeaned for whatever reason or headline.[7]

New Divides among Danish Muslims

The voyage of the party of Danish imams to Egypt received considerable and largely negative publicity, where in most cases the imams were assumed to articulate the opinions of Danish Muslims in general. However, according to Danish sociologist of religion Lene Kühle, the group of imams that took the initiative to appeal to the Muslim countries has its basis in a predominantly Arab, activist circle of mosques, organisations and individuals (Kühle 2006: 118–20). Its members have ties to primarily Arab globalised Islamic movements grown out of the environment of the Muslim Brotherhood, and they are not representative of Danish Muslims in general. A survey showed that during the crisis few – less than 7 per cent – of the Danish Muslims identified themselves with Abu Laban and associates or regarded these people as leaders or role models (Bræmer 2006b). For example, among Bosnian and Turkish/Kurdish immigrants there was little backing of the travelling imams during the crisis (Kühle 2006: 132–5).

---

[7] Translated from the Danish rendering of the Akkari–Laban dossier in Jerichow and Rode 2006: 43–6.

A couple of months after the imams' travel to Egypt, in the winter of 2006, a Danish Member of Parliament, Mr Naser Khader of Syrian background, and others formed an organisation called Democratic Muslims. Its programme is based on the separation of state and religion, and it opposes the bestowing upon sharia of any judicial status.[8] The timing was perfect, at the summit of the crisis.

The formation of this organisation, which has been regarded as controversial by some Danish Muslims, indicated that among Danish Muslims there has emerged a number of divides that do not correspond with ethnic background. Democratic Muslims is not the only such organisation; Forum for Critical Muslims is an intellectual example and part of the currents of Euro-Islam. Among other things, these groups stand for a reinterpretation of the Islamic idea about the two houses (the 'house of peace' and the 'house of war') merging into one 'house of faith', and they state that thereby they directly confront some of the radical Islamist movements.[9]

The formation of these new organisations runs parallel to the development in, for example, the United States, as discussed by Islamologist Christoph Schumann in 2007. In the 1970s, the discussions among Muslim students in the USA were often centered around their perceived situation as being in *kafir* (heathen) society, thus stressing the conventional Islamic distinction between the 'abode of Islam' and the 'abode of disbelief' (Schumann 2007). However, during the following decades with the increasing involvement of American Muslims in political life this distinction came to lose its significance. Intellectual Muslims subsequently expressed the view that they have the 'dual role' of striving for the well-being of the *umma*, as well as of the American nation (ibid.: 27). Schumann concludes that the 'political participation of Muslims in the United States can be described as a triangle between their community and its two homelands: the United States and the *ummah*' (ibid.: 27). It is clear from this quotation that Schumann regards these American Muslims as existing in a diasporic situation vis-à-vis the *umma*; in other words, that they constitute a religious diaspora.

Diaspora and *Umma* – an Ambiguous, Ascribed Connection

Sociologist Salman Sayyid has also discussed whether the Muslim *umma* could be called a diaspora in the West, and he interprets the concept of diaspora as a state of alienation: 'The logic of diaspora includes those who are articulated as homeless in this world. That is, for whom the global hegemonic order is not an echo of their subjectivity' (Sayyid 2000: 46). Thus, he links the diasporic situation of, in this

---

[8] See the home page of the organisation, www.demokratiskemuslimer.dk, accessed 18 February 2010.

[9] See the home page of the organisation, www.kritiskemuslimer.dk, accessed 18 February 2010.

case, Muslims to their alienation in Western societies that represent the global hegemonic order.

There is, of course, some variance among authors in the use of religious diaspora as an overarching description of the situation of Muslims in the West. By confining the term to Muslims supposed to be alienated by living in predominantly non-Muslim countries, as Sayyid does, large groups are left out. What about well-integrated, religious Muslims – if they do not feel alienated, are they then not included in the diaspora of the *umma*? It seems problematic if the label of diaspora is reserved only for those Muslims who cannot identify themselves with the country they live in; this risks arbitrary classifications with little analytical power.

I tend to lean towards a conclusion that the very concept of a religious diaspora is not particularly fruitful in a sociological analysis of different Muslim groups and movements in Western societies. It is generally observed that adherents of a particular religious tradition may feel some kind of solidarity and connectedness with their co-believers around the world. This is particularly pronounced for those who belong to transnational religious minorities, because being in a minority situation generally challenges a person's identity more than belonging to the majority, where identity is almost taken for granted. Among religious minorities some may rightfully be characterised as belonging to an ethno-religious diaspora, as for example the many Iranian Baha'is who fled from Iran after the revolution of 1979 (McAuliffe 2007). But the fact that Iranian expatriate Baha'is might be called a diaspora does not transform the more than 90 per cent non-Iranian Baha'is worldwide into a religious diaspora (Warburg 2006b: 12, 222–7).

Likewise, many Muslims of Europe constitute national diasporas, but there is no particular reason for regarding all European Muslims as a special case among the adherents of minority religions of Europe. By denoting them a religious diaspora, adherents of Islam are regarded as a special case compared with the adherents of all other minority religions of Europe. In the optics of the sociology of religion and comparative religions, this implicit postulate of the uniqueness of the position of Muslims in Europe is not convincing.

In his study of Turkish-Cypriotic immigrants to England, Talip Küçükcan concludes that adopting the view that European Muslims share an identity of being in a diaspora of the *umma* implies a risk of essentialising Muslim identity (Küçükcan 2004). In fact, I see this as one of the most problematic aspects of the concept of a religious diaspora, because it invariably puts the religious factor before all other factors contributing to a person's identity. In general, concepts should not essentialise the group under study (Schnapper 1999).

Mainstream Islam and New Islamic Movements – A Proposal for an Analytical Frame

Instead of operating with the problematic concept of religious diaspora for characterising Muslims of Europe (and of the West in general), I propose first to turn to historian of religion Bruce Lincoln's ideal-type dichotomy of religiously maximalist and religiously minimalist cultures (Lincoln 2006: 58–61). For the maximalists, religion is the central domain of culture, and religion is deeply involved in the ethical and aesthetic practices of the community. For the minimalists, it is rather economy and other secular matters that occupy the central domain of culture, and religion is restricted to the private sphere and to metaphysical concerns (ibid.: 59). The majority of Muslims in Denmark are to be placed more to the minimalist than to the maximalist side, which parallels the beliefs and behavior of Danes belonging to the national Lutheran Church or to the major Jewish congregation. The organisation Democratic Muslims is the most overt representative of the minimalist position.

Concentrating on those groups of rather few Muslims who are closer to the maximalist end, I shall then propose that such Muslim groups and movements in Europe should be analysed as any other new religious group or movement that has not been present in Europe for more than a couple of generations. Here, sociologist of religion Roy Wallis' 1984 typology of new religious movements is relevant. He distinguished between 'world-rejecting', 'world-affirming' and 'world-accommodating' movements in his study of new religious movements in the West in the 1960s and 1970s (Wallis 1984: 9–39).

Bruce Lincoln's dichotomy of maximalists and minimalists can be regarded as the first level in an analytical frame for characterising Muslim minorities in Europe. The second level concentrates on the maximalist end, and here Roy Wallis' three ideal types of new religious movements enable us to distinguish between very different relations with the non-Muslim majority society. The illustration below sketches this two-level analytical frame, which is proposed here for the first time.

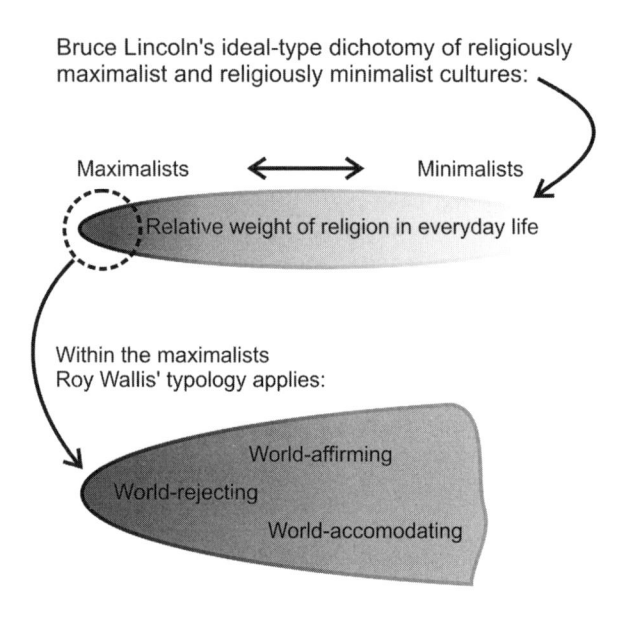

Bruce Lincoln's ideal-type dichotomy of religiously maximalist and religiously minimalist cultures:

Maximalists ⟷ Minimalists

Relative weight of religion in everyday life

Within the maximalists Roy Wallis' typology applies:

World-affirming
World-rejecting
World-accomodating

Characterising Muslim Minorities: A New Analytical Frame

According to Wallis, a *world-rejecting* new religion views the prevailing social order negatively, distinguishes sharply between insiders and outsiders, and has strong millenarian expectations. This type of movement opposes a distinction between secular and religious life; it seeks a spiritual transformation of society and offers the adherents a total institution regulating all of their daily activities. This description fits well with *Hizb ut-Tahrir*, for example. Among less radical circles in Denmark, the description also fits with the currents of activities associated with the mosques hosting the travelling imams and others who have connections to the Muslim Brotherhood. To the public this minority of Muslims is perceived as the most 'political' of the Muslim groups, receiving considerable publicity with its often provocative statements. For example, the spokesman (until 2008) of Islamic Society in Copenhagen, Kasem Ahmed, declared himself a supporter of Hamas and stated in an interview that all Jewish immigrants in Israel since 1948 should be expelled, in order to provide room for Palestinian fugitives.[10] There is little understanding among Danes of such views of ethnic cleansing.

The *world-affirming* new religion largely views the prevailing social order positively, and it disallows the dualism of the world-rejecting movement. It interacts with society and may have political reform goals, but seeks to realise them through the spiritual transformation of individuals. The representatives of Euroislam, such as Forum for Critical Muslims, are nearly all ideal-type world-affirming movements.

Both the world-rejecting and the world-affirming new religions see religion as having an important position in social matters. In contrast, the *world-accommodating* new religion draws a distinction between the spiritual and the worldly, and religion is taken to be concerned mostly with personal, spiritual development. Religion may be an asset in secular affairs, but this is not the justification of the religious practices. Neo-pentecostalism is a Christian representative of this; among Muslims it could be some of the Sufi-inspired groups. A well-known representative – although far from an ideal type – would be the native Danish imam and Sufi Abdul Wahid Pedersen, who converted to Islam in 1982 after first having been a Hindu for four years.

Conclusion

The perception of a Muslim religious diaspora in Denmark, whereby is understood that their diasporic position refers to an Islamic imagined commonwealth, the *umma*, seemed briefly to characterise the situation during the Muhammad cartoon crisis. In his analysis of the crisis, Ole Riis concludes that this brief

---

[10] 'Muslimsk talsmand', interview with Pernille Amnitzbøll, *Jyllands-Posten*, 1 September 2007.

skirmish accentuated a confrontation in Denmark between different attitudes towards the consequences of globalisation, including the space that should be permitted religion in an increasingly multi-religious society (Riis 2007). Among Muslims in Denmark in the wake of the cartoon crisis, movements arose to take a sharper public stance in this issue. This was expressed, among other things, through the formation of Democratic Muslims who clearly see themselves as a needed corrective particularly to the maximalist, world-rejecting groups, who are trying to advance the domain of religion further into secular society (Warburg 2007). Even if the conflict between minimalists and maximalists among Muslims may be important for the future position of Islam in Denmark and Europe, it is of more concern to watch the contest between world-rejecting and world-affirming currents among the maximalists. The outcome of this contest will be decisive for the accommodation of maximalist Muslims into societies, which heralds the secular foundation of the state after centuries of bloody experiences with political religion.

References

Anthias, F. (1998). 'Evaluating "Diaspora": Beyond Ethnicity?', *Sociology*, 32, pp. 557–80.
Ballard, R. (2003). 'The South Asian Presence in Britain and its Transnational Connections', in B. Parekh, G. Singh and S. Vertovec (eds), *Culture and Economy in the Indian Diaspora*, London: Routledge, pp. 197–222.
Baumann, M. (1995). 'Conceptualizing Diaspora. The Preservation of Religious Identity in Foreign Parts, Exemplified by Hindu Communities Outside India', *Temenos*, 31, pp. 19–35.
Baumann, M. (2000). 'Diaspora: Genealogies or Semantics and Transcultural Comparison', *Numen*, 47, pp. 313–37.
Bræmer, M. (2006a). 'Hver tiende muslim accepterer flagafbrænding', *Ugebrevet A4*, 10 (13 March).
Bræmer, M. (2006b). 'Toneangivende muslimer har kun få med sig', *Ugebrevet A4*, 11 (20 March).
Butler, K.D. (2001). 'Defining Diaspora, Refining a Discourse', *Diaspora*, 10, pp. 189–219.
Cohen, P. (1998). 'Welcome to the Diaspora: A Cure for the Millennium Blues?', *New Ethnicities*, 3, pp. 3–10.
Coleman, D. (1999). 'Internationale vandringer set i sammenhæng med den globale demografiske udvikling', in Coleman and E. Wadensjö (eds), *Indvandringen til Danmark. Internationale og nationale perspektiver*, Copenhagen: Spektrum. pp. 15–67.
Dørge, H. (2006). 'Min moske', *Weekendavisen*, 10 February, p. 1.

El Hamel, C. (2002). 'Muslim Diaspora in Western Europe: The Islamic Headscarf (*Hijab*), the Media and Muslims' Integration in France', *Citizenship Studies*, 6, pp. 293–308.

Foner, N. (1997). 'What's New about Transnationalism? New York Immigrants Today and at the Turn of the Century', *Diaspora*, 6, pp. 355–75.

Hassan, A.N. (2006). 'Dagbog', in L.F. Kaarsholm (ed.), *Muslimsk-Dansk dagbog. 19 dagbøger fra Muhammed-krisen*, Copenhagen: Information, pp. 27–33.

Jerichow, A., and M. Rode (2006). *Profet-affæren. Et PEN-dossier om 12 Muhammed-tegninger – og hvad siden hændte... Dokumenter & argumenter*, n.p.: Dansk PEN.

Kanter, R.M. (1995). *World Class: Thriving Locally in the Global Economy*, New York: Simon and Schuster.

Küçükcan, T. (2004). 'The Making of Turkish–Muslim Diaspora in Britain: Religious Collective Identity in a Multicultural Public Sphere', *Journal of Muslim Minority Affairs*, 24, pp. 243–58.

Kühle, L. (2006). *Moskeer i Danmark – islam og muslimske bedesteder*, Højbjerg: Univers.

Lincoln, B. (2006). *Holy Terrors: Thinking about Religion after September 11*, Chicago, IL: University of Chicago Press.

Lægaard, S. (2007). 'The Cartoon Controversy: Offence, Identity, Oppression?', *Political Studies*, 55:3, pp. 481–98.

McAuliffe, C. (2007). 'A Home Far Away? Religious Identity and Trans*national* Relations in the Iranian Diaspora', *Global Networks*, 7, pp. 307–27.

Modood, T. (2003). 'Muslims and the Politics of Difference', *The Political Quarterly*, 74, issue s1, pp. 100–115.

Modood, T., R. Hansen, E. Bleich, B. O'Leary, and J.H. Carens (2006). 'The Danish Cartoon Affair: Free Speech, Racism, Islamism, and Integration", *International Migration*, 44, pp. 3–62.

Pedersen, S. (1999). 'Vandringen til og fra Danmark i perioden 1960–1997', in D. Coleman and E. Wadensjö (eds), *Indvandringen til Danmark. Internationale og nationale perspektiver*, Copenhagen: Spektrum, pp. 233–84.

Qenawi, A. (2005). 'Danish Muslims "Internationalize" Anti-Prophet Cartoons', *IslamOnline.net*, 18 November; accessed 2 September 2007.

Riis, O. (2007). 'Religious Pluralism in a Local and Global Perspective: Images of the Prophet Mohammed seen in a Danish and a Global Context', in P. Beyer and L. Beaman (eds), *Religion and Globalisation*, Leiden: E.J. Brill, pp. 433–53.

Rose, F. (2005). 'Muhammeds ansigt', editorial in *Jyllands-Posten*, 30 September.

Rose, F. (2006). 'Why I published Those Cartoons', *Washington Post*, 19 February.

Roy, Olivier (2004). *Globalised Islam: The Search for a New Ummah*, London: Hurst.

Rudolph, S.H. (1997). 'Introduction: Religion, States, and Transnational Civil Society', in S.H. Rudolph and J. Piscatori (eds), *Transnational Religion and Fading States*, Boulder, CO: Westview Press, pp. 1–24.

Safran, W. (1999). 'Comparing Diasporas: A Review Essay', *Diaspora*, 8, pp. 255–91.

Saint-Blancat, C. (1995). 'Une Diaspora Musulmane en Europe', *Archives de Sciences Sociales des Religion*, 92, pp. 9–24.

Samers, M.E. (2003). 'Diaspora Unbound: Muslim Identity and the Erratic Regulation of Islam in France', *International Journal of Population Geography*, 9, pp. 351–364.

Sajjad, M. (2007). 'Ideal Culture', at http://www.oneummah.net/content/view/65/1/, accessed 18 February 2010.

Sayyid, S. (2000). 'Beyond Westphalia: Nations and Diasporas – the Case of the Muslim *Umma*', in B. Hesse (ed.), *Un/Settled Multiculturalisms: Diasporas, Entanglements, 'Transruptions'*, London: Zed Books, pp. 33–50.

Schmidt, G. (2002). 'Dialectics of Authenticity: Examples of Ethnification of Islam among Young Muslims in Sweden and the United States', *The Muslim World*, 92, pp. 1–17.

Schmidt, G. (2005). 'The Transnational *Umma* – Myth or Reality? Examples from the Western Diasporas', *The Muslim World*, 95, pp. 575–86.

Schnapper, D. (1999). 'From the Nation-State to the Transnational World: On the Meaning and Usefulness of Diaspora as a Concept', *Diaspora*, 8, pp. 225–54.

Scholte, J.A. (2000). *Globalization: A Critical Introduction*, Houndmills: Macmillan Press.

Schumann, C. (2007). 'A Muslim 'Diaspora' in the United States?', *The Muslim World*, 97, pp. 11–32.

Schwartz, J. (2003). 'Eksil, eksodus eller diaspora? *Prespa* i København som eksempel', in L.P. Galal and I. Liengaard (eds), *At være muslim i Danmark*, Copenhagen: Anis, pp. 33–47.

Sheffer, G. (1995). 'The Emergence of New Ethno-National Diasporas', *Migration*, 28, pp. 5–28.

Tölölyan, K. (1996). 'Rethinking *Diaspora*(s): Stateless Power in the Transnational Moment', *Diaspora*, 5, pp. 3–36.

Wallis, R. (1984). *The Elementary Forms of the New Religious Life*, London: Routledge and Kegan Paul.

Warburg, M. (2006a). 'Religion på globaliseringens betingelser', in L. Christoffersen (ed.), *Gudebilleder. Ytringsfrihed og religion i en globaliseret verden*, Copenhagen: Tiderne Skifter, pp. 102–14.

Warburg, M. (2006b). *Citizens of the World: A History and Sociology of the Baha'is from a Globalisation Perspective.*, Leiden: E.J. Brill.

Warburg, M. (2007). 'Globalisation, Migration and the Two Types of Religious Boundaries: A European Perspective', in P. Beyer and L. Beaman (eds), *Religion and Globalisation*, Leiden: E.J. Brill, pp. 79–99.

Index

Africa, growth of Pentecostalism 32, 52, 58
Agamben, Giorgio 53, 62
Akkari-Laban dossier (Cartoon Crisis) 219–20
al-Qaeda 44, 57
Ali, Shaheen Sardar vii, 119–39, 141–2, 156–8
Anglicanism 32, 153, 187–8
anti-intellectualism 52, 56–9
apologetics 104–9
Apostle Paul 62
atheism 51, 79, 86–7
atheists 47
    'belligerent' 62–3
    in Denmark 26
    increase in activity 145
    with interest in religion 53
Atkins, Peter 86–7
authority
    political-theological 212
    in religion and science 103–8
    religious 165, 179, 201

Badiou, Alain 53, 62
Baubérot, Jean 167–8, 173
belief, religious 76–8
    'believing without belonging' 20, 25
    and Enlightenment 70–71
    and foundationalism 75
    individualization and privatization 166–7
    nature of 105–6
    in religion–science debate 88–99
Benedict XVI, Pope *see* Ratzinger, Joseph
Benjamin, Walter 60–61
Berg-Sørensen, Anders vii, 207–13
Berger, Peter L 52–3, 164–5
Bernstein, Richard J 191–2, 201–2
Beyer, Peter vii, 37–50, 67, 74, 76–7
Bloch, Ernst 61

Brazil 31–2
Brecht, Bertold 99–100
Britain 32, 183–9
Bruno, Giordano 114
Bush, George W. 38–9, 51, 56, 67, 200
    Bush Administration 20, 58, 68

capitalism
    American 43
    Muslim attitude towards 58
Carter, Jimmy 39, 67
Cartoon Crisis 191, 207–9
    clash of mentalities 201–3
    in relation to globalisation and Muslim religious diasporas 216, 218–20, 225–6
    in relation to secularism 211
Casanova, José vii, 19–36, 76–7, 79–80, 163–4, 170
Catholicism
    and confessionalization 25
    and democracy 24
    global movements 31–2, 52, 187
    role in law and politics 146, 150–51, 155, 171
Christian Democracy 24
Christian 'fundamentalism' 38–9, 42
Christian Right 38, 42–4, 45, 58
    New Christian Right (NCR) 68
Christianity
    Anglican 32
    in Denmark 78, 85, 196–8
    Eastern 32
    global expansion 52
    as inspiration 62
    Pentecostal 32, 52, 58
    Protestant 31
    in Western Europe 30–31, 53
Church–State relations
    in Europe 23, 151–6

Islam's role 156–8
  in Nordic countries 143–4
  TAO measure 23n
Clayton, Philip vii–viii, 85–101, 103, 106, 111
confessionalization 25–8, 77
conflicts
  of early European era 21, 25
  of 'European short century' (1914–1989) 28
  religion as creator of 27–8
  in Scandinavian countries 144–5
  terrorist attacks 20, 135
  Two Frances Conflict 167–8
  see also Cartoon Crisis
cosmopolitanism 33–5
creationism 86
  see also Intelligent Design

Darwin, Charles 58, 75–6, 78–9, 107–8, 112–13
Davie, Grace viii, 67–72, 73, 165
Dawkins, Richard 47, 51, 62–3, 75–6, 87
de-privatization of religion 47, 76, 164, 170–72
  as challenge to secularism 19–24
  meaning of 177–80
  see also privatization of religion
de-secularization 40–42, 45, 47–9
democracy
  Catholic 24
  challenge to 56
  Christian Democracy 24
  Danish 185–6, 199–200, 209–10
    Democratic Muslims 210–11, 222–6
  Democracy and Tradition 108
  and folk churches 144
  French 167, 173
  in relation to European secularism 21–8
  religion in a democratic society 163–4, 172–3, 179–80
  twin tolerations model 23
Denmark
  Christianity 78, 196–8
  comparison with Britain
    geopolitical 183–5

music 189
religion 186–8
society 185–6
Danish Muslims 192–4, 201–3, 216, 218
  division between 221–2
  effect of cartoons on 220–21
democracy 185–6, 199–200, 209–10
  Democratic Muslims 210–11, 222–6
experiential centrism 199–201
intertwinement of religious and secular elements 78–9
Lutheran secularism politics 208–13
Lutheranism 78, 85, 143–4, 188, 196–8
mentalities of ethnic and immigrant Danes 192–6, 201–3
religious belief 26, 196–8
religious homogeneity 184–5, 187
religious legacy 85
and science 78–9, 85
see also Cartoon Crisis; Rasmussen, Anders Fogh
denominationalism, global 29–35
de-privatization of religion 19–21, 76–77, 179–80
  see also privatization of religion
Derrida, Jacques 61
diaspora and religious diaspora
  analysis of concepts 215–18
  as applied to Muslim immigrant groups 217–18
  Danish Muslims 220–22
  diffusion 32–3, 35
  in relation to Islamic legal tradition 128–30
  and ummah 222–3
Diderot, Dénis 63–4, 111
disenchantment 52–6
disestablishment 22, 153
dissociation 29–30
Drees, Willem B viii, 103–10

Edman, Stefan 64
Eisenstadt, Shmuel 69–70
emergence theories 113
enchantment 52–6, 63–4
Enlightenment
  critique of religion 25, 34

as freedom from belief 70–1
project 55
Entzauberung 52–3, 54
Europe 149
   Church–State relations 23, 151–6
      Islam's role 156–8
   confessional territorialization 25–8
   de-Christianization 53
   and governmentality 76–8
   impact of globalization 29–31
   individualization and privatization of religious beliefs 165–6, 171
   law 149–58, 171
   Muslim immigrants 26–7, 149, 215–18, 220–5
   religious pluralism 149–50
   republicisation of religion 170–4
   secularism 21–8, 41, 70, 165, 198
   Western
      Christianity 30–31, 53
      de-privatization of religion 19–21
      democratization 24
      secularism 21–8, 165
      views on religion 27–8
      views on religious mobilization 24
Evangelical Lutheran Church 78, 85, 143–4
Evangelical organizations 68
evolution 58, 78–9, 104, 107–8, 111–13

family values 42–3, 75
fatwa 132–5, 201–2
Ferrari, Silvio viii, 149–59
Finland 22, 143, 153
Foucault, Michel 77
foundationalism 75–6
France
   Church–State relations 151, 154
   laïcité 22, 46–7, 167–9
   'Muslim headscarf affair' 168–70, 211–12
   young Muslims in 166–70
free enterprise 43
freedom of expression 207, 209
freedom of religion 22–3, 30, 70–1, 77–8, 153n5
freedom of speech 68, 200
fundamentalism
   American 43–4, 58
   challenge of 39–41, 49
   Christian 38–9, 42
   Dawkins' view on 87
   and foundationalism 75–6
   Hindu 45–6
   Islamic 41–2
   meaning and use of term 40n, 67–8, 73–4
   and violence 44–5

Galileo 99–100, 107
Geertz, Clifford 92, 106
Gilkyson, Eliza 37–8
Glenn, H Patrick 141
globalization, impact of 29–35
God Delusion, The 51, 75–6, 87
governmentality 76–8
Great Britain 32, 183–9
Greece 22, 152–3, 184–5
Gregersen, Niels Henrik viii, 73–81

Habermas, Jürgen 53, 57, 63, 64, 71, 90
   on reason 60–1,
'headscarf affair' 168–70, 211–12
Herrmann, Robert A 86
Hervieu-Léger, Danièle 20, 25, 165
Hindu nationalist movement 45–6
Hoffmeyer, Jesper viii, 111–14
Huntington, Samuel 26, 29, 33

Iceland 22, 143, 153
immigrants
   Danish 192–4, 201–3
   as diaspora 217–18, 220–2
   integration in Europe 26–7, 149, 215–16
individualisation of religion 165–6
individualism 149–50, 156, 178–9
intellectual challenges
   atheism, belief and wonder 62–5
   capacity and limits of reason 59–62
   from religion 51–6
   to religion 56–9
Intelligent Design 58, 112n
Internet 52, 57, 134
'intertwinement' of religious and secular elements 78–9

Iran 39, 40–1, 48, 223
Ireland 184–5
Islam 27, 32–3, 51–3, 57, 59
   in Denmark 201–3, 207–8, 210–11, 218–23
   framework for new Islamic movements 223–6
   in France 166–70
   'fundamentalism' 41–2
   and Nordic legal culture 144–7
   struggle for authority 108–9
Islamic legal tradition
   fatwa 132–5, 201–2
   and Nordic legal culture 144–7
   overview 120–5
      history 124–5
      terminology 121–3, 130n16–19
   role in European Church-State relations 156–8
   Shari'a law 120–1, 124, 126, 141, 145–7
   transformative processes 125–30
      Ifta 132–5
      Islamic international law 126–8
      Muslim diasporic communities 128–30
      Muslim family law 131–2
Italy 150, 171–2, 216
Iversen, Hans Raun viii–ix, 191–205

jihad 32–3

Kalyvas, Stathis 24

laïcité 22, 46–7, 167–9
Latin American Pentecostalism 31–2, 52, 58n6
law
   in Europe 149–58, 171
   in Nordic countries 142–3, 144–7
   and religious pluralism 151–6
   see also Islamic legal tradition
Liedman, Sven-Eric ix, 51–66, 67, 74–5, 88n
Lincoln, Bruce 224
Luhmann, Niklas 33–4, 79
Lutheranism 185, 188, 196–8

Evangelical Lutheran Church 78, 85, 143–4
Lutheran secularism politics in Denmark 208–13

Madeley, John 23n
Man of God 37–8
Martin, David ix, 183–9
Marx, Karl 61, 178
Modéer, Kjell Å ix, 141–7
modernity 34–5
   enchantment of 52, 55–6, 61
   multiple 69–70
   Western 19, 26–7, 70, 163–4
morality 42–3, 64, 166–7, 170
Muslims
   American 222
   attitude towards capitalism 58
   Danish 192–4, 201–3, 216, 218
      division between 221–2
      effect of cartoons on 220–1
   Democratic Muslims 210–11, 222–6
   diaspora and religious diaspora 128–30, 217–18, 220–2
   in Europe 215–18, 220–5
   family law 131–2
   framework for characterising minorities 225
   in France 166–70
   'headscarf affair' 168–70, 211–12
   integration of immigrants 26–7, 149
   see also Cartoon Crisis; Islam

natural law 60, 113–14
naturalism 57, 61n, 63
Nordic legal culture
   Church–State relations 143–4
   overview 142–3
   secularism versus Islam 144–7
Northern Ireland 184–5
Norway 22, 27–8, 143–5, 153

'one-worldism' 43–4
Onfray, Michel 51, 62–3
'otherness' 26–8

Pannenberg, Wolfhart 94–5
Parwez, G.A. 120, 141

Paul, the Apostle *see* Apostle Paul
Peirce, Charles Sanders 96–8
Pentecostalism
   global expansion 31–2, 52, 58
   and Salafism 57–8
   and women 69
pluralism *see* religious pluralism
Poland 28
Polish nuns 69
political mobilization 24, 28
Pope Benedict XVI *see* Ratzinger, Joseph
privatization of religion 19–20, 163–6, 171–2, 179
   see also de-privatization of religion
Public Religions in the Modern World 19, 79–80, 164

Qur'an 108–9, 121n4, 124–5, 135–6
Qutb, Sayyid 44, 59

Rasmussen, Anders Fogh 200–1, 208–11
Ratzinger, Joseph (Pope Benedict XVI) 60, 61n, 64, 90n, 171n
re-enchantment 52–6
reason, capacity and limits 59–62
religion
   British and Danish comparison 186–8
   as cause of conflicts and violence 27–8, 44–5, 48
   in a democratic society 163–4, 172–3, 179–80
   individualisation of 170–4
   intellectual challenges 51–9
   as marker of identity 150, 168, 170, 177–9
   republicisation of 163–4, 170–74
   separation between state and religion 78–9, 154–5, 167–8
   Western European views on 27–8
   see also de-privatization of religion; privatization of religion
religion and science
   apologetics 104–9
   religion–science dialogue
      benefits of partnership 88–91
      change in mindset required 93–5
      critical religious reflection 95–8
      developments to encourage dialogue 98–9
      religious studies 91–3
   religion-science relations 85–7
   role in inter-religious disagreements
      Darwin and evolution 107–8
      Democracy and Tradition 108
      Galileo affair 107
      History of the Warfare of Science with Theology in Christendom 108
      Islam 108–9
      Mind and Life Conferences 108
   role of doubt 111–14
religious freedom *see* freedom of religion
religious pluralism 45–6, 48, 173
   in Europe 149–50
   and law 151–6
republicisation of religion 163–4, 170–4
Riesebrodt, Martin ix, 177–80
Rohe, Mathias 146
Roy, Olivier 52

Salafism 52, 57–8, 59
science 55–9, 78–9
   see also religion and science
Secular Age, A 76–7
secularism
   challenge of de-privatization 19–24
   Christian and secular Right in USA 38, 42–4, 45, 58
   de-secularization 40–2, 45, 47–9
   in Denmark
      Lutheran secularism politics 208–13
      in relation to Cartoon Crisis 211
      secular and religious elements 78–9
   in Europe 21–8, 41, 70, 165, 198
   versus Islam, in Nordic legal culture 144–7
secular believer 106, 109, 111
secular humanism 43–4
secularity, terminology, meaning and use 76–7
secularization 52–3
   within modernization process 70
   of religion and politics 172–4

separation between state and religion 78–9, 154–5, 167–8
Shari'a law 120–21, 124, 126, 141, 145–7
Stepan, Alfred 22n, 23
Stout, Jeffrey 108
Sunna 120, 121n5, 122n7, 135–6
Sweden 22, 27–8, 142–5, 153

Taliban regime 41, 48
Tank-Storper, Sébastien ix, 163–75, 177–80
Taylor, Charles 76–7, 80
television 52, 57, 133
terminology, meaning and use
    diaspora 215–16
    fundamentalism 40n, 67–8, 73–4
    religion (singular or plural) 103
    secularity 76–7
territorialization 25–8, 29–35
Tocqueville, A. 171–2
Traité d'athéologie 51
Turkey
    AKP government 41
    forming diasporas 33, 217
    joining the European Union 26–7
    laiklik 46–7

Tutu, Desmond 39, 76, 79
twin tolerations model 22n, 23

ummah 33, 215–6, 220–3
United States of America
    American Muslims 222
    Christian and secular Right 38, 42–4, 45, 58
    global denominationalism 33
    individualism 178–9
    New Christian Right (NCR) 68

violence, religion leading to 44–5, 48

Wallis, Roy 224–5
Warburg, Margit x, 185, 215–28
Weber, Max 52–3, 54, 178–9
Western Europe *see* Europe: Western
White, Andrew 108
women 68–9, 122–3, 131–2, 166–7
wonder 64–5
    see also enchantment

Žižek, Slavoj 53, 62
Zwischen Naturalismus und Religion 57, 61n, 90n